FIFTY WAYS
TO FLY BETTER

BRUCE GOLDSMITH
and friends

In the core, since 1988

About this book

Flying is our passion, and this book reflects that. It started life as a collection of the best learning articles published in Cross Country magazine since 1988, including Bruce Goldsmith's Icaristics column. But it evolved, was updated, revised and added to. The result is what you now have in your hands, 200-odd pages dedicated to the absolute core of what we do: the essence of our sport. It is aimed at anyone who has embarked on the remarkable journey that free flight is, from beginners to experienced pilots. It draws on some of the deep knowledge that is out there, held by some of the best, most time-served pilots in the game. You will find some theory in here, but mostly you'll find real-life practical experience, hard-won by pilots who have been flying and working it out for years. Read it closely – some of what's inside is absolute gold. See you in the air! *Ed, Marcus, Hugh, Charlie and Verity*

About Cross Country magazine

Cross Country was established in 1988 by Sherry Thevenot, an artist who married into the hang gliding scene and wanted to reflect the spirit of free flight through magazines. The magazine somehow just slotted right in, and it has grown ever since – it is now read by pilots in 75 countries around the world. It has always been edited and owned by pilots, and always will be.

www.xcmag.com

Publisher's info

Cross Country International
5 St George's Place
Brighton
BN1 4GA
www.cross-country-int.com

Author: Bruce Goldsmith and contributors
Editor: Ed Ewing
Designer: Marcus King
Editorial team: Hugh Miller, Charlie King
Sales: Verity Sowden
ISBN: 978-0-9570727-2-5
Second Edition (Printed June 2014)

"To have faith is to have wings." "

J.M. Barrie, The Little White Bird

THE BUCK STOPS HERE

FREE FLYING requires a dedication to the cause that is increasingly rare in our modern world. Unlike many other sports flying requires a large investment of time and money – but it doesn't stop there. To fly well, you need to be learning constantly and put in a level of commitment that may well put strains on other areas of your life.

But perhaps what makes free flying really stand out is the way it forces each pilot to take responsibility for his or her own actions. This bucks the modern trend of looking to blame others and hold them liable when things go wrong. We are increasingly taught that if you follow the rules, everything will be ok. That idea just does not work in paragliding or hang gliding. You will never be completely safe and fly far if you follow the rules.

Instead, you need to take responsibility for your flying and educate yourself as much as you can, to make sure you keep improving. The best pilots soak up tips from others and really absorb every experience they have in flying, so they just get better and better. The air is an ever-changing environment, and even flying the same site is different every day. Rigid rules just don't work.

In the end, you're up there on your own and it's you that takes the final decisions. Perhaps it is this that makes free flight the perfect antidote to modern life. It takes us back into the wild, where we have to live on our wits.

If you're ready for the challenge of flying better, then this book gives you a huge catalogue of ideas to draw on, enabling you to make better, more informed decisions. There are many new pieces, and also many updated chapters from my Icaristics column and articles by fellow pilots.

This knowledge has been earned the hard way: from real firsthand experience over several decades of surfing the sky. From windy days in the Alps to smooth thermals over the flatlands, from cliff soaring in England to the ripping dusties of the Mojave Desert.

The team from Cross Country have done a great job of bringing together some of the most important lessons in free flying. I sincerely hope this book will help you keep improving your flying.

Bruce Goldsmith

PS: The Buck Stops Here was a sign President Truman (term 1945-1953) kept on his desk to show he was ready and willing to take responsibility for his country. Taking responsibility for your own flying is the first step to becoming the pilot you want to be.

◄ **IN THE CORE**
It doesn't get better than this. Having fun
above the Dents de Lanfon, France.
Photo: Jérôme Maupoint

CONTENTS

◄ TEXTBOOK CONDITIONS
On track on a 150km flight through
the southern French Alps.
Photo: Ant Green

CONTRIBUTORS

Ian Blackmore
Cross country pilot, editor of Cross Country magazine from 2003-2005

Josh Cohn
Former US paragliding champion, PWC Americas winner and US team pilot

John Coutts
Standard Class gliding world champion 2003, started gliding in New Zealand aged 15

Bob Drury
Pioneering Himalayan adventure pilot and editor of Cross Country from 2005-2010

Jonny Durand
Multiple Australian hang gliding champion and pro pilot. World record holder

Ed Ewing
Editor of Cross Country since 2010

Kelly Farina
Alpine paragliding guide and former British team pilot, www.austrianarena.com

Will Gadd
Twice holder of the paragliding open distance world record (298km 1998 and 423km 2002)

Ant Green
Acro pilot, filmmaker, photographer and paraglider test pilot

Steve Ham
British paragliding champion 2002 and Piedrahita guru

Heike Hamann
Former Australian women's paragliding champion and psychologist

Greg Hamerton
Paragliding instructor, publisher, writer and author

Alex Hofer
European paragliding champion 2002, world champion 2003 and Red Bull X-Alps winner

Marcus King
Designer and associate editor of Cross Country magazine since 2005

Patrick Laverty
Hang glider pilot and altitude world record holder in powered hang gliding (5,348m)

Antoine Laurens
Himalayan adventure paraglider pilot

Horacio Llorens
Acro paragliding world champion four times, infinite tumble world record holder

Dustin Martin
Hang gliding open distance world record holder, 764km in 2012 with Jonny Durand

Hugh Miller
Former British paragliding champion and editor of Cross Country from 1998-2003

Russell Ogden
International competition pilot, former British champion, and test pilot

Honza Rejmanek

Red Bull X-Alps athlete and meteorologist, Cross Country magazine columnist

Adrian Thomas

Former British paragliding champion and a professor of flight at Oxford University

Jay Rebbeck

Sailplane competition pilot and member of the British gliding team

Jocky Sanderson

SIV guru and former international competition pilot

Pál Takáts

Leading acro pilot and three-time acro paragliding world champion

Karel Vejchodsky

Cross country pilot who runs www.xcontest.org

Godfrey Wenness

Former paragliding open distance world record holder (335km) and Manilla guru

Rob Whittall

Former world champion in both hang gliding (1989) and paragliding (1991)

Photographers

Andy Busslinger
Julian Cisterna
Loren Cox
Mike Endacott
Ed Ewing
Kelly Farina
Helen Gant
Bruce Goldsmith
Nick Greece
Anthony Green
Fred Gustafsson
Charlie King
Marcus King
Olivier Laugero
Jérôme Maupoint
Hugh Miller
Russell Ogden
Gudrun Öchsl
Tim Pentreath
Federico Rios
Martin Scheel
John Stapels
Vianney Tisseau
Roger Turner
Al Wilson

Cover photo

Tyr Goldsmith

Illustrations

Charlie King
Marcus King

► **WELCOME TO OUR WORLD**
Above the Roc d'Enfer in the Haute Savoie,
French Alps. Photo: Jérôme Maupoint

CHOOSING THE RIGHT GLIDER

By Rob Whittall

CONFIDENCE is often overlooked, yet I feel that it is the most important factor in glider choice. If you feel good on a glider, you will invariably fly better than on one that makes you anxious. If you lose confidence and get scared in a bad situation or rough air, you also lose the ability to make good calculated decisions. This is partly due to adrenaline and fear – they will cloud your judgement just when you need it most. On the other hand, if you really enjoy your wing and feel comfortable under it, then your discomfort threshold will be much higher and thus you have a better chance of making the right decisions all the time.

Fashion

First, I would ignore style or fashion, and I wouldn't be a slave to figures either: some crazy folk add up the results of the certification report and the glider with the best result is the one to buy (oh my God). I have also heard that pilots buy wings because their friend has one (isn't that sweet?). Or some are completely influenced by the top speed and manufacturer's performance figures (a recipe for disaster). Finally, some buy because it has a nice colour (matches their car!). I would avoid these points and simply make an honest assessment of your capabilities and then go for a wing which will give you that all-important confidence when in the air.

What type of pilot am I?

Now is the time to be completely realistic about your capabilities. If you are a leisure pilot flying less than 50 hours a year, then the choice is easy: an EN A or lower-end B wing will have the stability and handling to keep you confident even if you have the occasional lay-off of a month or more. Don't fall into the trap of dismissing these as 'beginner wings'. Nowadays performance is excellent and many long-time pilots say that they're getting their best-ever flights on them after unhappy experiences with hotter wings.

If you are lucky enough to fly most weeks and can keep current, consider stepping up. Only if you are already very confident, honestly extremely experienced, and fly all the time should you even think of any rating higher than an EN C.

This gives you the freedom to think: "So, I have decided that I am, in reality, an intermediate pilot nowadays rather than my previous image of myself being a hot cross country and competition pilot. Thank God for that!"

Remember, this is a flying machine you are about to purchase – your safety could depend on this decision.

Test fly

Once you have narrowed down the field to four or five models, go and take a test flight on them. This is what will tell you the most –

"What matters is that you have a great flight and go home with a big smile on your face "

don't listen to the sales pitch or think about the great offer the salesman will give you. Think about how each glider feels: Did it take off well? Did it feel twitchy or was it smooth as an oil tanker? Were you confident and comfortable every minute you were on it?

The one with the most yeses is probably the one for you. It does not matter if your friends are buying a different model at a cheaper price because at the end of the day it is you that has to fly the glider, not them. Remember, when you think about it, you are spending a lot of money. If the glider that really felt the best is a couple of hundred more, then you would be a fool not to buy it just because of the price.

Now, what size?

Size is always a problem, yet it's quite simple really. Just take your naked weight and add 15kg. This will give you your 'in-flight' weight. Knowing this, you can select the size of glider that puts you closest to the middle of the specified weight range.

If you fall on the border of two sizes, then just analyse what type of flying you do and choose accordingly. For example, if you expect to be flying in fairly strong winds quite often, then a little more wing loading could be a good thing to give you more speed, so the smaller size would be better.

On the other hand, if you are always flying in weak conditions, the bigger size might be a better choice as it will give you a slightly better sink rate, helping you to climb well. However, if you often fly in strong thermal conditions you may feel more comfortable on the smaller wing. Don't get too wound up about this: you will be safe on either of the sizes, so simply buy the one that feels the best to you.

The fun factor

Every pilot desires something a little different, but remember that fashion or fad is not important. Your comfort and confidence in the air is all that matters. At the end of the day it does not matter who was highest or who flew the furthest.

What matters is that you go home having had a great flight, with a big smile on your face, a headful of beautiful views and a fantastic feeling inside. Because that is what our flying is all about.

NEED TO KNOW

- Confidence in your glider is the most important factor in flying
- Be honest about your abilities
- Narrow down your options and go for a test fly
- Buy the one that gives you the most fun

CHOOSING THE RIGHT WING SIZE

By Bruce Goldsmith

HOW do manufacturers choose weight ranges, and what happens if you are too heavy or too light on your glider?

Look at the weight range

First, you should only look at the weight-range specified by the manufacturer and not the size of the wing. Different manufacturers measure their sizes in different ways, so just buying a wing that says it is the same size as the wing you had before (but from a different brand) can be a big mistake. The size could easily be different by as much as 10%, which is typically the difference between two sizes.

Secondly, what one manufacturer calls a medium could be called a large by another manufacturer, so look at the weight-range numbers rather than the descriptions.

What's the right size?

The answer should be simple: weigh yourself ready to fly, with all your equipment including the glider, then pick the size of glider where you are closest to the middle of the weight range.

"Glide angle is not affected by wing loading"

Typically I find that if you are a medium pilot your equipment will weigh around 13kg. If you are a large, your equipment will weigh slightly more, say 14kg and for a small, 12kg. However the weight of equipment can vary a lot. When I fly in competition I normally weigh in with 25kg of kit, largely due to the profiled harness. If you use lightweight equipment you can get your kit down to 6kg including reserve, which is great for walk ups, but means you may need to get a smaller glider.

How do manufacturers decide weight ranges?

I cannot speak for all manufacturers, but I can tell you the method I use. I design the medium size first and choose the size of the glider depending on several design factors, such as the profile used, wing curvature and intended use of the glider.

Typically the M will be 23m² projected area with a weight range of 80-100kg. When I have finished the test flying I have got enough practical experience of flying the glider to get a good idea if the weight range should be adjusted slightly from the intended design, up or down.

Other sizes of the glider go through a similar process, with each size being scaled up or down by 4% linear, giving an area change of 1.04 x 1.04 = 1.082, or 8.2% difference between sizes.

Experience shows that the wing loading recommended by manufacturers should not be exactly the same on each size of glider. The larger sizes are better with a slightly higher wing loading and the smaller sizes should have a slightly lower wing loading.

What happens if you are heavy on a wing?

There are both advantages and disadvantages to being heavy on a wing. The glider will fly faster. Stall speed will be higher as well as trim speed and top speed. The difference in speed between two different weights is normally 1-2km/h for every 10kg in weight added, although this does depend on the glider. You also get a slightly worse minimum sink rate. Brake pressure is also higher.

In general being heavy on a wing brings the following results:

- The glider flies faster
- Worse sink rate
- Higher brake pressure
- Lower spin tendency
- More resistant to collapse
- Less deep stall tendency
- More aggressive recovery from stalls and spins

And if you are light?

Everything is opposite to being heavy:

- You fly slower
- Better sink rate
- Increased deep stall tendency
- Less aggressive on spin and stall recovery
- Lighter brake pressure
- Higher negative tendency
- Less resistant to collapse

It's important to note that glide angle is not affected by wing loading. If you are heavy you get the same glide angle but at a slightly higher speed. However, smaller gliders tend to glide slightly worse than larger gliders.

Personal preferences

I personally like to fly heavy in summer and lighter on a glider in winter. This is because conditions are stronger in the summer and speed is more important than sink rate. In winter the opposite is true. So the perfect glider for me is one where I can be near the bottom of the weight range when I have little equipment, and when I have a bit of ballast and full competition equipment I can be right at the top of the weight range.

NEED TO KNOW

- Look at the weight range, not size
- Know your 'all-up' weight – you plus kit
- Aim to fly in the middle of the weight range – but don't get hung up about it
- Being heavy on a wing means you will go faster, and have higher brake pressure
- Being light on a wing means you will go slower, with lighter brake pressure

▶ **STRONG WIND SOARING**
At the beach in Jersey on a small wing. Flying a specialist
smaller wing lets you fly in stronger wind.
Photo: Marcus King

HOW WING LOADING AFFECTS PERFORMANCE

By Adrian Thomas

PEOPLE often ask how heavy they should be relative to the weight range on their wing. The aerodynamic effects of wing loading are fairly simple, but the choice of loading depends on where you fly, how you fly, and what you want to get out of your flying.

Wing-loading doesn't affect glide (unless the wing is distorted by the weight): you just go down the same glide angle at a higher speed if you are heavier.

Increasing wing loading increases speed by only the square root of the weight change. On any particular glider if you can double your weight without distorting the wing then your speed will go up by a factor of 1.41. So, if you are an 80kg pilot and you add the maximum ballast allowed under FAI rules (about 10kg), you will increase your speed by about 5%.

Optimisation for XC speed

In a four-hour competition task, that 5% increase in speed means that a given pilot on a given wing could finish (all other things being equal) 12 minutes earlier by carrying the maximum 10kg of ballast.

But all other things aren't usually equal. Flying XC means you need climbs as well as glides. The ballasted pilot gets about a 5% increase in both sink rate and flight speed. For any given turn-radius a heavier loaded glider has to bank more steeply, and sink rate in turn increases rapidly with bank angle. So a ballasted pilot loses out in turns from both the direct increase in sink rate and the increase in sink rate that results from the steeper bank angles. The total effect is roughly proportional to the change in weight.

So, if our competition pilot spends a third of his time during that four-hour task climbing in thermals, then by carrying ballast the higher speed on glides saves about eight minutes, but the total time taken to climb is about eight minutes longer.

If the conditions allow the task to be completed with only a third or less of the total time spent climbing then ballast could pay off. If more than about a third of total time is spent climbing then being light on the wing is more advantageous.

Stability and agility

But that isn't the whole story. Being heavy on the wing affects stability and agility as well. A heavily loaded glider is generally more resistant to turbulence-induced collapses, but collapses more violently when it does go. This is probably partly to do with internal pressure (dynamic pressure goes with speed squared, so it increases in proportion to any weight change), and with the angle of attack of the wing. A given wing at any given speed is at a higher angle of attack if it is heavily loaded than if it is lightly loaded. To get the lift to balance weight, the heavily loaded wing has to operate at a higher lift coefficient.

Tucks are (usually) produced when turbulence causes the local angle of attack at the leading edge to go negative, so the heavily

"Being the right weight on a wing is a delicate optimisation problem"

loaded wing is slightly more tuck-resistant. The angle of attack effect seems to be stronger than the internal pressure effect (which is the main reason why flying fast, with a low angle of attack makes the wing more likely to tuck). Collapses are probably more violent on a heavily loaded wing partly because the turbulence required to collapse them is more severe, and partly because the speed prior to the collapse is higher.

A heavily loaded wing is more agile because the pilot has greater roll authority – shifting all that weight to one half of a tiny wing will make it bank up quickly. This is probably why most comp wings feel like trucks if you are used to something with a shorter span, and why comp pilots end up wanging all over the sky on beginners' wings when they borrow them. It is also why acro pilots fly tiny wings.

There also seems to be something going on with pitch stability and the speed of transmission of information about turbulence, because heavier loaded wings tell you more about what the air is doing – but even I don't have a theory to explain that!

All this goes to suggest that if you want to float around at the top of the stack all day then you should be light on your wing. If you want to fly cross country or in competitions then you have an optimisation problem.

Small gliders suit mountains and deserts

If you expect to be racing spending one-third or more of your time on glide then it might be good to be heavily loaded on your wing. This would be particularly true if you expect the thermals to be turbulent (when the extra

agility and stability would help you core the thermal while lighter loaded wings get chucked about and thrown out of the core). It would be even more valid if you expect to be flying in straight lines in lift a lot. Alpine or desert flying is the natural habitat of heavily loaded wings.

If, however, you fly in circumstances where you're likely to spend more than one-third of the time climbing in thermals, where thermals are weak, or where just staying in the air is crucial, then you want to be lightly loaded. Every competition I've been in has had a task where staying in the air in weak lift was the key.

Big gliders have aerodynamic advantages

Finally, there is the question of big glider performance. Big sized gliders glide better (other things being equal), at least as I am told by some of the best pilots and designers around. The only reason I have been given is that it is to do with their higher Reynold's number (a fluid dynamics term). The Reynold's number depends on velocity, a characteristic length, air density ($1.225kg/m^3$ at sea level) and air viscosity (17.9×10.6 kg/m/s at normal temperature and pressure). For a paraglider flying at 10m/s Reynold's is about 10.6 times wing chord. So at a given speed a larger glider has a larger Reynold's number. As Reynold's number goes up, drag goes down, all other things being equal. For example, going from the Size-24 to Size-26 changes wing chord from 2.71 to 2.82m, which changes the Rc at trim speed from 1.85×106 to 1.93×106, giving a 4% increase.

The effect varies depending on the characteristics of the aerofoil. In general, for the sort of aerofoils used in paragliders the maximum lift and minimum drag both increase with Reynold's number. In other words, an increase in wing chord increases the maximum lift and decreases the minimum drag. The effect is small, but perhaps not insignificant – the large and medium-sized gliders do tend to have a noticeable performance advantage over the small wings.

The reason so many comp pilots can be bothered to carry around huge bags of ballast is that it allows them to fly a bigger glider that glides a little bit better and can fly a little bit slower and turn a little bit tighter in thermals. As far as I can tell there are no disadvantages for big gliders except for carrying them (and loads of ballast) up the hill.

The weight ranges that manufacturers quote are almost always the certified weight ranges – the gliders have been tested at the bottom and top of the weight range. If a glider is particularly benign it passes the tests at a wider-than-expected range of weights.

Personal viewpoint

I spent one year flying right at the top of my glider's weight range. As expected the wing was stable, the handling was rapid and speed was high, but I had to work to climb with people if thermals were less than 4m/s or so. The advantages of high loading meant that I thoroughly enjoyed the rough air of Castejon, Piedrahita and Garmisch, but I found it more difficult than usual to get away on XCs in the UK where even the best thermals are weak.

The next year I flew a medium wing right in the middle of the weight range (90-110kg). As expected, handling was good, speed was good enough and climb was very good indeed. I didn't find any detectable reduction in stability, but the improvement in climb rate was really nice. It was obvious that the optimisation involved trade-offs – I could

reliably climb through gaggles (even at the Worlds), but also found people overtaking me on final glide when I had the bar block-to-block.

A while back I also put a lot of effort into reducing the weight of my flying gear. By changing flying suits and dumping excess gear I managed to lose 2kg of useless weight. Weight is only useful as ballast if you can dump it when conditions get weak!

Is ballast worth it?

Being the right weight on a wing is a delicate optimisation problem, and the advantages are subtle. Carrying ballast to increase speed is almost always a waste of time in recreational flying. Even if you carry 10kg of ballast, your speed only goes up by about 3%. A 3% increase in speed means going from a trim speed of 36km/h to 37.08km/h. Not very dramatic – and certainly not enough to stop you being blown over the back of the hill if the wind picks up. However, in competition small differences matter, and the guns burning down final glide, block-to-block on speedbar, might give anything for a 3% increase in speed.

NEED TO KNOW

- Wing loading doesn't affect glide
- Increasing wing loading increases speed
- The maximum ballast allowed in competition is 10kg
- Heavily loaded wings resist collapse, but collapse more violently when they do
- Heavily loaded wings are more agile
- Lightly loaded wings will take you to the top of the stack, but you'll be slower on glide
- Ballast can make a difference in competition, where the margins are slim
- Flying with ballast in recreational flying usually isn't worth it

LEARNING TO FLY YOUR OWN WAY

By Bruce Goldsmith

WHEN I first started flying hang gliders I was told never to fly alone. The two reasons I was given for this sound piece of advice were that I was inexperienced and needed advice and guidance from other, more experienced pilots and secondly, if I had an accident it's always a good idea to have people around to help.

Flying alone

I stuck to the 'never fly alone' rule for the first five years of flying, until the day I was sent to work in Dunkerque, northern France. I was told by the locals that there were other pilots in the area, but on good days I kept arriving at the site and there was simply nobody else around. As far as pilots went, I think I saw one other hang glider pilot during the whole year that I lived there.

Eventually I decided that I would just have to break the rule and fly on my own, as the conditions just looked too good. Since that time, when I did the majority of my flying alone, I have never really looked back. I found that when I flew alone I was never worried, and more importantly I always flew. I was never talked out of flying by other, more cautious pilots, and I found as a result my flying improved greatly and my horizons expanded. I found that I could easily fly in conditions that, back at home, people would have said were unsafe.

I found also that I tended to always make the most of the conditions and get as high and as far as possible, instead of hanging around the home site with the rest of the gaggle. When flying alone like this I tried to do distances every time. Even if it was only 10km I did it, because I had no one to stick around with on launch and therefore no reason to stay there.

I realise that by the time I had moved to Dunkerque I had gathered quite a lot of experience in flying. I am not suggesting therefore that on your second day attached to a wing you go and jump off an unknown site on your own. Generally, flying with other people at first is a good idea.

The cheese up

However, I have noticed that the presence of a large crowd on launch will increase the chances of you not flying. It is all very well sticking to the 'don't fly alone' rule, but I have noticed that there are certain people in the flying scene who like to talk a lot about flying, but never actually seem to take off. It gets me really annoyed when I see a new pilot arrive on a new site and consult the 'locals' about the conditions. If he or she happens to encounter what I call a 'cheeser', then they will probably never get their glider out of the bag, even though the conditions may be perfect for flying. These 'cheesers' try to get other, less experienced pilots not to fly in order to make themselves look less conspicuous about not flying. In this scenario, the case of gaggle drag starts even before you take off.

I would say try to fly with other people, and always ask the advice of the locals on a new site when you arrive, as they might have something genuinely useful to say. However,

" If you look up to a perfect sky with puffy clouds, then take off "

bear in mind that there is rarely a 'perfect' flying day, and if the advice of your trusty local is that "it's a bit strong" or "it's pretty windy" or "this site can get really gnarly in this wind direction" but you can see other pilots flying around quite happily, politely walk away and go and fly before you get 'cheesed up'.

Gaggle drag

Another scenario is that you arrive on a new site. On the way there you get excited as the conditions look brilliant, the wind feels like it's on the hill and not too strong. However, you get to the site ready to tear your glider out of the bag when you encounter the locals sitting in a group, gliders still packed, looking sceptically at the conditions and no one is in the air!

You immediately think "What's wrong?" At this point, before you even speak to them, remember that there are people who actually dislike 'epic' days. This is fine, but you don't want to ask them about weather advice.

So, bearing this in mind, hear what they have got to say. If it's something like, "There's a helicopter arriving and we can't fly," then obviously don't fly. But, if it is something like, "The valley winds are a bit strong today," or, "There are thunderstorms expected and it's pretty unstable," and you look up to a perfectly blue sky with little white puffy clouds, then again, politely walk away, get out your glider and take off, is my advice. You will usually find that half an hour later they all take off too, having watched you have the time of your life.

I am not encouraging inexperienced pilots to ignore the advice of their elders and betters here, nor trying to encourage an 'outlandish' attitude to flying. What I am saying is that the more people you have on launch and the more they all discuss the conditions, the less likely they are to fly, as in most groups there are pilots who tend always to be negative about a perfectly flyable day.

Make your own decisions

My overall advice is this: if you feel confident about your own judgement, then feel confident about flying if the conditions feel good, even if the local advice is contrary to this. It is easy to get taken in by the 'cheesy chat' of other, less confident pilots. And if you happen to be on a site where the cheesers have won the day and nobody is flying, but the conditions are good, then my advice would be to break the 'never fly alone' rule and fly!

NEED TO KNOW

- 'Never fly alone' is good advice, but sometimes it's unavoidable
- Listen to advice on launch, but also make your own decisions
- Watch out for 'cheesers' on launch: people who talk a lot but never fly
- If you feel confident about your own judgement of good conditions, then feel confident in flying too

FLYING CLOSE TO THE RIDGE

By Bruce Goldsmith

WHEN you're ridge soaring and trying to get up in a thermal, how close in to the ridge should you be? You could be soaring in the morning, looking to get away on a big XC, or working an Alpine spine in the afternoon valley breeze, but the dilemma is the same: should you stick your wingtip right in among the grass blades, or should you be hunting way out front?

The Inn Valley study

In the mid-2000s meteorologists investigated the upslope thermal wind in the Inn Valley in the Austrian Alps. Often, people think that the closer to the ridge the better, but this study revealed otherwise. Thermal updraught is caused by the sun heating the sun-facing slope, causing convection up the slope. Close to the slope the friction between the slope and the air causes the updraught to rise more slowly. The study showed that the best distance is between 20 and 30 metres out from the ridge.

No such thing as average

On an average summer day in the Inn Valley I'm sure this holds true. However, the beauty of flying is that every flying site is different from one day to the next. Even if you fly the same ridge every day of the year (lucky you!) what can be true one day, can be completely false the next because the weather changes. This is particularly true of the distance you should fly from a slope. Some days you climb best by clinging as close to a ridge as you can, and other days the best thermals can be found 100-200 metres out in front of the ridge. But there are some main common factors to consider.

Slope smoothness

The smoother the slope the less the updraught will be slowed by the roughness of the slope. For example, if a ridge is tree-covered then the lift will be better further from the ridge. If the ridge is smooth grass, skimming along close to the grass could well be the best way to climb.

The features below

If there is a small break in the slope, or even a hedge-line or a line of trees, then this line of trees can kick off the thermals before they arrive at the part of the ridge where you are flying. Many ridges are double ridges, and the smaller lower ridge can often produce better thermals than the upper bigger ridge, therefore you can climb better by flying further from the main ridge.

So, imagine that you're thermalling over the peak of the lower ridge, rather than soaring on the upper ridge.

Small cliff bands

When a ridge has a small amount of vertical in it the lift is always much better precisely at this vertical part of the ridge. Typically, this would be a cliff or rock outcrop. Often you can stay up where the ridge is vertical,

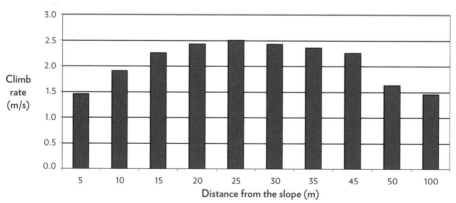

▲ **THE INN VALLEY STUDY**
The study showed that in this instance the best lift is 20-30m out from the hill

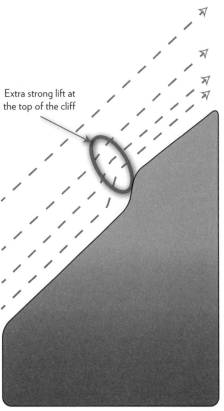

Extra strong lift at the top of the cliff

▲ **SMALL CLIFFS**
Cliffs, with their mini venturi, produce extra lift, and are also useful thermal triggers that you can often climb away from vertically

but you can't where the ridge is less than vertical. I think part of this is that you can get your canopy close to the area of best lift without the pilot being too close to the ridge. Little cliffs also create stronger lift because they produce a kind of mini venturi in front of the top of the cliff as the air accelerates past it. The result is you often find much more lift off a small cliff than you'd expect from its size.

The level of turbulence

Safety is always the prime consideration when flying and how close you dare go to the ridge must primarily be a safety decision. If the air's really rough then obviously you can't fly as close to the ridge as when the air is smooth. This decision also depends on your pilot skill and the kind of glider you have. You may feel happier to fly closer to the ground on a glider you feel more confident on.

When I fly in England in smooth dynamic ridge lift I feel quite safe and confident flying close to the ridge. As the thermals start popping then I venture away from the ridge and start hunting for thermals further out.

NEED TO KNOW

- Where to fly can depend on the ridge and on the day
- Ground cover matters: smooth grassy hills or covered in trees
- Look for breaks in the ridge-line lower down, thermals will kick off from there
- Cliffs are soarable when other parts of the hill aren't – tuck in close
- Stay safe: if it's rough, fly further out

◄ **GONE FISHING**
Resting a finger on the brake line lets the pilot feel what
the glider is doing, and respond.
Photo: Hugh Miller

ACTIVE FLYING

By Bruce Goldsmith

YOU may wonder how people ever manage to fly competitions, where you often fly a high performance glider in turbulent conditions at high speed! Good, active piloting is the answer. Active piloting is a method of feeling what is happening to the wing, and as you feel that a collapse is imminent, you apply the brakes to avoid the collapse.

Pulling on the brakes stops the wing collapsing in two ways. First, it slows the wing up because it reduces the performance and so increases the angle of attack. Secondly, it pushes air out of the back of the glider towards the front, so you can momentarily actually pump up the front of the glider with displaced air.

The technique

It is important to apply the brakes very quickly as well as just the right amount. I have a technique that I use to apply the brakes quickly that you may find useful. I often fly around with the weight of my arms on the brake just to keep a couple of kilos of pressure on them and I have my index finger resting on the brake line in the same way that a fisherman rests his finger on the line to feel for a bite.

By doing this you can constantly feel the pressure within the canopy through your finger. If the pressure drops at all on the brake line you can then instantly apply more brake and this will get the pressure back up again. But that sounds more complicated than it actually is. All you are doing is trying to maintain the same weight on the brake line, ie just resting the weight of your arm on the brake.

For bigger collapses you will need to do more than just rest the weight of your arm on the line, especially if the turbulence is strong or you are flying fast. In these cases you may need to actively jerk your arm down in order to be fast and effective enough to catch the collapse at an early stage. If you are using the speedbar you should always release it as soon as you feel that there is any chance that the glider may collapse. Weightshifting is another important part of active piloting.

How to recover?

For many years the most common cause of accidents in paragliding has been the asymmetric collapse. It is not so much the collapse that is the problem but the spiral dive

" Countering the turn is the first priority "

▲ **ASYMMETRIC COLLAPSE**
Maintain course, don't over react.
Photo: Gudrun Öchsl

▶ **EYE CANDY**
Above La Tournette, 2,351m, France.
Photo: Jérôme Maupoint

afterwards. (Note that following an asymmetric collapse you enter a spiral dive, not a spin.) But the primary cause of accidents is now changing as pilots become more aware that they should be countering the turn by applying opposite brake. Unfortunately this is now causing a new problem: stalling the remaining part of the glider by countering the turn too strongly.

Pump out the deflation

Countering the turn is always the first priority. This stops the glider from turning off course which could lead to you hitting the ground if you are very low, or having a collision with another pilot. It also stops the spiral dive from starting and picking up speed.

The way gliders react to an asymmetric collapse is one of the most important differences between school, intermediate and competition paragliders. School gliders should hardly change course even when 50% of the wing has collapsed. Intermediate gliders may turn but should come out quickly even if the pilot does nothing. Competition gliders may turn quickly following a collapse and unless the pilot reacts may never recover. The speed of the spiral dive can also be alarmingly fast.

NEED TO KNOW

- Active piloting is feeling what the wing is doing and responding to it
- The Fisherman's Technique helps you feel the pressure of the wing through the brake
- In case of an asymmetric collapse, weightshift away from it, counter the turn and pump out the deflation

UNDERSTANDING PITCH

By Bruce Goldsmith

WHEN you fly your paraglider, you sit in your harness at least seven metres below the wing – maybe as much as ten. This means that you are the weight of a huge pendulum. A large part of becoming a good pilot is learning to use this pendulum to your advantage and not allowing yourself to be thrown around by your own inertia or your glider.

Pilot-induced collapses

Controlling the pendulum effect is an essential part of flying safely. In extreme cases, failure to control it correctly can cause the wing to collapse, even in completely calm conditions. Many pilots believe that collapses come from turbulence, but some are directly caused by the pilot not controlling the pitching of the wing

correctly. I have often seen this when pilots first try to learn to do wingovers. If the movement of the wing is not timed correctly with the swinging of the pilot, the wing can get unloaded as it swings down when the pilot is still going up. When pilots are under training this does not usually cause problems because they should have been taught to expect the effect and how to handle it. However, a similar situation can occur when they start to venture into thermic air and the wing surges forwards and backwards. This can catch you out if you are not used to controlling the swing as the wing pitches.

Understanding the swing

As paragliders became more efficient, the pendulum effect became more significant.

◄ THE THREE STAGES OF PITCH
The glider pitches back (1), forward (2) and then the pilot
swings underneath (3). Photo: Marcus King

Older paragliders had considerably more drag which made it more difficult to start the pendulum swinging, and damped out the swinging once started. The race for ever-improving performance means our gliders now have less drag and more speed, so they need more pilot skill to fly them. This is one reason why an EN B glider used to be suitable for students straight out of school, but these more dynamic characteristics mean that today's hotter EN B gliders need a higher level of skill. They have become true intermediates.

Learning the swing

If you just fly around carefully keeping the wing stable over your head you will never get accustomed to the way your glider swings in pitch or roll. Imagine a child sitting on a swing without it ever moving. Suddenly someone pushes the swing! The child will feel scared and disoriented, and may well fall off. However, a child who is used to swinging will be completely at home and be able to control it with body and legs. Let's compare this to our pilot who flies around carefully keeping the glider stable overhead. Then the glider meets a thermal, and pitches and the swing starts. If you have never swung around on your glider your reactions may not cope with this situation. When you enter, the glider will first pitch back and then forwards again. If this coincides with the other side of the thermal, then if your reactions are wrong, the wing may well collapse, even though the thermal itself was not turbulent. Learning the swing, therefore, is an essential part of becoming a good pilot.

The pitching game

Start with pitching exercises on your glider. This is pretty safe and can be practised any time you go flying and get a reasonable amount of ground clearance – at least 200m (650ft). Warning: only do this in calm conditions. Fly straight and level and simultaneously apply both brakes to slow the glider down. Just pull them 20cm or so at first. Then release both brakes quickly and the glider will surge forward in front of you. You will then swing forward to follow the glider; as you do so you gently apply the brakes again. In this way you can get into a pitch oscillation and it can really be quite a fun game.

You can play around with the timing and amplitude of the swinging so that you train your reactions to understand the movements of the glider. Start slowly and gently at first and then as you get more and more confident let the glider go further and further in front of you. It is amazing how far in front of you it is possible to let it go before you get a front collapse. Be careful though: do not let the glider surge lower than about 45-degrees to the horizon. It is important to get used to starting and stopping the oscillation quickly and safely at will. The difference between getting it to start or stop swinging is just in the timing of the brake application. This is why practice is the only solution.

Swinging from side to side

The glider does not only swing in pitch forward and backwards, but also can roll from side to side. These two swinging movements are often linked when the pilot initiates a turn. A well co-ordinated turn is one where

▶ **PITCH PERFECT**
Understanding pitch will help when
it comes to flying wingovers.
Photo: John Stapels

66 When you enter a thermal the glider will first pitch back 99

the pilot controls the brake inputs – which are what make the glider turn – to coincide with body swing in both pitch and roll. With too much input too quickly you will swing out too far, and then rapidly back in again. The result is that it is easy to go negative as you try to get the glider to continue the turn while you are swinging back in the wrong direction. With practice you automatically learn to co-ordinate the brake movements with the pendulum effect to produce efficient and coordinated turns.

Practice your wingovers

Once you are confident with the pitching exercise, you are ready to start on wingovers. Learning wingovers is not just for show: it helps you to manage your glider better and to link the pitching of the wing with sideways swinging as well as the yawing of the wing. It all sounds very complicated, but fortunately our bodies have the ability to learn the way all these forces interact without the need to really understand them. Just practice wingovers and you will be rewarded with better coordination between yourself and the reactions of your wing.

The wingover is simply a series of turns left and right using the pendulum effect to help you to link each turn. It is the timing and amount of brake applied that is the most important, not the size of the turns. Be careful not to swing too high too quickly

when doing wingovers. I have seen over-keen pilots get too high too quickly and end up collapsing the wing. In extreme cases they have had to throw their reserves at low altitude. So be careful and take things one step at a time.

Each glider is different

Every model of glider has a slightly different swing, according to its size and the length of the lines. When you change gliders you need time and a little practice to let your reactions get used to the new one's swing.

You need to master the swing techniques to get your body used to the way you and your glider swings, so that you can use the brakes actively. When perfected this will result in a smoother ride through turbulent air, far fewer collapses and better landings.

NEED TO KNOW

- Your paraglider is a giant pendulum, you are its weight
- Controlling the pendulum is part of flying a paraglider well
- Enter a thermal, the glider pitches back
- Leave a thermal, the glider pitches forwards
- You can practice pitch exercises to learn how to control this
- Once confident with pitch, you can move on to wingovers

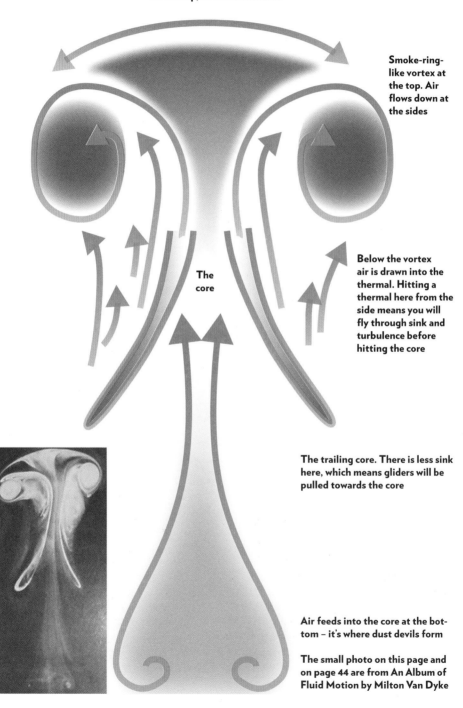

At the top, air flows outwards

Smoke-ring-like vortex at the top. Air flows down at the sides

The core

Below the vortex air is drawn into the thermal. Hitting a thermal here from the side means you will fly through sink and turbulence before hitting the core

The trailing core. There is less sink here, which means gliders will be pulled towards the core

Air feeds into the core at the bottom – it's where dust devils form

The small photo on this page and on page 44 are from An Album of Fluid Motion by Milton Van Dyke

◄ THE SHAPE OF A THERMAL

Studies using smoke show that thermals are made of a vortex at the top, a core surrounded by sinking and mixing air in the middle, and a trailing core below. What happens to you in the air will depend on where you hit the thermal.

UNDERSTANDING THERMALS

By Adrian Thomas

IN cross country flying the most important skill is your ability to find a thermal. When you are soaring along a ridge or flying at mid-level – halfway from ground to cloud – your only source of information about the presence of a thermal is the motion of the air and the movements of your glider.

Much has been written about thermal sources and triggers on the ground, but I'm going to focus in this article on finding thermals in mid-air by the movements and feelings they transmit to the wing.

Thermal structure

It helps if we can understand the kinds of movements involved in a thermal. Conveniently, the largest thermals known to man – atomic explosions – are marked by debris that reveals how they move.

Fortunately, the aerodynamics of these visible thermals and the invisible ones we ride are the same: only the scale and source of heating are different.

The thermals we use are formed from air warmed by contact with a hot surface. Initially the warm air rises as an unstructured blob, but very rapidly it rolls up into a smoke-ring-like vortex at the top, with a core connecting the vortex to the pool of warm air feeding the thermal. As air feeds into the core, any initial rotation is amplified so that the core rapidly adopts the familiar structure of a dust devil – dust devils are the bottoms of thermals.

At the top of the thermal – on top of the leading vortex – air flows outwards away from the centre of the thermal. At the sides the air flows downwards and below the vortex air is drawn in towards the thermal. What happens next depends on the size of the source feeding the thermal. If it is large, then it will continue to feed warm air into the column.

In some cases the source may be big enough (and the heating rate high enough) that the thermal forms a continuous column of lift. More often the column will be broken because the source will be insufficient to feed the thermal continuously and will be exhausted after a short time.

Once detached from the ground, the thermal continues to rise and the dust devil-like trailing core continues to roll up into the leading vortex, which may become hundreds of metres high. However, the trailing core also draws cold air from the surroundings with it, which can reduce the buoyancy so much that its lower parts get left behind.

Thermals vary in size, but the largest ones can be huge – several hundred metres across and stretching from ground to cloudbase. As a cubic metre of air weighs just over a kilogram, a small thermal 100m across and 200m tall will weigh over a thousand tons.

When you remember that the air that initially formed the thermal was in contact with the ground and therefore stationary, or at least moving slower than the wind, you can see that once they get going, thermals have enormous momentum.

41

Useful features

Five useful features of thermals are:

- At the top of the leading vortex air is moving outwards away from the centre of the thermal.
- At the side of the leading vortex the air outside the core is descending.
- Below the leading vortex air is being entrained into the trailing core of the thermal.
- At the centre of the core the air rotates about a vertical axis like a dust devil.
- Thermals initially drift more slowly than the wind, but the wind pushes against them, distorting and accelerating them.

Encountering the top of the leading vortex

The only place where we regularly encounter the top of the vortex is when a new thermal pushes through a site where we are slope soaring. If you are tracking along a hill as a new thermal comes through, it can feel as if a giant hand has grabbed your wing and pushed you aside.

In this case the correct response is to turn to oppose the giant hand. However, this situation is rare – if you had been beating back and forth along a ridge with no thermals and then encountered the giant hand, you might reasonably assume a new thermal was pushing through.

In general, though, it is more common to hit the side of the leading vortex, or the trailing core of the thermal. The movement of the wing and the air is completely different (in fact opposite) in those cases, compared with the top of the thermal.

Hitting the side of the leading vortex

At the side of the leading vortex the air is descending. This means that the first sign of the presence of a thermal may be sink rather than lift. The leading vortex may have a regular structure but shearing between the 'up' and 'down' air produces turbulence. Therefore, as well as sink, turbulence may be the first thing you detect when passing a thermal.

The turbulence generated by thermals is, however, not entirely unstructured. Often there appear to be regular patches of lift and sink radiating from the thermal core like the ripples that spread out from a stone hitting water. These ripple-like disturbances can provide information about where the thermal is – if you hit the ripples at an angle, then they affect one side of the wing first. Turning towards that side will take you towards the core of the thermal.

In practice you often hit sink and then lift, and then sink again. Keep going through this sink to find the core. Often it will feel as if one wing hits the sink first and you should turn towards that wing to find the core. The weak lift surrounding a strong thermal can cause considerable confusion and pilots often end up circling in this weaker lift rather than pushing on to find the much stronger lift in the core – especially if the thermal is stronger than usual.

The best way to avoid this problem is by building up a picture of the expected thermal strength on any given day. If you are flying on a day during which the previous best-climb rates have been around 7m/s, then it is likely that a patch of 3m/s lift is the weak stuff surrounding a core rather than the core itself.

Hitting the trailing core

Below the leading vortex there tends to be much less turbulence, and the thermal is less likely to be surrounded by sink. Instead, air being drawn into the thermal can actually cause the glider to be pulled towards the core.

Again, it feels as if a giant hand has grabbed the glider and is pulling you sideways through the air. In this case you have to go with the flow of air to find the core. The sideways drift can be difficult to detect if you are high

"Thermals are difficult prey – invisible and elusive "

and it is essential to monitor ground drift carefully all the time. GPS can help with this. However, many gliders will tend to follow the flow of the air – to some extent anyway. Top pilots, including British team member Russell Ogden, advocate allowing the glider to follow its own path and go with the flow, rather than forcing it along a straight path.

Whether you hit the leading vortex or the trailing core of the thermal, its centre will be marked by a rotating core like the middle of a dust devil – though with less concentrated energy. Flying through this rotating core provides a unique feeling when the wing twists briefly as you hit the rotating air and then recovers. It can almost feel as if the wing has been punched. A bit disconcerting – but at least it tells you that you have found the core of the thermal.

Thermals in wind

Thermals can have enormous mass and it can take some time for this mass to accelerate laterally to the speed of the prevailing wind. This allows some thermals to block the wind. While this is happening they can adopt a rolling structure, as the upwind edge is blown downwind round both sides of the thermal. This means that the strongest lift is often found at the upwind edge of the thermal.

Thermals in strong wind get blown over – like smoke out of a chimney. In these conditions as you circle you descend through the thermal, but because the thermal is tilted you descend towards its lower, downwind

edge. It is not uncommon to fall out of the downwind side of a thermal, and since the strongest lift is often at the upwind edge of the thermal, it pays to extend the into-wind part of your 360s so that you stay near the upwind edge of the thermal.

Thermals blocking the wind can also provide temporary lulls. If you are soaring along a slope and suddenly find it much easier than usual to push upwind, that may be a very good sign that there is a thermal kicking off somewhere out in front of the hill. A search upwind may well pay off.

How steeply should you bank?

You should bank as steeply as necessary to stay in the strongest part of the lift. In general, inexperienced XC pilots do not bank enough, and it is often possible to climb through gaggles because pilots are not turning steeply enough to stay in the strongest part of the core all the way round a 360.

It often pays to crank the glider round steeply in the lower parts of the thermal where the core is particularly narrow. Bank angles of well over 30 degrees are entirely reasonable. When you rise with the thermal and it becomes bigger and better structured, it may be possible to make flatter turns, but that rarely seems to provide any improvement in climb rate. It always seems to be much more important to concentrate on finding the strongest core than to worry about bank angles.

Does the wing fall back or surge forwards as you enter a thermal?

Depending on the strength of the thermal, where you hit it and the glider you are flying, it can do either! If you are fortunate enough to hit the rising air directly, most wings will feel as if they are trying to 'bite' forward. If you enter the raggy part, it may well feel as if it is trying to hang back. However, there are no hard and fast rules: gliders have their own habits. If the lift is extremely strong, then your glider may fall back as you meet it and you then may have to wait for it to dive so that you can turn into the core.

In the UK where we fly very small hills, a good way to find thermals on days when the wind is too weak to soar is to stand kiting the wing above your head on the edge of the hill. As a thermal arrives, the wing will surge forwards and even with full brake on will sit in front of you trying to pull you off the hill. That is the time to launch – in fact if the thermal is strong you may not have any choice.

Senses

There are always clues to where the next thermal is going to be found. Visual cues such as thermalling birds, other gliders, thistledown or airborne debris of any kind are important. However, sight isn't the only sense that can help us in the thermal search: feeling the motion of the air through the risers is at least as valuable because large-scale air movements can push you away from the core if you are near the top of the thermal, or pull you towards it lower down.

Sense of smell and touch play a part too. Thermals often carry smells up from the ground and they are sometimes so warm relative to the surrounding air that your skin can easily feel them. Turbulent mixing can mean that both the smells and the warm air extend out some distance away from the thermal itself. Even sound can help: thermals

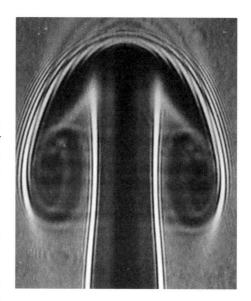

may even also make a noise – a sort of rushing sound – particularly as they break through an inversion or as they pass through foliage up a ridge.

Thermals are difficult prey – invisible and elusive – but that is probably why they are so much fun to chase. And, as you can see, there are all sorts of clues.

NEED TO KNOW

- For flying XC finding thermals is the most important skill to master
- It helps if you understand how a thermal moves
- Usually we hit the side of thermals, not the top
- That means we fly through sink first, and turbulence
- That turbulence is not unstructured – it has ripples of lift and sink radiating out
- Keep going until you find the core
- Once in the core, stay in it. Turn, bank up, lean in, turn tighter
- Stay alert – use your senses

THE LIFE OF A CUMULUS CLOUD

By Tom Bradbury

RESEARCH suggests that in a field of cumulus cloud only about 10% of the air contains useful lift. When there are a lot of moderate-sized cumuli one can expect at least half the clouds to have little or no lift under them when you arrive. Here are some suggestions meant for cross country pilots looking for lift under cumulus.

The ideal cumulus is distressingly rare. Most people know what it should look like. It has a flat level base, a crisply-defined bubbly top with no hairy bits or fuzzy patches, and a cross-section rather like an equilateral triangle. It is neither too tall nor too flat. Taken together they are evenly distributed, like trees in a well-kept orchard. If high resolution satellite pictures are any guide, this state of affairs is uncommon in many places.

To get these ideal cumuli requires a moderate depth of instability, air which is relatively dry and a wind field with little vertical shear. For most of the summer we have to put up with an inferior brand of cloud and learn to make the best of it.

Shallow cumulus

- If cloud centres fail to work well look for edges that show the most rotation or movement.
- Only search the areas of the cloud that are clearly growing
- If a cloud shows signs of decay, look to the sides for signs of new wisps forming, especially upwind or downwind in breezes stronger than 15km/h
- When low, finding heavy sink can be a good sign: look carefully at the cloud for a building edge and the corresponding lift
- Allow for wind drift: when low, search slightly upwind of the cloud
- Prepare to leave before cloudbase due to small latent heat generation (heat energy released by vapour condensing into cloud forming water droplets).

Bigger cumulus

- Stay high to use latent heat effects
- Look for the darkest, most defined base with a concave shape
- Look for tendrils of cloud and centre directly underneath them
- When there is a recognised step in cloudbase, always search on the higher side
- Be very wary when there is no sun underneath a promising cloud, especially if you are low: watch out for cycling.

Life of a cumulus

Judging by the radio chatter, some pilots have an exaggerated idea of how long a thermal lasts. One pilot will call a partner from many miles away to give the location of a thermal. Most thermals will usually have changed or died out long before the partner gets there. But with luck another may grow in the vicinity to support the laggardly pilot.

It is well to be aware of the life span of cumuli; one can get badly out of phase by sticking too long in a weak thermal, planning to step across to a better looking cloud after gaining a little more height. By the time you at last make the move the next cloud has grown tired of waiting and has shut up shop.

Cumulus clouds often look better from the side

If you look back at the feeble cloud you have just left it may appear much better now. Perhaps it had a new injection of thermals since you left it. Be warned – many cu look much better from the side than from below. Some apparently well-formed clouds look fine from a distance; when you arrive below them they turn out to be badly decayed. However, if your last cloud had lost all its lift before you left, it will usually be dissolving into shreds when you look back.

What controls the lifespan of a thermal?

The lifetime depends on:

1. The mass of air in the cloud and the number of thermals which continue to refresh it. The bigger a cloud grows, the longer it takes to dissolve but it may

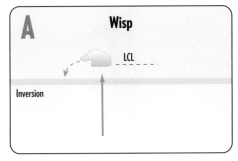

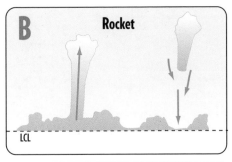

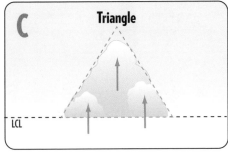

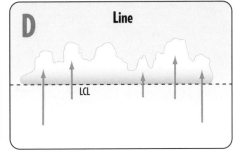

▲ **Cumulus clouds form when medium-level air is lifted above a different condensation level (LiftedCL)**

A: It is common for the ephemeral puffs or wisps of white which appear just above a strong inversion to disperse in under a minute. By the time you have spotted them the thermal is almost finished. With luck there will be another one along soon. If the puff formed just below the inversion (where the air is usually more moist), it often marks a new thermal which lasts just long enough to give a climb.

B: Tall narrow cumuli nearly always have a brief life. These 'rocket clouds' shoot up in five minutes or less and dissolve two minutes later. The proper name for these towers is 'castellanus'; I think 'rocket' says more.

C: Cumuli with a roughly triangular shape have a moderate lifetime; many seem to survive 10 or 15 minutes but they may be revived by fresh thermals. When this happens you can watch them start to decay and then rebuild in a different shape.

D: Cumuli which form a line often consist of several turrets side by side. These may last half an hour or more, especially if they have formed over a line of hills with sunny slopes.

become almost inert for the last part of its life.
2. How dry the surrounding air is. Evaporation is slower in moist air so the cumuli take longer to evaporate. In contrast cu which penetrate into very dry air (often found above an inversion) disperse very quickly.

In the morning there is seldom a large reservoir of warm air waiting to form thermals. As a result clouds may only receive one or two thermals. The poor little cumulus is starved of energy and soon decays.

In the afternoon cumuli are usually fed by many more thermals so their lifetime is longer. Timelapse films show these cumuli are maintained by several new surges of life. Any one thermal has a short life but the general effect is to produce a moderate-sized cloud with a lifetime of 15 to 30 minutes.

It takes practice to tell if a cloud is building or dissipating. Curls and horns of cloud are one sign that the cloud is building and there will be lift. The curl is formed by the wind blowing over the top and shows that the thermal is pumping energy into the cloud. "Looking at these clues gives me some idea what to expect from the climbs," says Helen who took these photos, "Fingers of cloud suggest little tight cores you need to hang onto."

Life of a cloud ▶

Helen Gant (UK) captured this sequence of a cumulus cloud building as she headed towards it while on glide during a cross country flight in England.

It's a fizzing spring day, with some overdevelopment and quickly building clouds. Helen has her eye on the small cloud left of centre.

Drifting as she climbs she takes a mental snapshot of the cloud every couple of turns. It's growing, developing a small cloud on its right.

As Helen takes another climb and tops up the the cloud on the right looks like it is becoming bigger. Sunlight shows the expansion.

With sun shining on the other side of the cloud and on the ground it continues to grow. The cloud on the right is starting to dominate.

Cloudbase is darker, becoming slightly ragged and there is an indent. This is where the strongest lift will be.

The same scene a few minutes later. The short-lived curl is now on the wane, which means the energy is less. However, now the most active bit looks like the right-hand side – you can sense the expansion. Looking further afield you can see much more evolved clouds. Expect this one to turn into one of those quite soon. It's time to go hands-up, push the bar and get there.

The two small clouds are consol-idating, with better bases and a definite step between them. She sets off on glide.

Both clouds are building quickly, growing in height and bulk with the start of a domed undersurface and a more pronouced step.

Getting closer and it's still building. Vertical development is increasing on the left while the right-hand side is expanding in bulk too.

Now clearly dominant you can sense the lift powering through. Sunlit wisps show it's active all around. Lift at base will be strong.

Helen lines up her approach so she is aiming for the right-hand and sunny side of the cloud, avoiding any potential cloudsuck.

She's there, arriving high and close to base she doesn't even need to turn, simply straight-lining it and going up. Time to pick the next.

Cumulonimbus clouds are taller than they are wide.
They're too strong to fly near safely.
Photo: Professional Flying Team (www.profly-images.org)

Long-lived clouds

A cumulonimbus large enough to produce a substantial shower can grow to maturity within half an hour and, if no fresh supplies arrive, collapse into shreds soon afterwards. Monster cu-nim which develop into 'supercells' no longer depend on a stream of individual thermals. These clouds form in a type of wind shear which separates the warm moist updraft from cold, rain-bearing downdrafts. The lift becomes a continuous process like a steeply sloping conveyor belt. Near the top the conveyor belt becomes almost vertical. At the top it turns horizontal as it encounters a much stronger wind which blows the air away as a long anvil-shaped cloud. The strong wind seems to act like an extractor fan carrying the air away instead of letting it fall back as sink. (But there are still areas of ferocious sink elsewhere!) As a result these monsters have a lifetime of many hours; they can persist through the night and keep going even if the storm moves over the sea.

▶15 minutes in the life of a cumulus

A is at minute one, a few seconds after the puff forms. If you are nearby this is the cloud to aim for because the thermal is usually fresh and vigorous.

B is at minute three; a second thermal has shot up to produce another little cu alongside. It usually appears on the upwind side.

C at minute six shows the second thermal becoming dominant and making a taller cloud.

D at minute nine shows this taller turret curling over in the wind aloft and perhaps forming a short-lived hook. Meanwhile a new thermal has produced another cell, sometimes with a small step between the two cloudbases.

E at minute twelve shows the first signs of degeneration. Hooklets, spiky prongs and fuzzy edges are usually signs of the dry wind aloft twisting the cloud top over and evaporating the bubbly domes into spikes or hairy bits.

F is the last stage before the cloud disappears. All sign of the cumulus has gone, leaving a wispy mess with only sink under it.

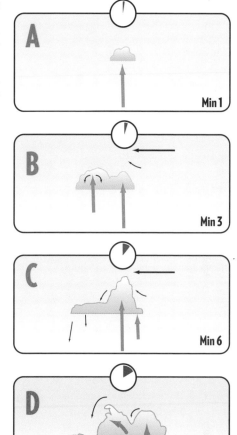

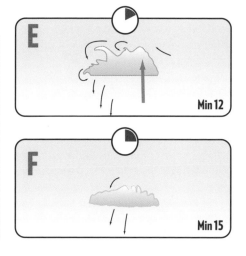

NEED TO KNOW

- On a good XC day 10% of the air is lift
- Perfect cumulus are rare
- A working cu lasts around 15 minutes
- But new thermals can feed into the cloud, making it work for longer
- Clouds often look better from the side than they are
- Cumuli in the afternoon are better for us than in the morning
- Watch clouds and learn their life-cycle

THERMALLING TECHNIQUES

By Bruce Goldsmith

FINDING the best lift in a thermal is one of the most vital skills in flying. Half of competition flying is about climbing the fastest, the other half is about gliding. For the recreational pilot, flying around above your friends is always a kind of private competition, but it's not easy; lift is invisible and there is no easy way of knowing where to find the best core.

The classic technique

When you approach a strong thermal you can actually feel it sucking you in. You can feel the air flowing in towards the thermal. If you are flying into a headwind then it is suddenly easier to penetrate into wind, or if you are going downwind your groundspeed increases as the thermal sucks you in. This sucking only happens with really strong thermals, but it can be used to feel if there is a strong thermal off to your side when you suddenly feel yourself being pulled sideways. The sucking happens before you actually enter any lift, and tells you this is going to be a really good thermal.

When you first enter lift and the vario starts to beep, pay careful attention to the feedback you get through your harness from the air as the wing rides the thermal. You are going to have to turn one way or the other, so from the very first beeps of the vario you should be trying to decide which way you are going to go. If you feel more lift under one side of the glider, and you feel it lift that side of the harness with pressure building in the respective brake line, then the centre of the thermal will be off that way as well.

The ideal way to thermal is to turn around the core where the lift is strongest. Normally when you enter a thermal the vario will indicate weak lift. Don't turn right away: just relax, concentrate on visualising the shape of the thermal, and try to make your first turn where you guess the core will be. As you fly towards the core the lift will get stronger and stronger and the vario will sing out.

Wait until you have flown past the place where the lift is the strongest before turning. In a strong core of 4m/s plus, usually two seconds past the core brings you back to circle around it. Remember to use the feedback from the wing to decide how tightly you turn. If the pressure is uniform, then you can afford a large circle, but when it feels punchy and rips up one half of the wing, then don't be afraid to really crank it up. One wrong move at this stage can mean you drop out of the side of the thermal and lose it completely!

> " Don't turn right away: just relax "

The turn reversal

There is another useful trick I sometimes use. When I first enter a thermal and am unsure as to which way to turn, it often means I am exactly in the centre of the core. Whether you do a left or a right 360 doesn't matter: either way you are going to fall out of the side (especially if it is a small thermal). So I make a quarter turn to the left as I enter the core then reverse the turn, leaning hard right to immediately make a right-hand 360. The quarter turn enables you to alter course just before the core so your first 360 can be better centred on the core.

Keep working

Once you have made your first guess as to where the core is, it is not over. Thermals constantly change shape and strength as they thrust their way skyward through wind, temperature changes and small inversions. The process of re-centring your 360 should continue constantly. Keep feeling the feedback from the glider as you turn and try to work out if the lift is better in one part of the turn than another. When you get a surge of lift, straighten up for a couple of seconds and then turn again around this new core. Often new bubbles of air join the main column and push through, creating a new core.

Picking a winner

When you are looking for the best core in a thermal, it is not as simple as trying to find the winning horse in a horse race. The winning horse is simply the one that crosses the line first. Thermalling is more complicated. When trying to climb as fast as possible in a thermal you always want to be on the leading horse, and the leading horse at the start will probably

53

▲ CLASSIC TECHNIQUE
Half the circle falls outside the lift

▲ THE TURN REVERSAL
Ensures that the complete 360 is in the lift

not be the same horse that crosses the line first at the end. So if you were doing the same thing in a horse race as you do when you are flying you would be jumping from horse to horse, always trying to be on the the fastest.

Never be outclimbed

If someone outclimbs me in a thermal I take it as a personal insult! There should be no reason for someone to outclimb you from below, not even a bird. Paragliders and hang gliders all have pretty much the same sink rate, so if someone is outclimbing me then it is because they are in faster rising air. So I would immediately go over to join them.

When I say join them, I mean exactly that. Not three metres to the left or right, I mean exactly the same circle. It is important because they have already been climbing, trying to find the best place for some time, so a very good place to start is where they are. When you are in exactly the same circuit as them, then you can try to search for better lift.

Try upwind

If you have been in a thermal and have either lost it or want to find the core, and there are no other indicators around (birds or gliders), then searching upwind is a good bet. When a

thermal is released from a source it will drift with the wind. Weak thermals will drift more than strong thermals. For this reason if you are in a weak thermal, then it is quite likely that looking upwind will give you a stronger thermal from the same thermal source. When flying upwind the lift may increase and increase – I normally keep going upwind until the lift starts to decrease again, then I turn back to turn in the area of strongest lift that I have just flown through. It is surprising how often this thermalling trick works.

THERMALLING ON A STABLE DAY

By Bob Drury

THERE is simply nothing worse than a stable day with weak thermals and lots of turbulence. They are generally lots of stress for little reward, but if you want to be a good all-round pilot you have to learn to fly in all conditions. So here's what to do.

First, understand why it's rough on stable days. Stable days are caused by high pressure systems where the air particles are generally sinking earthwards. That alone makes a thermal's ascent more difficult, but in mountains you generally need to be in a high pressure to get good flying conditions; low pressure produces too much instability and it storms. Worse still, sinking air particles cause adiabatic compression which creates heat. This forms bands of warmer air which we call inversions. Inversions trap air beneath them which then warms up more than on unstable days where the upper and lower air gets mixed more by thermals.

The net result is that it is harder for thermals to form and harder still for them to rise once they have enough buoyancy to actually break free of the ground. As the air is warm and stable there is a low temperature difference between the thermal and the air it's travelling through, so the climb rates are weak. As the air surrounding the thermal is almost the same temperature as the air inside the thermal it doesn't take long until all the weak lift dissolves into the surrounding air. All that is left are tiny hotspots or micro cores. Sharp edged and rocket-like in comparison to the soupy air you're flying in, they hit you like missiles out of the blue and you're through them and out the other side before you've had time to think "What the hell was that?" There's the roughness on an otherwise weak day.

Success on these days requires a combination of two separate tactics.

Search mode: wide and slow. Covering as much ground as possible with the best sink rate. The chances are you'll encounter wide areas of weak lift in the general stable ambiance.

Climb mode: tight and fast. When you hit the micro cores crank as hard and tight as you dare and hang on for your life. You might only get half a turn in lift, but crank it round the whole 360 and see if you hit it again. Often you can climb like this in little surges with only half your circle in lift. Watch your averager to see if it's working.

▲ Unstable day: large area of more consistent lift and large, smoother cores

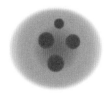

▲ Stable day: area of weak lift with tight, 'bullet' cores

THERMALLING ON WINDY DAYS

By Bob Drury

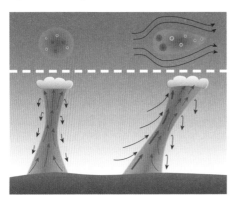

▲ WIND POWER
The difference between a thermal on a nil-wind day and a windy day from the side, and from above.

IN NIL-WIND thermals form like mushroom clouds with a main core dotted with hotspots, but in the wind it all changes. Wind distorts the column of lift, tilting it at an angle. Because a thermal has its own mass the wind blows around it and up it rather like a mountain face. That airflow produces dynamic lift. If you have ever soared up the outside of a cumulus cloud you will have experienced this.

The airflow around the sides and behind a thermal also gets disturbed in the same way it would if the thermal was more solid, like a tall building. This causes turbulence and can be a cause of those unexpected whacks you sometimes get on thermic days.

Inside the thermal are hotspots, or micro cores, the stuff we love. They are formed by hotspots on the ground. Cores travel upwards faster than the rest of the thermal. They have a greater vertical velocity than the weaker lift so they are less affected by the horizontal wind.

The cumulative effect is that the weaker lift gets blown to the downwind side of the thermal, while the stronger cores remain at the upwind side. This is why we should always work the upwind side of the thermal to find the strongest lift. Do this by extending your 360s slightly when facing into the wind. When you reach the edge of the thermal you sometimes get an extra surge in lift as you hit the dynamic lift on the outside of the thermal. Push too far and fall out of the upwind side of the thermal and you only have a quick downwind dash straight back in.

In comparison, the downwind side of the thermal is bleak. The lift is weaker and should you slip out of it you fall into the leeside sink and have an upwind struggle to get back in. When you do, you arrive back in the weakest lift. If you've ever been thermalling with another pilot and seen them plummet like a stone, you know they've found the downwind edge of the thermal for you.

NEED TO KNOW

- Wind distorts the thermal, tilting it over
- Weak lift gets blown to the back of the thermal
- Stronger cores punch through and stay upwind
- Find the strongest lift by working the upwind side of the thermal

LEARNING TO CLIMB FASTER

By Bruce Goldsmith

THERMALLING is probably the most important part of flying, as well as the most pleasurable. The feeling of using the natural energy of rising air is a pleasure similar to surfing an invisible wave. But the pleasure of thermalling like a bird is also closely linked to the feeling of being connected to the air through your wing. The better you are in harmony with your equipment the more you will enjoy the feeling of thermalling.

In this article I will explain how to climb faster, using Feeling, Observation and Understanding. Any textbook can give you the beginners' theory, but these are slightly more unique tips, from firsthand experience.

Feeling

Feeling is what a bird uses to thermal better. It is an instinct, a way of feeling the air and using the information you get to better use the thermal. It is hard to put this into words because it is instinctive. Some pilots naturally have a lot of feeling for the air – they just seem to be born with it. It is all about the decision to search out new, stronger areas of lift or to stay and climb in the strongest lift you are in. This balance of whether to search or to stay is super important and is one of the factors that defines a great pilot.

Observation

In your search for the best lift, observation is one of your most important tools. There can be many different visual clues as to where the best lift might be. The most obvious is other gliders or birds climbing better than you, but also insects being swept up in the core of the thermal or even a few stems of grass, a plastic bag or a single dry leaf can give you the vital clue to where the best lift is. My favorite is swallows: they fly super fast and are hard to see, but they constantly search out the best lift, flipping from one updraught to another in their endless quest for insects to eat. I often try to follow their wavy path through the sky, more out of interest to try to understand how these incredible birds fly rather than just to find the best lift.

Understanding

Having an overall understanding of the thermal is also an important part of thermalling. This means understanding the overall picture. Try to understand where the thermal came from, what was the thermal source. Also look at where the thermal is going to. By that I mean look at the cloud formations above you and try to understand if your thermal will form a new cloud or if it is going to join part of an existing cloud formation. Looking at what the clouds have been doing over that area in the last 15 minutes will give you some good clues about how to answer this question. You will have seen those speeded-up films of cloud formations bubbling up – try to picture your thermal in that speeded-up film and this will give you some clues as to where to look for the best lift.

Hints on climbing

1. Use little brake and more weightshift

Modern gliders have changed significantly from their older counterparts and the way you need to fly them in thermals has also changed. Because the wings are more efficient, the speed to achieve the best sink rate has gone up. In the old days you could boat around with lots of brake on and float your way to the top of the stack. Nowadays the min sink is very close to trim speed and so applying as little brake as possible gives the best sink rate. This means that weightshift is a more efficient way of turning than using the brakes. This also means that you will be flying faster in thermals which makes it harder to stay in the core, so more concentration and skill is required to stay in the core using this technique.

2. Do not use trimmers in the slow position

If you are flying a glider that is equipped with trimmers, you may automatically think that applying the trimmers to the slowest position gives the best sink rate. However, this is often not the case, particularly if the thermal is strong or rough. The trouble is that you lose handling and bite when you apply full slow trimmers. The reduction in handling means that it may be harder to core the thermal efficiently. By 'bite' I mean the tendency of the glider to surge forward and fly again when it encounters turbulence or strong lift. If you have your trimmers on slow then the glider may tend to sit back a little sometimes and you will not get the best climb rate out of it. The only time I use full-trimmers-slow is when the lift is extremely weak and smooth, such as in the evening. In this case you do not need great handling and there are no gusts to stall the wing either so you can gain from the slightly improved sink rate the slow trim position brings.

3. Try to turn in the best lift

It may be a rather obvious statement but you should make every effort to try to turn the sharpest when you are in a surge of lift. This means that you will spend longer in the lift. Also, the surge of lift will go some way to compensate for the reduced sink rate you get when you turn. I often try to imagine that I am grabbing hold of a lump of rising air with my brake when I turn sharply into a bubble of lift.

4. Never be content with the lift you are in, continually search for better

Thermalling is a never-ending search for stronger lift using all your senses. Never be content with the lift you are in, continually search for better, and search for new areas of lift using all the information at your disposal, what you see and feel through your harness as well as through the brakes. Thermalling is a kind of state of mind, each thermal is different and an invisible puzzle to explore so you get the fastest climb out of it. That's what makes thermalling such a pleasure.

NEED TO KNOW

- Some pilots have a natural feeling for thermalling, others need to develop it
- Observation is key: birds, other gliders, things in the wind, even smell
- Understand the thermal: look at ground sources and the clouds
- Use weightshift
- Turn in the best lift
- Never stop searching

▲ **DIP IT IN HONEY**
Thermals, like honey, are fairly sticky. It takes imagination to
work out where they will come from and where they will go.
Photo: Ed Ewing

PREDICTING WHERE THERMALS WILL BE

By Bob Drury

AT SOME point in your training you've probably been told about the 'syrup theory'. Take a 3D map of the terrain you fly over, cover it in syrup, turn it upside down, and the syrup will drip off from the same places that the thermals would leave the ground. This is a very accurate, if messy way of understanding thermal routes, because thermals, like syrup, are fairly sticky.

Despite their inherent buoyancy, thermals are still reluctant to leave the ground. Instead they prefer to roll along or up the landscape, until they are either triggered or run out of ground to stick to. In the mountains, thermal routes are fairly easy to work out as the valley winds and anabatic circulation tend to move the thermals along and force them up the terrain.

Low down you should look for any big, steep slope that faces into the valley flow. Don't worry about the thermal's source – it's not as important in the mountains as it is

in the flats. If there's wind on the face and a cloud above you, you're almost certainly OK.

If the face is in the sun too, there's even more chance of finding good lift. The slope will not only be channelling thermals up, it will probably be producing thermals itself. This helps to pull even more air towards your slope, and increases your chances even further.

On a good thermic day with decent convection, you can often soar in the dynamic lift of the valley flow until a thermal comes along – even if you happen to be low at the time. Once a thermal does come along and collides with a face, it will start to rise, so hop in and start circling.

Low down, gullies that face the wind are good places to find lift – they act like collection points for the wind and thermals that are channelled into them. Once dragged in and climbing up a gully, a thermal will try to take the most direct and vertical route possible to cloudbase that still keeps it in touch with the terrain. So unless the gully is very steep, the thermal will soon climb out of the back of the gully and try to take a more direct route to the sky.

Often a thermal will roll up the side walls of a gully until it finds a spine to follow. Spines offer thermals an easy route to the sky, and once rolling up one, there is often no other possible route to take. The thermal will then stick to the feature until it either reaches a peak, or the feature sharply decreases in angle, causing the thermal to break free.

However, if you are flying in a crosswind from either a valley flow or meteo wind, the thermal's route might well take it diagonally across the face until it reaches a 'breakaway' point. This is where the terrain turns, and causes the thermal to let go. Any sudden change in angle of the terrain along the thermal's route is a potential breakaway point.

When you're trying to predict a route, you

should study the terrain very carefully for breakaway points. They can be hard to spot, and to the untrained eye the best breakaway point can sometimes look like the worst place in the world to go, as they are quite often not dynamically soarable.

Once high on mountainous terrain, you should try to fly over the points on the landscape that the thermals break away from. As mountains are often complicated structures, there might well be several 'obvious' points to go for, so check the airflow that supplies each one. One that faces straight into the sun and the valley flow will be good, but a peak with spines and gullies that drop into two or three different valley flows will be

"Low down, gullies that face the wind are good places to find lift"

even better.

The more routes a breakaway point can take air from, the more likely it is to work. The clouds will prove this by showing you which points on the mountain are working better than others. The best lift will be producing the best cloud and even from a long way off you should be able to judge the points on the mountain that are working best.

Because wind likes to gather in gullies whilst thermals prefer to run up spines, the pilot who glides on to a spine stands a better chance of catching a proper 'moonbeam'. However, they do also carry the risk of finding nothing.

The pilot who glides to the back of the steep gully will almost certainly be able to soar and stay up, but is less likely to connect with a ripper that blasts them straight to base. The choice is yours, but given any height, it is generally better always to go for the spine, saving the gully for when you are really low and in need of something dynamic to wait on.

An interesting point to add to your growing picture is a thermal's inability to go back downhill. Any type of col, no matter how slight, will cause thermals to trigger. Sometimes the vaguest of cols can end up producing fantastic lift, if a decent valley wind blows over it, particularly if the valley wind has just blown over terrain that's producing

good thermals – such as a town. This is a fantastic flatland trick too.

Finally, once you've identified the best thermal route and committed yourself to it, then believe in it. If you're in the best spot to find a good thermal, there is no point in panicking and charging off to a worse place. Just sit tight and pray that a cycle with your name on it comes through and carries you out. Only move if you can definitely reach a better place with enough height to climb, or if you see a definite sign of good lift like another glider climbing.

NEED TO KNOW

- The syrup theory is a good starting point for working out where thermals will drip off the landscape
- Thermals like to roll along the ground until they hit a trigger, or run out of terrain
- Wind likes to gather in gullies whilst thermals prefer to run up spines
- Look for breakaway points – any change in the angle of terrain
- Look for triggers downwind of towns – the air warms up and can easily trigger
- Believe in your decisions – go there, now
- Only move if you can definitely reach a better place

▲ PREPARE TO SUCCEED
And you will. Photo: Al Wilson

LEARNING TO FLY CROSS COUNTRY

By Patrick Laverty

THE KEY is attitude and confidence. Start by eliminating all potential excuses not to fly XC. Be well prepared before going to the hill:

- Personal items: wallet and mobile phone

- Car prepared: money, petrol and SatNav. Also, most important, keys in the car if you're organising a shared retrieve.

- Navigational items: GPS, good XC map and pen. You should be able to navigate

without a GPS – spend time studying your map on those winter evenings.

- Comfort and warmth: dress as if you will spend hours at cloudbase, even on hot days. Warm clothes and gloves. Does your helmet tip forward into your eyes? Will your balaclava restrict vision? Does your harness pinch anywhere? Eliminate any irritants.

- Equipment: good batteries in your vario and GPS? Hitching sign. Mine is a folded

"Everybody has to make the short hops first"

card with 'Glider pilot. Lift Please!' – it works every time.

- Bladder: empty it before take-off. The damp and cold at cloudbase reaches the bladder very quickly. Many pilots use catheters, like the XCPee system.

- Drink: carry a drinks bladder, or at least a carton of juice. Dehydration causes tiredness and destroys concentration.

- Communication: Sort phone numbers out with your mates before take-off.

Just go

Many pilots develop such an affinity for their mother flying site that they can't leave its security and head off into the unknown. This can be a huge psychological barrier but it can be broken down by repeated short hops over the back. Everybody has to make the short hops first, and the sooner they are out of the way the better. Don't expect 50km on your first XC. Plan for 10km and then your confidence will not be dented.

Think for yourself

With all the preparation done you should be cruising up and down your home site like a hungry shark looking for escape. The first thing to learn is to start operating on your own – don't follow others around the sky. By all means use them as thermal indicators and take advantage if they find lift within reach, but if you chase others, often you get there just in time for the sink.

Independent thinking is called for on the ground as well as in the air. I have noticed that many pilots will spend the majority of a flyable day sitting on the hill. If you are apprehensive then it is very comforting to join a group of like-minded individuals and stay put on terra firma. Unfortunately, lethargy and negative thinking thrive in this environment. There is usually some part of the day when you can get away and it is best to be waiting for it, preferably in the air. If you just do the odd five-minute hop, you will be lucky to meet a decent thermal. If you fly for a few hours you will be unlucky not to.

Make your own luck

Hunting for thermals way out in front of the ridge is often a waste of time. But fairly poor thermals get a nice kick-off from the ridge and often really lift off just behind it. So be prepared to thermal back, even when low, especially on a good flat-topped site. You will be amazed how often a scrappy broken thermal becomes bigger, smoother and better-formed behind take-off. To follow your thermal, keep your glider in steady smooth turns and don't let it tip you out. You may alter the radius to incorporate better areas of lift, but still keep your steady circle going. Some pilots develop a tendency while thermalling on a ridge to throw a quick 360, straighten for a while into wind, then another 360, etc. Do not do it! This leads out of the front of the thermal.

Bank it over

Get used to banking your glider over and leaving it there. This steady thermalling shows you the thermal drift and allows others to join in, thus marking out the limits of the thermal. Low down, thermals are rough and try their best to boot you out. Grit your teeth and fight and higher up you ought to be rewarded with a smoother, more pleasant climb. The better they are, the harder they fight, low down. Incidentally, don't forget to turn the same way as the first person in the thermal.

Heading for base

If you are climbing at a steady 2m/s up on average, you are probably heading for cloudbase. Thermals often have lots of little cores with less lift, or even sink between them and your circling may be like a rollercoaster ride. Keep it going and you may be rewarded when the cores get together to give one nice smooth area of lift. If the lift starts to die off, open your turn out much wider and often you'll find another area of lift nearby. On days of moderate wind you should be able to thermal to cloudbase and still make it back to mother ridge if you wish.

Keep going

But why go back? There you are in nice smooth lift which is surrounded by big sink. Straighten up even for a little while to decide and all your valuable height will disappear. So keep the monotonous circles going, calm down and try to relax. When experienced XC pilots depart from a hill they will often still be turning the same steady way 20 minutes later when they reach cloudbase. Do not rush about like a headless chicken. Don't worry about outlanding and remember that it may be harder to fly back to the ridge than to keep on going.

Have patience

On nearing cloudbase in active lift, don't go racing off downwind because there will be equally active sink. If there is wind, your thermal is drifting and so are you. It won't feel as if you are making much progress because of the height you are at, but you will be covering the miles. So work a drifting thermal or cloud until it dies, then head for the next likely-looking one.

As you climb to cloudbase, keep an eye on the cloud itself. In the old days we flew as close to cloud as possible! If it was very black and nasty looking we knew we had to avoid being sucked into it, so we would head towards the sunny side. We knew that the lift would be weaker at the edges and occasionally we could climb up the side, turning half in clear air and half in cloud. This was not as risky as it sounds because it was obvious where the sun was and the lift was usually very smooth. The sight of your 'glory' reflected on the side of the cloud is wonderful and emerging from the grey into clear air can be one of the great joys of flying.

Another way of dealing with vigorous clouds is to fly out into the sink, turn around tightly and back into lift, in a stretched 360. The transition from lift to sink at altitude is usually smooth. If your cloud is joined to another in the direction you want to go, try feeling your way along under it but do not fly past the end. Rather, sit under the last bit and try to spot the cloud marking your next thermal downwind.

Close to cloudbase it can be difficult to see the development downwind as there may be

▲ **ON THE DECK**
A well kitted-out cockpit. Photo: Al Wilson

bits of cloud hanging down obscuring the view. Cloud shadows on the ground are good indicators, but remember to allow for the angle of the sun. While all this is going on, your own cloud will be getting less active. You may be able to spot its shadow on the ground getting thinner and breaking up. If it is a day which is overdeveloping and the clouds are not decaying, then don't fly under large dark masses of cloud. You will not find lift. Go to wispy, straggly bits hanging down near the edges and search under them.

The next cloud

By the time you have milked your first thermal dry you should be able to pick the next part of the route. This will not necessarily be straight downwind. You may do better to go crosswind to an active cloud – the best ones are dark

underneath and look like milky cauliflower on top. Don't be put off by a sky which does not look 'classic', as some amazing-looking days are useless and others, with hardly a wisp in the sky, are super because more sun can get to the ground.

Follow the clouds

When flying XC, the clouds are our main guide; ground thermal sources and ridges are only of interest when getting low. Avoid flying into large blue areas if possible. Often, when you are flying out of high ground into lower flat land, you will find large blue holes where descending air suppresses thermals. These can be hard to cross. It is often worth deviating to keep over high ground as it works better than flatlands or valley bottoms. To improve your chances of connecting with your next cloud,

" Don't follow others around the sky "

try to fly under it from directly upwind. If you are forced to approach from the side, make allowances for the fact that the thermal is probably leaning downwind.

Gliding efficiently

When travelling between clouds, fly at maximum glide speed, but if there is no cloud to aim for, use minimum sink, as you will cover more ground and, therefore, more possible thermal sources. If in sink, speed up. When gliding to another cloud, do not be so determined to reach it that you ignore little blobs of turbulence you may meet while in apparently clear air. Often you can work such a little patch of lift on the way to your next cloud which develops into an even better cloud. Lovely! Also, you catch it at the start and not halfway through, like the one you were originally aiming for. Remember the rule: never leave lift! Between thermals, get your head down level with your shoulders and your feet up towards the keel to reduce drag on a hang glider. Stay absolutely still and do not move your body around. Try not to tense up or stuff your toes into the bottom of your harness when thermalling or gliding. It just wastes valuable energy.

Hang on

Between thermals watch your vario. If the sink starts to decrease or goes to zero, then do a large smooth 360. If you do not connect, elongate your 360 downwind. Hang on to a zero; quite often it will lift off and develop into an 'up'. If not, you are still travelling. Even a -0.5m/s thermal is worth a few 360s to see if a core is lurking nearby.

When you start getting below 650m above ground level start looking for thermal sources or soarable ridges. Thermals, low down, will probably be small and very vigorous. They do not want you aboard. So stay high and go far.

NEED TO KNOW

- The key is you: your attitude and confidence
- Prepare your gear so your mind is free to think about flying
- Make a plan and set a small goal
- Get high and drift with your climb – suddenly you'll find you're going cross country
- Stay with the lift – if the cloud is still working, drift, don't race off
- Head downwind towards something – a climbing glider, cloud or bird
- Stay high and go far
- Even if you only go a few kilometres, celebrate your success

▶**FIRST STEPS**
Flying a good, basic glider will free up your mind and
allow you to focus on making decisions.
Photo: Nova Gliders

FLYING XC ON AN EN A GLIDER

By Hugh Miller

YOUR first wing is your most important one. It is the bedrock of your flying career. You need to be totally comfortable on as safe a wing as possible as you slowly become familiar with the strange, turbulent, ever-changing world of the sky.

And with a modern EN A glider, you have the perfect wing to do just that. EN As climb as well – if not better – than other classes of wing, and I believe offer better 'real' performance for early pilots than any other. Simply put, they look after themselves and let you get on with the job of learning to fly really well. They're brilliant fun, too. I've flown recent XCs on an EN A, EN C and competition wing: the EN A was by far the most enjoyable wing, dispelling all my ideas of dull handling. It was pure joy.

Some would say you shouldn't move on from your first wing until you've perfected your launches, thermalled it to base, set off on your first cross countries and finally wrung the life out of it on an SIV course.

The reasoning is this: as a new pilot, your workload in the air is phenomenally high. You have so much to think about to stay safe. During your first 200 hours, you're looking to convert as much of that workload to intuition as possible, so the basics – ground-handling, glider control, thermalling and gliding efficiently and safely on speedbar – become second-nature. This'll allow you to free up some mental space to deal with decision-making, route-planning and so on – and only

then are you ready to fly a higher aspect wing.

Indeed, most pilots move on from their first wing far, far too quickly, sold on the empty promise of 'better performance', when in reality they would progress far quicker and become more natural pilots by flying their first wing to the absolute limit of their capabilities first.

Here are some pointers on flying a lower performance wing really well.

1. Learn to climb well

Low aspect wings climb tighter in the core than higher aspect wings. You can spin them up on a sixpence (and that's a figure of speech – no spins on my account, ok?), and crank them inside their higher aspect counterparts. That's why paragliders can outclimb sailplanes, despite their much poorer sink rates. We fly right in the strongest centre of the thermal core, while the sailplanes fly orbits around us in the weaker lift. The same principle applies to EN A wings. The right pilot should be able to outclimb competition wings with them.

2. Learn to ride low saves

Low aspect wings are easier to catch low saves with. Because they don't move about much, you can concentrate on the feel of the thermal. There's less 'wing' between you and the air. Rather than being busy managing a higher aspect wing, you're free to feel where your wing is being pulled and go with it. EN As can

help you find the core more easily. They're trimmed so they're really pitch stable, so you don't get so buffeted around in turbulence, meaning you can dial in really steady 360s. You'll need to learn to ride low saves, as you may well end up lower than your friends after each glide – but it's an essential skill.

3. Fly good lines

Your glide and speed won't be as good as pilots on high aspect Bs and Cs, so you have to learn to feel 'lifty' lines of air. They do exist. Competition pilot Nick Greece has this to say: "Following lines requires a feeling that is so 'black art' that it is impossible to put down in words what we are doing on a line sniff." Intrigued? Get practicing! Some hints: listen to your vario, and glide hands-up. Feel the subtle shifts through the risers and make very

tiny movements with your brakes to feel your way into lifty air.

Instructor and alpine guide Kelly Farina has been flying for years and chooses to fly low aspect wings over competition wings, and reminds us that "a good line on an intermediate paraglider will outperform a high performance glider on a bad line every time." Go downwind as much as possible and definitely don't race the others. Just concentrate on yourself and picking the right lines for your wing. You can overtake competition wings with the right lifty lines. And that's satisfying.

4. Climb right to the top

You won't be able to glide as far, so altitude is way more important than distance. The trick then is to really learn to work each climb right

66 Low aspect wings climb tighter 99

to the top. It's like the last few hundred feet to base are your golden time. Though it feels time to rush off, you have to really soak up the best of the climb on an A before picking a really close next target. Spend your time coring the climb, and in time you'll free up some space to think about your next move.

5. Avoid sink

Stay high and under cumulus, or milky patches to stay in good air, and stay on the upwind side of clouds. You don't get so many plan B, C or Ds because you don't have the reach, so fly conservatively. In lifty air paragliders are amazing – they glide for miles. But in sink it's a different game. I keep forgetting just how slowly we fly, and how quickly the clouds we head for can turn from mushroom dead certs to fat lumps of decay. Really, at 35km/h, we're not going any faster than a road bike. And when you're spending time in horrible sinky air, it really hurts. That's why high performance wings have such an advantage – they can cut faster and flatter through the slabs of sink, which drag lower performance wings down like weights of concrete.

6. Keep learning

To keep learning, make it your goal to keep learning. A lot of us get lazy, and think we'll get better just by going flying. We don't. We need to learn from our mistakes and set ourselves goals. Some might be, 'stay in the air for two hours', 'get right to cloudbase' or 'practise gliding on half speedbar'. Jot down some thoughts after each flight, and read them before your next one, so your learning is a continuous thread.

When you think you're ready to change to a higher performance wing, stop and ask yourself which of these you haven't yet done... and ask yourself again if you're really ready. Have you flown a few cross countries? Done an SIV course? Ridden a leeside thermal that feels like it wants your wing anywhere but in the core? Glided on full bar at cloudbase? Because you're only holding yourself back if you haven't yet mastered these skills on an EN A first.

NEED TO KNOW

- Your EN A wing is very capable of being flown cross country – the pilot is the deciding factor
- A good pilot on a basic wing will always outfly a bad pilot on a higher performance wing
- Feeling comfortable on a wing means you will fly it better – without a doubt
- Don't feel pressured to 'upgrade' too soon – put 100 hours on your first wing, SIV it, go XC on it

READING THE SKY AHEAD

By Jay Rebbeck

WHEN we're flying cross country, the picture as we look ahead is packed with potentially useful information to help us decide where to point the glider. While a fat cumulus cloud lying bang on track might seem the obvious place to go, that won't always be the best decision. If a hard right avoids that juicy cloud, but takes you to a cloud street or mountain ridge that runs for 20km and arcs back onto track, then which option would you choose?

The point is that we need to make decisions on two levels. As well as short-term decisions based on the weather immediately ahead, we also require a long-term strategy. This article looks at how short-term and long-term decision making might come into play when we're going places on ridges, in thermals, and, rarer for paraglider pilots but useful for hang glider and sailplane pilots, in wave. But before we decide where to go, we should first evaluate what's lying in front of us.

Types of cloud

Orographic cloud: any low-level, scuddy-looking cloud is bad news. A sign of very moist air, it offers little chance of soaring. Makes for interesting photos though.

Cumulus: the size, shape and colour of a cumulus tells us how good the lift will be. In general, look for the firmest, whitest clouds, with the flattest and best-defined bases. When arriving under a solid cloud, look directly up for discontinuities: a wavy line in the base where the cloud is darker on one side than the other. In Holland they call this the 'eye of the cloud'. It is the best indicator of excellent lift when seen in clouds that already looked very good. Don't confuse it with holes forming in deteriorating cu!

There is also a relationship between the vertical development of a cu and its life span. Assuming it's still active, with a well-defined base, the rule of thumb is that the deeper the cloud, the longer it will produce lift. When there are towering cumulus clouds ahead, you can expect lift to last for much longer than when they are very shallow. This should be considered when deciding whether to make a long glide to distant clouds.

Stratus (layer cloud): the problem with middle-level cloud is that it cuts out the sun's heating effects. There are often days where cu feed the stratus layer. The sun then burns holes in the stratus, allowing convection to start again, only for cu to fill the holes again. The trick is to monitor the cycle carefully and remember that on these days, sunshine is king. When there is sheet cloud cover ahead without sun on the ground, always get high. Only get low when arriving under developing cu being fed by strong sunshine!

Altocumulus: these are totally useless to us. They are formed from middle-layer instability and not by thermals rising from the ground. Watch out for them though: on a couple of occasions I've mistakenly headed off for a distant cu only to realise it's a deceptive alto cu.

Cirrus: this is highly relevant as it may move quite rapidly, has a big impact on the amount of sun reaching the ground, and hence the overall strength of thermals. This is probably the single most overlooked factor when pilots evaluate the sky ahead. Although the picture may look uninviting because of ragged cumulus and little sunshine, the root cause is thickening cirrus (or 'top cover'.)

Lenticulars: these are not always the classic elliptical shape as seen in New Zealand, and are not, of course, always accessible from low down. However, if you spot them, think about the influence they may have on thermals or ridges: when in phase with thermals they can produce unexpectedly good climbs, but,

when out of phase, can even stop ridges working at all!

Terrain

Watch out for any ridges facing into wind and avoid flying downwind of these. Also, observe whether the ground is conducive to good soaring. For example, when flying in Holland I found that rivers and their surroundings were always difficult, and I needed to get high in order to cross them.

Wind direction

When interpreting the sky ahead, your awareness of what the wind is doing is critical. Various indicators help us work out the wind direction on the ground: chimney smoke, for starters. It can also be gleaned by

66 Always have a game plan 99

observing the pattern or ripples on lakes; the upwind edge will show an area of flat water parallel with the upwind bank. This is the side of the lake in wind shadow. The wind can also be worked out at higher levels by looking at your GPS's ground speed. Above the clouds, look for tops being blown off by differing upper winds.

Short-term decisions

Having considered all these factors, how do we decide where to go?

As my opening example showed, we need to make decisions both for the short and long term. The trick is to have an overall long-term strategy based on the 'big picture', within which you have the flexibility to make good short-term decisions.

Always have a short-term plan. Knowledge of the wind direction will help you locate lift under clouds, and help you decide whether a ridge will work. Remember to constantly monitor the wind strength and direction: it may alter due to a change in the weather (eg an approaching front) or terrain (bending as it funnels up a valley).

An example of a good short-term plan would be: 'I'll go to the upwind side of the cloud ahead, then I'll try the two beyond it. If they don't work, I'll try soaring the ridge facing into wind, and if that doesn't work I'll land in the good area of fields at the bottom.' Always try to plan a few steps ahead. It's always a worry when your last option doesn't work out and you're left with nothing but a 'think bubble'!

Follow the best line

When thermalling, try and 'join up the dots' to fly under the best lift whilst still moving forwards. When ridge-running, pick the best line of lift – when very low, close into the crest, but when higher, move out from the ridge slightly. When tracking along a wave bar, experiment with your distance in front of the bar until you find the strongest lift. Then try to maintain that distance. Similarly, try and find the height in the wave where the lift is strongest, and adjust your speed to stay at that height as you proceed across country.

Continually re-evaluate

Watch clouds carefully. I try to use a 'freeze-frame photography' technique, taking regular snapshots in my mind of the sky ahead to see how it's developing. There is no point pressing on to a decaying cumulus cloud just because it looked good ten minutes ago when you were in decision-making mood.

Delay final decisions

Sometimes, when you look a reasonable way ahead you can't decide which looks the best. It sometimes pays to point between them, while you closely monitor options. Only commit to one when you're sure it's the better choice or you have to decide.

Long-term decisions

Get a feel for the day from the forecast. Approaching fronts or expected thunderstorms should make you think of starting earlier rather than later. The

"Your awareness of what the wind is doing is critical "

forecast also gives an idea of an appropriate task to set. Work out your expected cross country speed, a conservative estimate of the day's duration and hence a good distance to fly. In competitions with a fixed distance, your speed estimate tells you the approximate time required. Consequently, you can work out what start time enables you to fly in the best part of the day.

Change gear

One of the keys to cross country flying is to spot when the weather is deteriorating ahead, so as to climb high in the last respectable thermals. Similarly, when you see a marked improvement ahead, it's critical to save time by pushing into the better weather.

Work out the day's puzzle

Before you start, and on task, try to closely monitor all the factors outlined above, and piece them together to solve the puzzle.

Summary

To make good decisions, we must first look at the picture ahead and pick out the relevant factors. Having evaluated wind, terrain and clouds, we must constantly make short-term decisions within the framework of an overall strategy. By doing this, we should avoid running out of ideas. Always have a game plan: if you don't have one, you can't change it.

NEED TO KNOW

- Know your clouds
- Know what the wind is doing, it's crucial
- Plan ahead, short- and long-term
- Follow the energy
- Evaluating wind, terrain and clouds helps inform your decision-making

PLANNING YOUR LINE

By Jay Rebbeck

TO FIND the best lift we need somehow to judge what the invisible currents of air around us actually look like. We have to analyse the clues available in the sky and on the ground, integrate all these scraps into one holistic picture in our minds, and then decide where to point the glider.

The first part of this three-stage process – absorbing information – demands a real thirst for knowledge. When you first get among really successful pilots you will see that they devote much more energy to looking around than you had previously ever thought necessary. They are always the first to notice birds circling or tendrils of mist being sucked into cloudbase. An acute awareness of the wind direction is equally important. Try to assess the local wind direction using whatever indicators are available. This will help you to imagine the wind flowing like a fluid over the terrain below. Then you can visualise what it is doing and create a mental picture of it squeezing through narrow valleys or spilling around ridges.

The Sun

Another thing to look for is the angle of the sun to the ground. What might the effects be of the sun passing from east to west through the day and of its height at different times of year or in different latitudes? For example, have you ever experienced an inexplicable lull in thermals in the early afternoon, just as you get into the rhythm of a good flight? Multiple sailplane world champion Justin Wills suggests that this is because when the sun is at its highest, the cooling shadow cast on the ground by 'your' cloud falls directly upon the very area of hot buoyant air that is feeding your thermal. Later in the day, the angle of the sun avoids this effect.

Building the picture

Once you've gathered your information about the effects of the sun's heating and monitored the wind, you then have to process this material to build a mental picture of what's going on.

I remember reading in textbooks that convergence is the lift created when two opposing airmasses meet. So a sea-breeze convergence is set up when sea air flowing inland meets the overland air. However, what I had always assumed was that these would have to meet each other in diametrically opposing directions.

Experience in Spain, though, has taught me that surprisingly good convergence lines can form even when two air masses meet at quite shallow angles. So, noticing a change of wind direction of as little as 20 degrees could be enough for you to exploit a developing convergence line.

The comfort zone

Where we search for lift depends on our height. When we're cruising along in contact with cloudbase – what is commonly known as the comfort zone – our outlook is quite different from when we drop to lower levels. But height is relative, so how do we define the height below which we are uncomfortable, and why is this important?

A really useful distinction is to imagine splitting in two the operating layer – the height band in which you plan to fly – with the divide at half the height of cloudbase. This allows for the fact that how comfortable you are about your height depends on how close you are to cloudbase.

While you can frequently push down to 700m in the UK and be relatively confident of climbing away, attempting the same tactic on a storming South African day with a 5,000m cloudbase will almost certainly end in tears. The thermal which is feeding that booming cloud might have left the ground as long as half an hour ago, and there's no guarantee it's still sucking down low.

Put simply, when we are cruising along

◄ **FIELD OF VISION**
Wind, clouds, ground features, trees, snowline, lake.
Which way would you go?
Photo: Andy Busslinger

Searching at cloudbase

Use your time climbing to pick your route ahead. At cloudbase, the deterioration in horizontal visibility makes it difficult to choose the best direction. If, however, you are forced to make a decision at cloudbase, rely on the shadows cast on the ground ahead. This will show in which direction the clouds line up best. When deciding which clouds will give the best lift, it is more important to concentrate on what the bases look like than the tops. Search for the darkest, flattest bases from the side, but when you arrive under cumulus look for the discontinuities in the base.

When picking your route, try and work out if the lift is located consistently relative to the cu on a given day. This will be more predictable on some days than others.

Even when you can reliably find lift, the effect of the sun moving from east to west may cause the thermals to shift. Remember, too, that the picture looks completely different when you change directions. To avoid disorientation after rounding a turnpoint, spend time looking down the next leg before you turn.

When you've decided where you think the strongest lift is, what's the best way to search under the cloud? To maximise the number of thermals you sample, fly to the side of the cloud you think looks best, and then turn towards the middle. I often S-turn three or four times under a cloud before I decide either to press on or to stop to climb.

in the top half of convection, we are nearer the clouds than the ground, and so should pay more attention to features we note at cloudbase.

However, as we descend into the bottom half of convection, ground features become more relevant to our decision-making. So we should search the sky differently at different heights.

Getting low

Below half the height of convection, I start feeling low! I find I don't have the capacity for so much long-term planning, and am more occupied with the short-term problem of climbing again. It often pays to take larger deviations to get a climb out of trouble. When you get low, your options are more limited and a weak climb (with associated swearing) frequently ensues.

As you are now nearer the ground than cloudbase, it pays to study it more closely for thermal sources. The key factor to search for is differences in surface heating. Thermals are formed by bubbles of air, warmer than their surroundings, escaping from the ground, so anywhere that encourages good temperature differentials will facilitate thermal formation. Good examples include:

- Hot-spots, such as small towns on blue days; working power stations; motorway service stations

- Edges between cloud shadows and sunlight, especially on the upwind side, as the sun starts heating an area that was previously in shade

- Borders between ground features of

66 It is more important to concentrate on what the base looks like than the top 99

different heating capacity. For example, mountainous snow lines provide good trigger points for warm bubbles to break away from the mountainside.

- Ridges facing the wind obviously boost thermals, but lee ('wind shadow') thermals can also form on the downwind side of ridges in relatively light winds. Here the ridge itself provides shelter for warm bubbles to heat up, before they break away in the turbulent air behind the ridge.

As well as paying close attention to ground features, another key to getting out of low scrapes quickly is good preparation. Firstly, choose your landing options as early as safely possible, so that when you get really low you can concentrate fully on soaring.

Secondly, prepare yourself, mentally and emotionally. When low, you often have to go into survival mode and take a weaker thermal to climb out of the hole you're in.

Whatever mistakes got you into this mess are history now – forget about them. As you glide to a low point, combat the frustration by mentally rehearsing a patient climb. Avoid the strong temptation to leave a weak climb sooner than is sensible because your rhythm has been broken.

Work the energy

In order to get the most out of the sky when flying cross country, you need to practise. The best way to do this is by racing against friends on similar gliders.

I have learned how to choose routes through the sky by flying my own flight, but watching others around me. At competition level you will see relatively small differences in climb performance. However, in the glide, the good guys can pull out surprisingly big leads by working the energy efficiently. My advice to any pilot hoping to make the most of the weather is to race, compare, and learn.

NEED TO KNOW

- Look around you and notice everything: clouds, wind, birds, gliders, weather.
- Know where the sun is and where it's going. Ditto for the wind
- Divide the sky into two, or use the 'thirds rule': in the top third of the sky fly the clouds, in the bottom third look to terrain, when in the middle use both
- Plan your route while climbing

OBSERVATION

By Bruce Goldsmith

FLYING, to a large extent, is a guessing game – even in order to safely do a top-to-bottom you need to gather a lot of information, and make some important decisions. But isn't that what makes flying so fascinating? That the air is invisible, so you have to watch its effect on visible objects to work out what it's doing. Clouds, the terrain, the sun, the wind and, of course, other flying objects all bring us invaluable information. It's no wonder that your ability to observe and absorb information is key to understanding what the air is doing, and ultimately, the key to flying well.

This sounds simple enough, but in reality, most pilots who don't fly regularly need most of their concentration to control their gliders, and for this reason don't have the spare mental capacity to look around and observe the world. As flying becomes more automatic, your mind has the freedom to pay more attention to your surroundings. To a large extent this is what makes experienced pilots better pilots. To help accelerate that process for you, here's what I'm looking for when I'm flying in different situations.

The weather

The most important thing to observe and understand in this sport is the weather. It's not only paramount to your success, but also your safety. You should constantly assess the wind direction and strength to work out where the dynamic lift will be, where there might be dangerous rotor, and the direction thermals are drifting. The Sun's position in the sky and any shadow from clouds will have a big influence on thermal production, as will changes in the air mass or upper clouds. It's important to be aware of any changes that are forecast, and then to monitor them.

Clouds

Cumulus clouds mark the tops of thermals. They grow and die as thermals arrive at cloudbase and are a definite sign that there is lift. Day-to-day, clouds form in different ways, from large growing cauliflowers to nothing more than wisps. Noting how they grow and comparing them with the other clouds you can see will allow you to identify the best areas of lift, and assess whether a cloud is becoming dangerous.

80

Thermalling

One of the situations where observation, or lack of it, is most evident is when we are thermalling. A good pilot is constantly watching the other pilots around. If someone else starts to climb faster, then they recognise that the lift is better there, and immediately move closer. There is simply no excuse for being outclimbed by someone or something – gliders, birds, bags or debris – lower than you. You should have flown over and joined their thermal long before they passed you. Thermalling should always be a quest to climb as quickly as possible, so you need to watch the relative climb rates of everything around you. If you suspect someone is climbing faster than you, readjust your 360s to benefit from the air they are climbing in.

Gliding

Watch the pilots around you to see if anyone is in better air. Watch their heights relative to your own, and that of pilots around them. In competition seconds count, and the earlier you react the better. If someone else hits lift I often start gliding towards them before they've even started to turn. You can see when someone is about to hit lift because their glider starts pitching around as they enter the turbulence around the thermal. If you're behind a gaggle you'll get a great view of how all of them move relative to each other. Not being the pilot out front is sometimes highly advantageous.

Ridge soaring

Observation isn't just a skill you need when cross country flying. It's as important when you're just ridge soaring a hillside. You should be noting what every other pilot on the hill is doing. Hillsides work in different ways and, if someone gets up, you need to know where they got that lift. Watch other pilots' strategies and see what works and what doesn't. If it's weak and people are sinking out, you might be able to save yourself just by remembering where all the best lift has been in the last half an hour. Remember to include the weather, and note how the sun, shadow and wind are affecting things.

Competition

Nowhere are your observation skills more tested than in a competition. The best pilots know exactly what everyone in their field of view is up to and why. If I see a pilot fly off in an unusual direction, I immediately question why. What's he or she seen? A bird? Another pilot climbing in the distance? Sometimes, if it's a pilot whose decision-making I trust, I might even follow before I have spotted what he is after. As you observe other pilots don't forget to assess the outcome of their decisions too. Is their plan working for them, and if so, why? Don't let them out of your sight for more than a few seconds, especially if you are gliding or hunting for thermals, even if it means really stretching your neck to look above and behind.

Getting low

Eventually, even the best pilots land, and when we do we enter one of the most dangerous moments of our flight, the bit when we're close to the ground. Observing the wind speed and direction when landing is a crucial skill all cross country pilots need to master.

Obviously windsocks and streamers help, and we can all tell which way the trees are blowing, but did you know that the upwind sides of lakes and ponds nearly always have a ripple-free area close to the shore, whereas the downwind side doesn't? And that standing birds always face into the wind? They just hate having their feathers ruffled.

Keep your eyes open

If you want to become a better, safer pilot you'll do a lot for yourself just by keeping your eyes open. Consciously make a decision to look around continually rather than wandering around aimlessly daydreaming. And watch others close to you like a hawk – if they vanish or head off ask yourself why. Don't wear a helmet or glasses that restrict your field of vision, and don't spend all your time with your nose buried in that new GPS / vario unit. Finally, get plenty of airtime on a glider you're comfortable with so you can relax and free up as much of your mind for the task of observing as possible.

NEED TO KNOW

- Observation is key to flying well
- Flying a comfortable glider means you have more time to observe, therefore you will fly better
- Watch the weather throughout your flight, including wind, shade and the sun's position
- Watch the clouds, where they are and how they are developing
- Watch other pilots, how fast they are climbing, where they find lift
- Watch your height, know where you can land and what the wind is doing
- Get your nose out of that GPS!

USING YOUR SPEEDBAR

By Adrian Thomas

WHEN you start out flying XC you often hear people talk about 'half-bar', or 'three-quarters bar'; others talk about 'standing on the bar' and going for it 'full bar'. I admit, it can be confusing for the new pilot.

When someone talks about full-bar they mean block-to-block, with all of the speed-system travel used up so the pulleys are touching – the absolute top speed of the machine. Half-bar means half way through the speedbar range – half way from trim speed to full speed. Often, people set up their speed system with multiple steps, so that with legs straight on the top step of the speed system you are at full bar, and with legs straight on the first step you are at something like quarter-bar, on the second step you might be at something like half-bar.

It's worth considering what exactly the speed system does. The speed system makes you go faster by lowering the angle of attack of the glider. On most gliders the rear risers stay the same length, and the speed system shortens the front risers, pulling the nose of the glider down towards you. At a lower angle of attack the glider has to go faster to generate enough lift to balance your weight.

When pilots start out they often only use the bar when they get pinned to a ridge or very tentatively on a glide. But the speedbar is just another control on your glider. If you aren't using it you are missing out. In sink, or in a headwind it can make a huge difference to performance. If you were pinned to a ridge

and didn't use bar you wouldn't get anywhere. The same thing happens in a headwind – you have to fly faster to get anywhere; and in sink using speedbar just means you spend less time in sinking air. In a tailwind using bar doesn't make all that much difference, but even with a tailwind if you are in sink you really need to get on bar to get out of it.

Today's gliders are so good on bar that you don't really sink all that much – basically they are all limited in top speed to get through certification, and the glide polar is pretty flat all the way up to top speed. In fact, with their shorter span and lower line-area some modern EN B gliders outperform some modern EN D gliders at full speed – the sink rate goes up but the speed goes up more than enough to make up for it.

Stability at speed

You hear so many pub stories that start 'There I was, on bar, when whack! Full frontal!' that pilots can be scared of the bar before they've even used it. But in fact a lot of gliders stiffen up and become more solid and tuck resistant when you go on bar. I've had several gliders that were more comfortable in turbulence on quarter-bar than at trim, and one or two that were more tuck-resistant at three-quarter-bar than at trim. It varies from glider to glider, and the only way to find out is to try it.

One reason some gliders get more stable at speed is that their structure is designed for a lower angle of attack than trim speed. As you pull the nose down it shortens and the trailing edge lengthens (it's inherent in the geometry of an arc-shaped wing), so the designer has to choose the angle of attack at which the wing structure is spot on and the nose and trailing-edge lengths are correct. At lower speeds (higher angles of attack) the nose will be over tight, which can help performance a little, but the trailing edge will be slack, which can make the wing wobbly, but can also help handling. At higher speeds the trailing edge goes tight, stiffening the wing.

When the wing does go whack (and there is turbulence out there that can collapse any wing, even a hang glider or a 747), well, at high speed you have more kinetic energy than at low speed, but that isn't necessarily bad – deep stall (and cascades) are less of an issue, and the glider may recover more quickly.

When do you use the bar?

There isn't a hard-and-fast rule to when to use it or not, but you will find that the more experienced pilots rarely glide without using the bar. If you are aiming at maximising your average cross country speed, then as a rule of thumb if the thermals are giving you an average climb rate of 3m/s (ie any reasonable day), and there is any sink or headwind around then the correct theoretical speed-to-fly is likely to be full speed, even on an EN B. There are some outstanding pilots around who use the speedbar like that – flying with two modes – full-bar or thermalling.

Personally, I generally go to quarter-bar as I leave the thermal and then move up from there, rarely gliding below half-bar, often going full speed – on my Boomerang X full speed is very comfortable – but for me speedbar isn't an on-off thing, I use it very actively to control pitch, pushing hard as the glider pitches back, and coming off the bar

completely when the glider dives forwards through rough air.

One tip: the load on the legs is very much less if you push the bar with the ball of your feet rather than having it sit in the notch of the heel – the biomechanics work much better – like standing on tiptoe. And you can do fine pitch-control with the calf muscles, which are fast, strong and have great endurance.

Rear-riser control

The normal advice when on speedbar is to put your hands up and release the brakes. You can use the brakes when you are on bar but it isn't a good idea. When you apply brakes you load up the rear of the wing, removing any designed-in reflex (and the pitch stability that gives) and tilting the nose down, making it more collapse prone.

I don't think there are any current gliders that do it but there were a few really popular three-line EN B and EN C wings around not too long ago that would take a front tuck instantly if you touched the brakes on full bar. It's much better to reach up high so the brakes are unloaded, and hold onto the rear risers so you can feel what is happening.

Steering and pitch control is much more effective on the rear risers than on the brakes when you are going fast and it doesn't break the profile in the same way the brakes do, allowing you to maintain reflex and pitch stability and keep the glider flying at full performance.

It is an important skill to be able to control your glider with the rear risers – what else can you do if you break a brake line? The main thing to remember is that the rear risers are much more effective than the brakes, so you only need to make small movements. I find it easier to use the small movements that are needed by pulling the risers back towards me – putting an angle in the run of the rear set of lines rather than grabbing the risers and pulling down on them.

66 Speedbar isn't an on-off thing, I use it actively to control pitch 99

Being smooth on the bar

The other advice always given is to be smooth on the bar. That is often easier said than done. Lots of steps on the speedbar will help. I find it really helps to have the first step relatively small so that you can gently ease the bar on.

The thing to avoid is pushing so fast on the bar that the wing pitches down and you end up in an oscillating flight path – that really hurts performance. Smooth and easy acceleration is your aim.

Of course, if the wing has already pitched out in front of you there is no downside to smoothly applying the bar as you swing down so that you are at speed in stabilised flight just as the wing comes above you.

Pitch control

This brings me onto one key aspect of speedbar use, which is pitch control. There is an easy way to train at pitch control on the bar – get high, go on glide, get on the bar, then use rhythmic applications of bar to get the glider surging. Push hard and fast so that the glider dives in front of you, then when it is out there in front let off the bar quickly so that it surges behind you. Get the wing dolphining in a surging waveform and then use the bar to stop the glider exactly above your head.

You will be very surprised how far the glider can get out in front of you while staying stable, and how much surge, dive and pitch oscillation the glider can tolerate.

Obviously do this at height, and build up slowly. If you work really, really hard you can eventually get the glider so far in front of you it takes a frontal... and that gives you the chance to practice frontals!

NEED TO KNOW

- The speedbar is simply another control on your glider – use it or lose out
- Use it in sink or in a headwind when on XC
- Push the bar with the balls of your feet, it's much easier
- When on bar, keep your hands off the brakes. Use rear risers for control
- Lots of steps will help you be smooth on bar and avoid oscillations

◄ **GOOD STYLE**
Controlling the glider using the
rear risers while on bar.
Photo: Martin Scheel

REAR-RISER CONTROL

With Russell Ogden and Adrian Thomas

WHAT is rear-riser control? "Rear-riser control allows you to keep contact with the glider while gliding, especially when using the speedbar," explains test pilot Russell Ogden. "For exactly the same reason you use your brakes to keep contact with the glider at trim speed in turbulent air – to keep active control, pressure control, to feel the glider – you can use the rear risers to achieve the same thing while on glide."

Although the technique has been used by many pilots for many years, it has only become more common practice in recent years. "I've taught it on SIV courses for 10 years," says Russell. "I do it by keeping the brakes in my hand – but ensuring I'm not applying any brake – whilst taking hold of the rear risers near the maillon or in a position that is comfortable for me, normally somewhere lower."

So what are the benefits, compared with using the brakes? "If you're gliding somewhere, whether at full-speed, half-speed or trim-speed, using the rear risers helps you feel the back of the wing; to control the pitch and maintain the pressure in the nose," he explains. "If the air is turbulent, pulling a small amount of tension allows you to feel the pressure inside the wing and it also means that your hands are in a ready position to effect pitch control if necessary. If the nose suddenly loses pressure, a quick input on the rear risers can keep it open, it gives you a little bit more information than just working with your feet on the speedbar alone. If the air is smooth, of course you can just release all the pressure to allow the glider to fly normally."

Rear-riser control gives you the maximum amount of information and the maximum control with the minimum amount of input, he adds. "It also creates less drag than brakes and is more efficient than always coming completely off the bar and then accelerating again." It's useful in 'mid-level' turbulence. "If the air starts to get really rough then of course I come off the speedbar and use the brakes as normal.

"The technique is especially useful for high performance wings in competitions when maximising efficiency is the main aim, but it is also applicable to XC and everyday flying on recreation gliders. I use it all the time."

Wing-watching

Russell admits to being "a closet wing-watcher". "I look at my wing a lot, especially if I'm gliding at speed because my priority is the leading edge and keeping it inflated," he says. "So I use a combination of the pressure through the speedbar on my foot, my eyes on the leading edge, and the feel through the rear risers. That way I have as much information as it is possible to gather."

If you start to see and feel the leading edge collapse, you can do a combination of coming off the bar (slightly, not all the way) and pulling the rear riser (as much as necessary) to keep the wing inflated, Russell explains. "The input is not like a brake input, it's a smaller, faster one – there is a risk of stalling if you are too heavy-handed. I find it gives you more feel, more control, and it gives you a quicker warning of any imminent collapse."

Collapse recovery

So do you go onto the brakes to sort the
collapse? "You can open a glider with the rear
risers. If you take a full frontal, you come off
the bar and pull the rear risers immediately to
open the glider. For side collapses, or frontals
that develop further it is better to go back on
the brakes to regain control."

Competition pilot Adrian Thomas says
the few times he's had frontals his reaction
has been to let go of the risers and go for the
brakes. "And the lesson has been obvious –
letting go of the rear risers and going for the
brakes is the wrong thing to do," he says. "It
de-stabilises the wing just when you want
to leave it alone, and it is far too easy to put
in too much pilot input – to overcontrol the
paraglider."

It's much better to stay on the rear risers
and wait until you see something recognisable,
he says. "One thing that works is to pull down
sharply on the rear risers as the front riser load

goes slack – to try to keep the load even."

He adds: "One extreme thing that also seems
to work is to pull in on the rear risers and cross
your arms once the wing has frontalled."

This, he explains, keeps the tips from going
forwards and encourages the middle to recover
first. "I've not done it often but if you pull the
risers towards each other you slow the tips
more than the middle of the glider. That can
be extremely useful if you need to stop the tips
going forwards after a collapse."

NEED TO KNOW

- Use it on glide when on speedbar
- You can feel the back of the wing, can
  control pitch and maintain pressure in the
  nose
- It gives you the maximum amount of
  information and the maximum control with
  minimum input

SPEED-TO-FLY THEORY

By Adrian Thomas

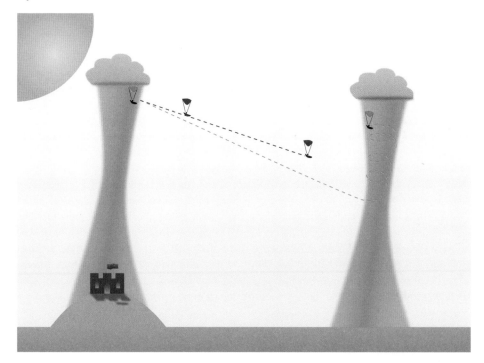

'SPEED-TO-FLY' is a theory that enables pilots to fly as fast as the day's conditions allow to maximise their cross country speed. You put it into practice by gliding between thermals at a speed appropriate to the average thermal strength of the day.

When thermals are strong you can forget about trying to fly at max glide, and instead fly at warp speed because the height you lose on the glide is easily made up for by the speedy climb in the next thermal, giving a fast average speed. However, when thermals are weak, you have to glide at a slower speed (closer to maximum glide speed) so you arrive in the next thermal as high as possible, avoiding wasting time in the slow wallowing climb.

Surprisingly, according to speed-to-fly theory, on a modern performance paraglider on a good day (with climbs of 3m/s or better) the optimum speed to fly on glide in order to maximise the day is full speed all the time. For a modern competition paraglider, speed-to-fly suggests that the optimum speed is full speed even on an average day.

This is good news: competition pilots can forget about speed-to-fly theory and concentrate on where to go and on keeping the wing open at full speed. But it's worth looking into how speed-to-fly is calculated, and also some of the situations when the theory can be thrown out of the window, in order to gain a full appreciation of the best times to use the theory.

Speed-to-fly in practice

It was a spring day and I was cranking my way to base in a 4m/s climb out from Oliver's Castle, a small XC site in the west of England. Fellow pilot Jim Mallinson was also in the climb somewhere a few hundred metres below me.

I reached the white stuff and, spotting a nice-looking cloud 5km downwind, I sat back, let go of the controls and relaxed, cruising at trim speed. Looking behind me, I saw Jim reach cloudbase about 200m behind me and set off in pursuit.

Jim had just had speed-to-fly theory drummed into him on one of Jocky Sanderson's courses, and I could see his legs stretched straight, pinning the bar out on full speed. About 3km later, Jim passed right below me, about 100m lower. Five minutes later and I saw Jim hit the next thermal out in front. By the time I got to it he was already at cloudbase, with me scurrying frantically around underneath for any last scraps of lift.

That was the first speed-to-fly lesson I learned, and it was by no means a subtle one. Jim had made a major gain by making a better choice of speed on the glide.

Glide polar

The starting point for speed-to-fly theory is the glide polar, which is a graph showing the sink rate at different speeds. If you don't have a glide polar for your wing (and few manufacturers publish them), then try searching online. But measuring a glide polar isn't hard to do: just measure your sink rate and speed at top-speed, half-bar and trim-speed and then plot the curve. It works regardless of altitude, air pressure or wing loading. **Figure 1** is a polar curve I made of a paraglider a few years ago.

Speed up in sink

Figure 2 shows how to use the glide polar to predict the best speed in the sink that occurs between thermals. For example in 2m/s sink, taking a tangent with the line starting at 2m/s gives a best speed-to-fly at 45km/h. In sink of 3m/s or more, for this glider at least, the best speed-to-fly is full speed.

The complication in practice is that your vario can't easily separate out the sink caused by the air descending from the sink caused by pressing the speedbar ('total energy' varios are the exception). My solution to this problem is to go straight to full-bar when I leave a thermal. Once settled on this full-speed glide then if my vario is reading 5.5m/s sink or more I am flying at the right speed. If it is reading less I slow down to half-bar where the vario should read 3.5m/s. If the vario reads more I speed up a bit, if it reads less I slow down a bit.

Speed up in a headwind

Figure 3 shows how to use the polar to select optimum speed in a head or tailwind. Again in practice the problem is that when you leave the thermal you don't know what the wind speed is.

My practical answer is again to leave on full-bar and then look at the GPS to read groundspeed. If the groundspeed is 22km/h or less I am in a 30km/h headwind (not optimal) so I stay at full speed and try to figure out a better way to go.

If groundspeed is higher still I slow

down to half-bar where I expect a 23km/h groundspeed (roughly). If the groundspeed is higher than that I slow down a bit more. In a tailwind it can make a small difference to fly slower than trim speed (to get a better sink rate) but the advantage is so small that it isn't worth worrying about.

If (as usual) you expect sink and a headwind then just move the origin up for the sink, and across for the wind: basically, go faster.

Follow the energy

When travelling cross country, a glider extracts energy from the air. The bigger the difference between the thermal climb rate and the inter-thermal sink, the more energy there is available. The more energy there is, the faster you can go.

If you are flying on a day where the thermals give an average 2m/s climb rate (common) and there is no sink between thermals (lucky), then the best speed to fly for maximum average cross country speed is the same as in 2m/s sink – 45km/h in this example. If (as usual) there is a 1m/s sink between thermals, then full speed is optimum.

Too fast is better than too slow

You lose more by going slower than speed-to-fly dictates than by going too fast – at least in terms of their effect on your average speed across country.

Even in the relatively weak 2m/s thermals in the example in **figure 4** (over the page), the pilot using 'get high and boot it' as a flying strategy loses only 5% compared to a pilot who selects the ideal speed-to-fly. Cruising along at hands-up, max glide is hopeless – even with only 2m/s thermals it is 14% slower than speed-to-fly.

If the thermal strength was 5m/s in the previous example then the best speed to fly (top speed) gives almost 30% higher cross country speed than flying at best glide speed.

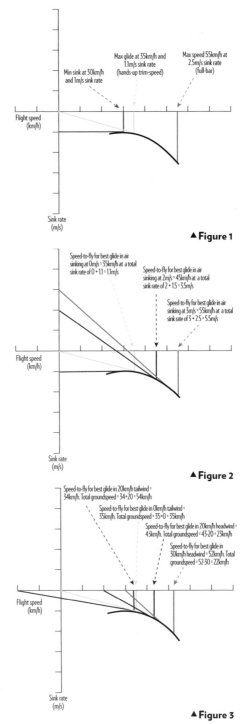

▲ Figure 1

▲ Figure 2

▲ Figure 3

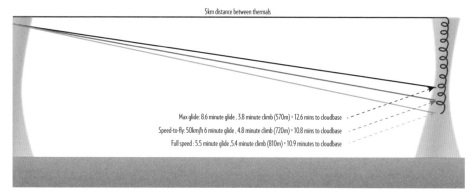

5km distance between thermals

Max glide: 8.6 minute glide , 3.8 minute climb (570m) = 12.6 mins to cloudbase
Speed-to-fly: 50km/h 6 minute glide , 4.8 minute climb (720m) = 10.8 mins to cloudbase
Full speed : 5.5 minute glide ,5.4 minute climb (810m) = 10.9 minutes to cloudbase

▲**FIGURE 4**
'Get high and boot it' works almost as well as speed-to-fly speed. Too slow is much worse than too fast.
Illustration: Charlie King

Hang glider pilots can pull in the bar and dive at speeds that are essentially limited by drag – close to terminal velocity. On a paraglider, stability limits top speed (paragliders can't dive out of the sky like hang gliders or their leading edges would collapse), so modern paragliders just don't get to the sort of high speeds where performance drops away dramatically. Indeed, the improvements in paraglider design over the last few years mean that modern paragliders have enjoyed increasingly flat polar curves all the way up to full speed.

The flipside

Full speed is the correct speed to fly on a modern performance or competition paraglider if conditions are even vaguely good. Except of course that there are situations when you should recognise that speed-to-fly theory doesn't apply and take that vital decision to slow down to maximum glide because the next climb just might not be there.

Although speed-to-fly gets you across country in the fastest average time, it requires you to glide at high speed with a steep glide angle. Those steep glides cover less distance so they reduce the chance of hitting the next thermal. The stage when you have to slow down to glide further and reach the next climb – or just stay in the air – comes sooner on a sports

wing than on a competition wing, because the glide performance is lower at speed.

Real-life XC

Speed-to-fly theory then strictly applies only to an ideal flying day where:
* You are so high that the ground doesn't matter
* You always find the next thermal
* All the thermals are the same strength
* All glides are the same, with the same sink

Unfortunately this isn't practical for the real world of flying XC. So how should pilots fly in real life? A few examples point the way:

1. You're flying at speed-to-fly glide speed when pilots 2km out in front of you hit a rocketing climb. How fast should you fly to get there? The answer is obvious: you speed up to get to the strong lift as quickly as possible, because you can see the gliders charging skywards. Your extra information allows you to go faster than speed-to-fly based on the average thermal for the day.

2. You have been flying speed-to-fly for 150km, you come to the top of the next thermal and set off at speed-to-fly speed on glide only to realise that the sky has gone

completely blue and you have just taken the last climb of the day – how fast should you fly? Obviously maximum glide speed – because you can see that there aren't any more thermals, you have extra information that allows you to go further than if you stuck to speed-to-fly.

3. You have been flying speed-to-fly for 50km with a 20km/h tailwind when you come to a lake. Speed-to-fly speed gives a glide that won't get you to the other side – how fast should you fly? You slow down to a speed lower than max glide speed (but higher than min sink) so that the tailwind and your glide get you to the other side high enough to get the next thermal. Because you can see the lake you know there won't be any more thermals for a while.

4. You are flying speed-to-fly along a weak and broken cloud street gliding, then stopping to top up in the strong lift. Pilots flying along the next cloud street over to your left are not having to thermal at all – how fast do you fly? Speed-to-fly theory can't help here – probably you should fly across to the other street. Whether that is a good idea depends on how far it is to the other street, how reliable that street is, and how much time you will lose by crossing streets. Perhaps a good idea would be to look at the sky two thermals further ahead and see whether the other street is still better than the one you are under.

5. You are circling at cloudbase at 800m. There is a line of low hills ahead and to your left, a decaying cloud in front of you and a wisp that might be a forming cloud ahead to your right, but the ground looks a bit damp that way. How fast do you fly? Well, it depends, doesn't it? Perhaps the best thing to do is stay at cloudbase and assess the situation – if that developing cloud looks like being really good, that might be the way to go, but maybe the drier ground over the hills

will pay. Decaying clouds are usually a bad thing – but what if it recycles? In any case, with a cloudbase as low as 800m, dribbling along in light lift may be the only way to get anywhere. Speed-to-fly becomes irrelevant when staying up is the only concern.

In each case, a little thought allows you to fly further or faster than strict application of speed-to-fly theory would allow.

Summary

What's the answer? Well, if you know where the next thermal is and how strong it is going to be, then you can't really do any better than fly at speed-to-fly speed. Full-speed on a half-way decent day, and the assumptions of the theory are all met.

However, for most of us, in most circumstances the assumptions of speed-to-fly are not fully met. Either we don't know what strength the next thermal is going to have, or we don't know where the next thermal is, or we don't know if there is going to be another thermal. For real pilots flying real skies, slowing down to think about where to go can make the difference between staying up or going down.

NEED TO KNOW

- Speed-to-fly is a theory developed by a sail plane pilot
- Assuming good conditions, it works: the best speed to fly is full-speed
- Speed up in sink
- Speed up in a headwind
- Flying too fast is better than too slow
- Understanding speed-to-fly is good because it helps you decide when not to use it and why
- Slowing down can help you think things through – flying full speed to the deck is not the game

FLYING AT THE RIGHT SPEED

By Adrian Thomas

GLIDER pilot and aeronautical engineer Paul MacCready is usually credited with developing mathematical principles for optimising the speed at which to fly when flying cross country. This is called the speed-to-fly theory.

The theory allows the optimal flying speed between thermals to be computed, using thermal strength, glider performance and other variables. It accounts for the fact that if a pilot flies faster between thermals, the next thermal is reached sooner.

However at higher speeds the glider also sinks faster, requiring the pilot to spend more time circling to regain the altitude. The MacCready speed represents the optimal trade-off between gliding and circling.

Many glider pilots still use a MacCready Ring, a rotatable bezel on the glider's variometer, to indicate the best speed to fly. Others use a flight computer.

This article builds on that 'classical' speed-to-fly theory with work done by Helmut Reichmann (a German sailplane pilot who co-founded the Barron Hilton Cup alongside millionaire hotelier Barron Hilton) and applies to paragliders and hang gliders.

The puzzle

Speed-to-fly theory seems to puzzle even expert pilots. The reason is that classical speed-to-fly theory makes many impossible assumptions. First, it assumes a pilot has perfect knowledge – even precognition. It assumes the pilot not only knows where the next thermal is, but also knows how strong it is. Secondly, standard speed-to-fly theory assumes that the strength of thermals is constant from the ground to the top of the climb. Thirdly, it assumes flight in the open atmosphere, ignoring such complications as wind or ground.

Those assumptions don't really match what we experience on XC flights. Thermals are different strengths and change strength as you climb up them. You aren't always sure you will get to the next climb; the ground may get in the way, either because it is too far to the next cloud to glide at the recommended optimum speed, or because a ridge gets in the way.

Real XC rarely happens in windless conditions, and any decent flight crosses areas where conditions change radically, sometimes scarily booming, sometimes boringly slow.

Fortunately, the sailplane theorists recognised these problems years ago, and some even managed to convince grant-awarding bodies that the problems of speed-to-fly theory were important enough to be worth three years' PhD funding. One of these was Helmut Reichmann, who won the world sailplane championships three times. He wrote the fantastic book Cross Country Soaring and, along with Rene Comte and Anthony Edwards, came up with a grand unified general theory of optimum speed-to-fly so simple it can be stated in a single, simple paragraph (although he, of course,

proved it mathematically – you have to do something for a PhD). They concluded:

- Fly so that your final climb rate equals your initial climb rate. Then glide at the speed-to-fly for that climb rate.

In practice this means in each thermal notice your climb rate in your first properly centred 360. (A good pilot will centre within four 360s). Keep climbing until, at the top of the thermal, your climb rate drops off to that initial climb rate. Then set off on glide at the speed-to-fly for that final climb rate, and glide until you find another thermal with at least that climb rate. At any time if you can reach goal, or some other target (such as crossing a ridge), or a stronger thermal at the glide and speed-to-fly for your current climb, then go.

That paragraph summarises a lot of fairly abstract algebra, but it provides a speed-to-fly rule that can be proved to be optimum in all sorts of conditions.

When conditions are ideal

If, as does very occasionally happen, conditions are so good that classical speed-to-fly theory is appropriate, then a pilot applying the general theory described above will fly in complete accordance with the classical theory because the thermals are of constant strength and speed-to-fly has to be selected for that strength.

For example, in really strong racing conditions you just thump along at classical speed-to-fly with no need for thought or variations – mechanical flying, PWC style. The general theory becomes equivalent to the classical theory when the strict assumptions of that theory are met.

The general theory says do your scratching high up

What is more interesting is what happens in more complicated and realistic conditions.

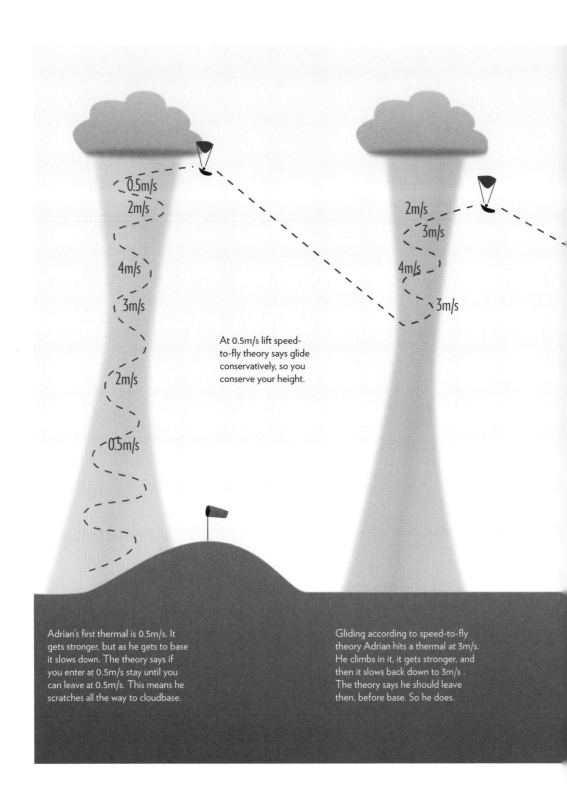

0.5m/s
2m/s
4m/s
3m/s
2m/s
0.5m/s

At 0.5m/s lift speed-to-fly theory says glide conservatively, so you conserve your height.

2m/s
3m/s
4m/s
3m/s

Adrian's first thermal is 0.5m/s. It gets stronger, but as he gets to base it slows down. The theory says if you enter at 0.5m/s stay until you can leave at 0.5m/s. This means he scratches all the way to cloudbase.

Gliding according to speed-to-fly theory Adrian hits a thermal at 3m/s. He climbs in it, it gets stronger, and then it slows back down to 3m/s . The theory says he should leave then, before base. So he does.

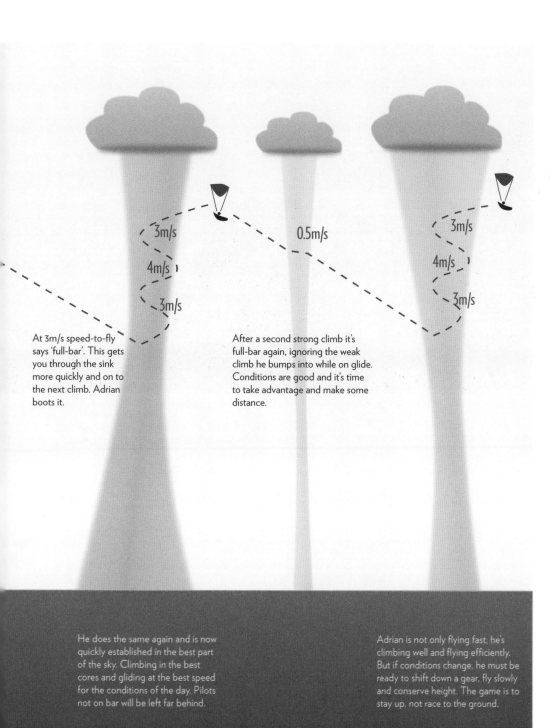

3m/s

4m/s

3m/s

0.5m/s

3m/s

4m/s

3m/s

At 3m/s speed-to-fly says 'full-bar'. This gets you through the sink more quickly and on to the next climb. Adrian boots it.

After a second strong climb it's full-bar again, ignoring the weak climb he bumps into while on glide. Conditions are good and it's time to take advantage and make some distance.

He does the same again and is now quickly established in the best part of the sky. Climbing in the best cores and gliding at the best speed for the conditions of the day. Pilots not on bar will be left far behind.

Adrian is not only flying fast, he's climbing well and flying efficiently. But if conditions change, he must be ready to shift down a gear, fly slowly and conserve height. The game is to stay up, not race to the ground.

Normally, thermals are disorganised at their bases, stronger in the middle levels and then often weaker as you approach their tops – either as you bounce off the inversion, or as you approach cloudbase.

Applying the general theory and arriving at the bottom of a climb you will probably be in the disorganised bottom of the thermal, multi-core madness and all, so your climb rate in the first centred 360 is probably relatively slow. The rule then requires you to climb to the top of that thermal, scratching just as hard at the top of the climb as at the bottom (unless you can obviously reach a stronger climb). That means you do your scratching high, and then glide relatively slowly to the next climb.

The obvious advantage is that while the penalty for scratching high is wasted time, scratching low risks landing. Typically, if conditions are reasonable, having scratched high you will arrive at the next climb relatively high where thermals are better organised, so the first centred 360 will be better in the second climb. Applying the rule, you do less scratching at the top of that second climb, leave slightly earlier and fly slightly faster to the next climb, which you arrive at slightly lower. Very quickly, applying the general speed-to-fly theory gets you operating only in the levels where the thermals are strongest, and gliding between climbs at a speed that is the highest that can be achieved while staying within those levels. That is where the rule really wins.

Slower optimal glide speeds

The general theory says you should glide at the speed-to-fly for the final climb rate

"Keep climbing until, at the top of the thermal, your climb rate drops off to that initial climb rate "

in the thermal, whereas most applications of classical speed-to-fly theory suggest you should base your glide speed on the average climb rate in the thermal.

Indeed, in practice, many pilots actually choose speed-to-fly based on the climb rate they see on their varios when coring properly about half way up the climb. Most varios either report an instantaneous climb rate, or a climb rate averaged over 20 or 30 seconds (about the time of one 360). So the climb rate varios report is often much higher than the average climb rate for the thermal because the average climb-rate should include the whole of the climb from the moment you stop gliding and start to thermal, until the moment you leave and go on glide.

If you fly according to the classical theory, then quite weak thermals require you to glide at full-speed because paragliders' top speeds are limited to only 65km/h, or thereabouts – paragliders cannot dive. With the relatively flat polar curves of current paragliders this means that applying classical speed-to-fly theory we all ought to be gliding at full-speed if the thermals are 3m/s or more, not rare in decent XC conditions.

Under the general theory, full-bar only becomes the optimum speed once the initial and final climb rates in thermals are equal to 3m/s, which is far less often the case.

Don't waste time with weak thermals

The time that can be saved by flying a little bit faster is small. Real overall average speed gains are achieved by minimising the time spent climbing and, particularly, by avoiding wasting time climbing in weak thermals. The general theory suggests you should only climb in thermals that are at least as strong as the initial and final climb you experienced in the last thermal.

The real advantage to applying this principle is that you start out by climbing high in your first thermal, staying in that climb until you have done as much scratching at the top of it as you did at the bottom when you arrived. By applying 'initial climb = final climb and gliding at the speed-to-fly for those climb rates', you optimise your use of the climbs by starting out high (which minimises the risk of going down after the next glide), and then progressively gliding faster and deeper until you are operating with as fast and long a glide as possible and climbing in the strongest parts of the thermals.

Obviously, you shouldn't use thermals that are weaker than expected. Avoiding weak thermals is what saves the most time.

Expect exceptions

The general theory includes a rule to be applied in exceptional situations. Where there is a target ahead, then you should continue to climb in the current thermal until you can just reach the target when gliding at the speed-to-fly for the current climb.

The reason is, if you go earlier and glide closer to best glide ratio, then a pilot who stays and climbs to the optimum glide slope can speed over the top of you gliding at optimum speed to fly for your current thermal, and climbing any higher than the optimum glide slope is obviously a waste of time.

This rule works for final glides or for any glide to a fixed position (such as gliding over the crest of a ridge). It also works when you know that there is a stronger climb ahead of you – you should only climb just high enough to be able to reach that climb by flying at the optimum speed for your current climb, even though the next climb is stronger.

Of course, if you are already high, then you should leave immediately because you are already on the glide-slope and have already wasted time getting high in your current climb.

Theory in practice

The main thing to do is be aware of how your climb rate changes as you ascend in a thermal. You need to make a mental note of the climb rate that you achieved as soon as you centred the thermal, because that determines how long you hang on in the top of the climb.

During the climb you need to decide whether there is another climb out there and, if so, where. If there isn't a next-climb then you might need to climb as far as the thermal takes you. In XC conditions that is not a rare situation – particularly early or late in the day. In racing, it is much less common, but still happens.

Assuming there is an obvious climb to go to, and knowing your initial climb rate, you now have a definite indication of when to leave – you just climb until your current climb rate decreases to your initial climb rate in the thermal. Then you glide off at the speed appropriate for that climb rate, and keep gliding until you hit a climb with the same or better climb rate. Obviously, it makes sense to have a minimum altitude below which you switch to survival mode, in case your expected thermal fails to materialise.

All this assumes you already know the polar curve of your glider and your glider's optimum glide speeds. However, the effect of errors in speed-to-fly theory is quite interesting. Flying too fast turns out to have very little effect on average speeds round a course – so long as you don't land you only lose a relatively small amount of time by flying too fast. On the other hand, flying too slowly is not a good idea. In particular, the losses get quite large if you fly as slowly as maximum glide speed.

NEED TO KNOW

- Classical speed-to-fly is good if conditions are perfect
- This general theory says you should leave a thermal when your climb-rate at the top of the thermal is the same as your climb-rate was when you entered
- Between thermals you then fly at speed-to-fly for that climb rate
- It means if you scratch into a thermal, you scratch out of it at the top too
- It also means if you boom in, you boom out
- The result is you fly the best part of the sky at the best speed
- You fly fast when in strong conditions and slow down when it's light
- Always be aware of your climb rate in the thermal
- Flying too slowly is bad, but flying too fast isn't really a problem
- Unless you land
- There are always exceptions – if you can reach goal or can cross that ridge, go

FLYING FAST AND EFFICIENTLY

By Bruce Goldsmith

MANY pilots are under the illusion that racing and flying fast is all about pushing harder on the speedbar. Nothing could be further from the truth. Flying fast isn't simply about gliding fast. Other things are far more important, like finding and climbing in the strongest lift as quickly as possible, and not getting stuck.

Spend a moment thinking about the amount of time that can be gained or lost from each activity to understand what I'm talking about. Let's consider a pretty normal XC task, one where you climb 1,000m in a 2m/s average climb and then glide to find the next climb. It then takes you between one and two minutes of searching to find the climb. Let's look at a few different options.

Gliding faster

First let's say that you push a bit more bar and glide at 50km/h instead of 45km/h at about 8:1. From 1,000m you will glide 8km, which would take 10 minutes 40 seconds at 45km/h and 9 minutes 35 seconds at 50km/h. Flying 5km/h faster would only save you a minute, but your glide angle would be worse at the higher speed. This may well negate the advantage, but is something, for the ease of the example, that we will disregard for the time being.

Finding the next climb

If, after the next glide, Jack finds the next climb straight away, whilst Jill takes two minutes to find it, then Jack will instantly gain an impressive two minutes on his rival. If you have other pilots around you then they will help you locate the thermal quicker.

The rule of thumb here is that if you are not sure exactly where the next thermal is coming from then don't accelerate to arrive there first, as you may then be forced to spend time looking for the climb.

It's better to fly a little slower with a better glide angle, arrive a little higher, and use the other pilots just ahead to find the climb for you. That way you'll stand the greatest chance of arriving straight into the best lift with the minimal amount of time lost.

If you have been pressing the speedbar more than the others, then you may arrive first, but lower too, so, unless you find the thermal immediately or the rest of the gaggle all get stuck too, you are on to a loser!

Climbing better

If you don't thermal efficiently your overall climb rate can be considerably reduced. Analysing tracklogs of members of the British team at one European Championships I found that the better pilots were actually climbing at twice the average climb rate of the weaker members of the team in the same climbs – something that will make a huge difference as I show later.

Using the average climb rate as opposed to the peak climb rate is crucial. The peak climb rate is what you boast about when you see your vario scream 5m/s for a few seconds. This is very different to the actual average

▲ **FAST AND FURIOUS**
On a ridge like this there is no need to spend time
turning. Just fly along it. Photo: Ant Green

climb rate achieved by the pilot. Normally the average climb rate is less than half the peak climb of the thermal.

Let's say, in a 1,000m climb, Jack manages an average climb rate of 2.5m/s (which is really good) whilst Jill is less efficient and averages at only 1.5m/s. Then Jack will take only 6 minutes 40 seconds to reach base, whilst Jill will take 11 minutes seven seconds.

Jill will lose four-and-a-half minutes over her faster-climbing rival, a massive difference and one you could never possibly make up just by gliding a bit faster.

Getting stuck

Worse than spending time looking for a thermal is getting stuck. Often, getting stuck can cost you anything between five minutes to an hour, or even your entire flight. To simplify

our analysis let's assume getting stuck will cost you 30 minutes. Half an hour when compared with the two or four minutes lost by climbing inefficiently, or not finding the climb instantly, can be the end of your race.

If you arrive just a bit too low, maybe just below the level you can get up easily from, those few metres can have an even heavier cost – getting stuck can mean you never get out and your day is over. So when gliding towards an unknown area where lift isn't assured, then minimise the risk and avoid going in first, and certainly not alone.

In summary

So let's summarise how much time you can lose from our four different strategies:

- Gliding slower: 1 minute
- Finding the climb: 2 minutes

- Climbing slower: 4.5 minutes
- Getting stuck: 30 minutes

One very important exception to my advice not to glide too fast is when conditions are just so good that there is little risk of going down. This can be the case when you are flying at the best time of the day and in the best season of the year at some of the best competition sites in the world. This is often the case in major international competitions, and in such conditions the chances of getting stuck or not finding the thermal are greatly reduced because you are gliding along south-facing ridges pumping with enormous thermals. In such conditions, clearly the faster you glide the better, but such conditions are not the norm in every competition or on every flight.

Don't dither

Part of flying fast is to make fast decisions and act on them quickly. If you see a pilot or bird climbing better than you within reach, or a cumulus building just ahead, then don't wait a few more 360s before making up your mind to go – go there, go now, while it's happening. Those few extra 360s might cost you a minute or so and you may miss the lift. Do this a few times each flight and you'll very quickly lose a lot of time.

On glide

If you've thermalled up and you know where the next climb is then get there quickly. Now is the time to use the bar. However, using the speedbar to fly fast isn't simply a case of just pushing on it. The speed and timing of the application is crucial to reducing the pitching movements of the glider as you accelerate, and also to damp out pitching movements of the glider induced by thermals or turbulence.

Hang glider pilots do this all the time as they glide through the air by moving the control bar, constantly making minor adjustments to the glider's pitch. This movement feels very easy and natural on a hang glider as the speedbar is just floating around under your fingertips. On paragliders the same movements don't come so naturally they are harder to coordinate with the pitching movements of the glider as we are so much further from the wing.

Pitch control is of immense importance on paragliders and by constantly adjusting how much speedbar you apply you can actually improve your glide performance by a considerable amount. This is one major reason why some pilots always seem to glide better than others, even though they are on the same glider.

Get it right, all the time

To be a top competition or XC pilot you need to get everything right even when conditions are not perfect. You need to find climbs instantly, climb at the best rate and never get stuck. If you do all these things perfectly, then gliding a bit faster can make the difference between winning and losing.

Flying fast takes a lot of experience and practice and isn't something that comes naturally even to gifted pilots. It takes a lot of training and the best place for that is in competition. Because the speed and efficiency of pilots changes according to the different levels of competition the only way to learn how to fly really fast is to fly in competitions at ever-increasing levels.

NEED TO KNOW

- Flying fast isn't simply about pushing the bar
- It's about flying efficiently and climbing at the best rate
- And thinking ahead so you don't get stuck
- Glide fast when conditions allow, otherwise it can be a risk
- Use the speedbar to control pitch
- To learn to fly fast, fly competitions

HEXAGON THEORY

By Bruce Goldsmith

I FOUND out about the hexagon theory in 1992. It helped my own understanding of the sky and improved my XC flying significantly. Since then I have always had it in the back of my mind when looking at cloud formations.

The Sahara conclusion

In the 1980s a group of French meteorologists went to the Sahara to study the way that clouds form. The desert they studied was covered with small sand dunes, with no other significant features. The sand was a uniform colour and there were no mountains or hills to form or trigger thermals.

When the atmosphere was unstable the thermals still set up as expected, but the scientists reached some rather astounding conclusions: in nil-wind conditions, the thermals form along the edge of hexagonal patterns. These hexagons are regular in shape with the length of each side being 6km.

Cell circulation

Imagine a saucepan of water on a stove to boil. As the water boils it will form bubbles that rise in the same way thermals rise through the atmosphere. These bubbles will rise in some areas and the water will also flow down to the bottom of the pan in other areas, thus forming cells of water that circulate.

In the atmosphere the same type of thing happens on a much larger scale. The exact length of the sides of the hexagons will of course vary according to the density and viscosity of the air. The height of the cloudbase and the strength of the thermals will also be important factors, but you can understand the principle.

Wind effect

Here comes the interesting part. When there is wind, the theory says that two sides of the hexagon will line up automatically with the wind direction, and these two sides will then become longer. The stronger the wind the longer these two sides will become. The other four sides of the hexagon will remain 6km long. These long sides of the hexagon are of course cloud streets.

Implications for pilots

This has important implications for pilots flying in cloud streets over flatlands. Firstly it means that cloud streets do not go on forever, but are of limited length and fit together into an elongated hexagonal grid. Secondly it means that if you are flying downwind and come to the end of your cloud street, then you should not continue to fly directly downwind to find lift. The theory suggest that you should turn 60 degrees away from your downwind flight path and fly cross-wind for approximately 6km where you should find the beginning of the next cloud street, if all is going according to theory.

Blue holes

The hexagon theory also explains why you get blue holes. These are simply the middle of the hexagons. I used to think that if you flew into an area of blue sky where the sun was heating the ground strongly then you would

▲ WARM AIR RISES

Hexagon and polygon patterns formed by the clouds in Namibia. The theory is also called open cell convection.
Photo: Vianney Tisseau

inevitably be rewarded with a nice thermal. I soon found out that this idea did not work well and I ended up too many times on the ground looking downwind at amazing skies due to landing early. The hexagon theory says that the air is flowing downwards in these blue holes and so even though the sun is heating the ground it cannot overcome the downward flow of the air.

Mountains

The hexagon theory should only be applied over flatlands. Mountains are such strong thermal sources that they destroy the application of the theory. But what I find interesting is that it explains why some thermal sources may work and why others may not. If you have two thermal sources of the same strength, then the one that lines up with the hexagon pattern is going to be the one that works and the one in the blue hole will not work, even though it looks so great

NEED TO KNOW

- The Hexagon Theory applies to flatlands
- In still air, the air 'bubbles' like water in a saucepan
- The bubbles are clouds, and they form a hexagon pattern
- Each side is 6km long
- In wind these get elongated into cloud streets
- The theory says when you get to the end of a cloud street, turn 60-degrees and fly 6km to find the start of the next cloud street

FLYING CLOUD STREETS

By Honza Rejmánek

ON windy days over flat surfaces clouds no longer tend to form the fishnet or polygonal pattern that they do on light wind days.

Instead, the wind tends to organise lift into long helical rolls that extend through the depth of the boundary layer (the bit we fly in). If sufficient moisture is present for cumulus clouds to form then the upper portions of these helical rolls become visible. We call these cloud streets.

On windy, cloud-free days lift will also organise in this pattern – invisible thermal streets.

Post-cold-frontal days

Cloud streets tend to occur when there is a cold air outbreak, such as behind a cold front. The wind in the convective boundary layer needs to increase at least 10-20 knots from the surface up to cloudbase. A strong capping inversion caused by generally sinking air keeps individual cumulus clouds from growing tall and disrupting the cloud street pattern. This is usually the case when the surface pressure is increasing (a building high pressure). As the boundary layer isn't very deep after the front the streets are tightly spaced at first. Then they

◄ **STREET LIFE**
Late evening flying in England with a cloud street
stretching to the horizon. Photo: Al Wilson

"Keep an eye on the cloud shadow"

gradually increase in width as the boundary layer deepens.

Low down

At the surface, wind can make for more challenging conditions since the lift is likely to be constantly shredded by wind shear. So getting low on streeting days should be avoided even more than on other days, as the climbs are likely to be rough, disorganised and difficult to climb in. These weak and shredded thermals coming off the surface will grow stronger as they better organise in the mixed layer in the upward part of the helical roll.

Spacing

The spacing between streets tends to be about 2.5 to three times the boundary layer depth (eg, if cloudbase is 2,000m above the ground, cloud streets will be typically 6km apart). The sink between streets tends to be organised into long lines too, and tends to be stronger than would be typically found under similar convective conditions on a light wind day.

At base

At cloudbase darker patches of cloud usually mark stronger lift. If the lift is strong enough then it is possible to fly in a straight line, slowing down slightly in areas of stronger lift to go up. In weaker conditions it is necessary to occasionally thermal in the stronger lift in order to remain near cloudbase. When near cloudbase it can be hard to discern how far a street runs. In this case it is good to keep an eye on the cloud shadows ahead.

If the street ahead is ending or your route dictates that you switch streets it is best to top up with as much height as possible, then turn 90-degrees away from the street you are under. When you take into account the wind you are flying in, your actual track between the streets will probably be more like 45 degrees as you get blown downwind.

In summary, cloud streets can make for very straightforward flying conditions, especially if you are near cloudbase.

NEED TO KNOW

- Cloud streets form when the lift is organised by the wind
- At the surface climbs will be shredded by the wind, avoid getting low
- At cloudbase darker patches of cloud usually mark stronger lift
- When high look at cloud shadows to spot the streets
- The spacing between streets tends to be 2.5 to 3 times the height of base
- When flying a street, speed up in sink and slow down in lift – this is dolphin flying

CONVERGENCE

By Bruce Goldsmith

WHEN I started flying I remember learning about a strange phenomenon called 'convergence'. In the books, convergence was always discussed as something unusual, as though it only occurred in certain places such as on the coast, or in certain rare conditions.

Yet to my surprise I discovered that convergence appears all over the place: in mountains, flatlands, coastal sites and valleys. And that during an average distance flight you are likely to encounter it at least once if not more. In the Alps I'd say I encounter convergence during at least 50% of all my flights.

What is convergence?

It is basically the meeting of two winds of different directions. Normally, providing that the air masses in each wind direction are different, one will ride up over the other, thus creating lift. However, if both winds are the same in temperature and density, then they will both ride up together, also creating an area of lift. In convergence zones, the thermals are generally more concentrated and are often stronger because the air around is already going up.

1. Sea-breeze convergence

This is perhaps the most obvious type of convergence. It occurs usually when you have a relatively straight coastline, a prevailing, offshore wind and thermal activity inland. As the land warms up and convection starts, cool, high density air from the sea is drawn inland in a line. At the point where the cool sea air meets the warm inland air, convergence occurs, almost forming a soarable ridge in the sky.

You will find the best and most usable lift on the inland side of the sea-breeze convergence, as the dense, cool air from the sea is typically stable. The convergence line moves constantly inland throughout the day until the thermal activity stops: how far you are from the coast will determine the arrival and departure times of the convergence zone at your site.

What does it look like?

You can spot a sea-breeze convergence in a number of ways. First, by the change in wind direction on the ground. The windsock will switch from blowing offshore to onshore in a matter of minutes. The air will also feel cooler.

Secondly, by looking at the clouds. Look for where the cumulus clouds stop in a consistent line, with blue stable air beyond.

Thirdly, if there are clouds in the sea-breeze air the base will be lower than the inland cumulus clouds. There will also often be a vertical curtain of cloud connecting the two cloudbases. Along the edge of the convergence zone this 'curtain' may look like darker, wispy bits of cloud hanging below the flat base of the inland cumulus clouds. If there is a range of hills near the coast expect to find the convergence zone situated over and along the higher ground.

These three indicators can sometimes all appear at once making spotting the convergence zone quite easy, especially if tell-tale clouds are present. On blue thermal days however, both sides of the convergence may be clear blue sky, so the change in wind

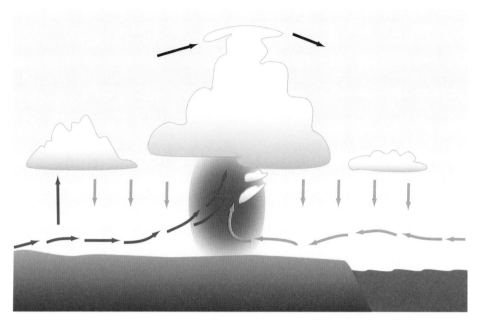

▲ SEA-BREEZE CONVERGENCE
A step in cloudbase, change in wind direction and a ragged cu 'curtain' are all signs to look for. When flying sea-breeze convergence stay on the landward side in the red zone and don't fly into the stable, sinking sea air.

direction on the ground may be your only sign of the sea breeze. My experience of flying in these conditions however has taught me that with blue sky sea-breeze convergence, the sea air mass is often a slightly hazier blue than the inland air mass, creating a faint 'line' in the air. This is enough – if you look carefully – to tell you where the convergence zone is.

How to exploit it

Once you have spotted it the next thing is to use it. The first rule is to fly on the inland side of the sea-breeze convergence line. There are then two techniques of flying the convergence line, depending on the type of lift.

The first method, provided that there is thermal lift in the convergence zone, is to use the thermals in the normal way. The second method, when there is a weak line of ridge lift along the convergence line but no thermals, is to treat the line like a ridge-soarable hill and maintain height by doing beats along the line

of convergence. The most important thing in this case is to pay careful attention to stay on the inland side. It is easy to accidentally slip into the sea air side, in which case you will go down very quickly.

The only way to make distance flights in these conditions is to fly along the convergence line. If you try to fly away from it in either direction, then you either encounter stable air or a headwind. But staying in the convergence line is not always as simple as it sounds. Often the 'line' is not straight, and tends to get pushed inwards in some places and stick close to the coast in others. It depends on the nature of the coastline and the landscape. Sea breezes often flow up small valleys near the coast more easily than over the small hills, so the convergence line is often very irregular.

Places renowned for their sea-breeze convergence are the whole south coast of England when there is a northerly prevailing

111

wind (John Pendry once flew 250km here in sea-breeze convergence). The west coast of California is famous for brilliant sea-breeze convergence when the prevailing wind is easterly. And the east coast of Spain near Barcelona is another good sea-breeze convergence zone in an easterly.

2. Lee-side convergence

As air flows around an obstacle it divides on the upwind side (this is called the stagnation point), flows around the sides and then collides together again on the downwind side. This meeting of airflow on the lee side from two directions is of course convergence. But be careful here – downwind of an obstacle you can also find rotor, sink and turbulence. It is a refined skill to try to identify whether there is lift or sink downwind of an obstacle.

Generally, if the obstacle is relatively small (by small I mean less than 5km across or lower than 1,000m) or the wind is strong, then downwind you will just find rotor. On the other hand, if the obstacle is large or the wind is light, then you are more likely to find convergence downwind, particularly if there is sun on the ground in the downwind zone to give the air a bit of extra warmth to get the converging air to produce lift.

3. Valley wind meets meteorological wind

During summer days convection in the centre of the Alps draws air towards it. Because the air always takes the easiest route, it flows up the valleys. These are valley winds and they can vary in strength up to 50km/h.

Often the valley winds may be in the opposite direction to the meteorological wind. When this occurs there will be a point where the two opposing winds meet. This is the convergence zone. I have seen this many times in the southern Alps in Italy north of Trento. Here, the northerly meteo wind

▼PLAN VIEW OF LEE-SIDE CONVERGENCE
You can find sink, rotor, turbulence or convergence downwind of a hill or mountain.

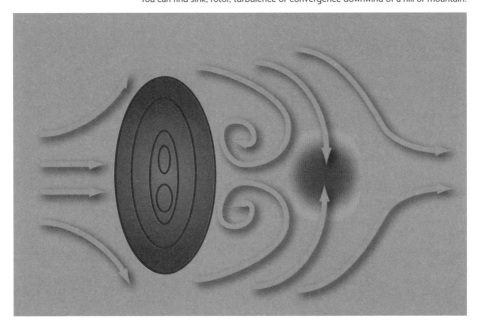

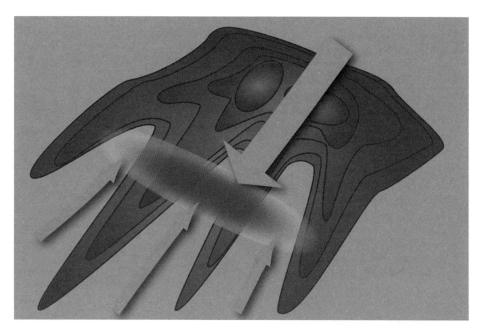

▲ METEO WIND MEETS VALLEY WIND

The resulting convergence zone shifts during the day as the valley winds strengthen and push into the mountains.

pushes south from the north of the Alps, and opposes the strong southerly valley wind. The result is a line of convergence cloud extending right across the valley. This zone of convergence starts quite far south in the morning, but as the strength of the valley winds increase it moves north during the day approaching the centre of the Alps.

I once flew in convergence in the Les Saisies and the Megeve valleys during a competition. Normally the wind flows up each side of this ridge and produces thermal lift over the peak. However, on this particular day the prevailing north wind reinforced the upslope wind on the Megeve side of the ridge and pushed it over into the Les Saisies valley. So a convergence zone was formed halfway down the ridge on the Les Saisies side. I flew in this convergence zone for 15km, while several pilots flew to the normally reliable south face of the ridge. They went straight down, not having understood what was happening at all.

4. Valley wind meets valley wind

It is a little difficult to separately classify these different types of convergence. The example in Les Saisies could also be classified as valley wind/valley wind convergence, for example. But it is the effect of the meteo wind on the convergence that makes it something unusual.

The area to the west of the Cheval Blanc (20km north of St André-les-Alpes, southern France), is very special. There are often good thermals and light unpredictable winds with strong thermals originating in the flat valley in front of the mountain. In fact the thermals are frequently better in the valley in front of the mountain than on the impressive Cheval Blanc itself. Why is this?

Well, the area is a zone of valley wind/valley wind convergence. The wind flows into this area from the southern route from St André and Lambruisse, and also from the northwest

113

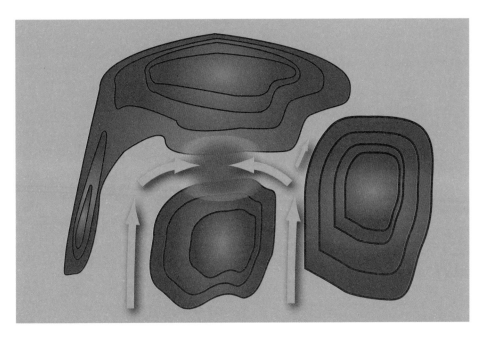

▲ VALLEY WIND MEETS VALLEY WIND
A plan view of how two valley winds can meet, creating a convergence zone that can last all day.

from Digne and the La Javie valley. The two valley winds are separated by the massif of the Montagne de Coupe.

The exact location of this convergence zone will be influenced by the meteo wind of course, but it generally stays in this location all day without moving. This convergence zone has, in the past, enabled tasks to be set that take pilots directly west from the Cheval Blanc to the Montagne de Coupe, normally an exceptionally difficult leg as it involves flying directly upwind into the lee/shadow side of the Montagne de Coupe.

Conclusion

Convergence, rotor, lee-side thermals and valley winds are all closely connected. It is impossible to say exactly when one ends and when another starts, but being familiar with this complex mixture of influences is the key to understanding airflows in mountains.

Every pilot who flies should be aware of the type of things that can occur. Fly with your senses as highly tuned as possible to the little clues that nature provides to reveal the unique meteorological situations that can exist.

NEED TO KNOW

- Convergence is two winds meeting
- The convergence lines that set up can be flown, often very far
- Different types of convergence exist: sea-breeze convergence, valley wind convergence, lee-side convergence and valley wind/met wind convergence
- Signs of convergence can be wispy cumulus clouds, different levels of cloudbase, cumulus clouds in 'odd' or unexpected positions
- Convergence can be very useful, providing lifty lines through the sky or 'bridges' across difficult valley crossings

CLOUD FLYING

By Bruce Goldsmith

ALMOST every experienced cross country pilot has a tale to tell: the time when they sneaked another 300m inside a cu and popped out the side in orbit; when they glided for half an hour on a compass bearing without losing a metre and flew so far they didn't recognise where they were when they finally broke free; the time they got sucked in so deep with no instruments and came back out facing the same way they went in.

Cloud flying can be everything from a magical moment, to an absolute necessity, through to downright terrifying. In competition flying it is highly illegal, and rightly so, for both sporting and safety reasons. When free flying, though, in certain places, and at certain times, you can seriously enhance your flight with a bit of well-planned and well-executed cloud flying.

Preparing to go in

Before we even look at the 'how to', let's look carefully at the 'when to' of cloud flying. Firstly, if you're on a hang glider simply forget it. Due to the way a hang glider is controlled almost any attempt to fly without visual reference will result in you getting into a serious and, potentially, very dangerous situation.

The pendular stability offered by a paraglider offers us the ability to fly without visual aid. It helps us calculate our attitude to the horizon – if left unchecked in smooth air a paraglider pilot will swing back under their wing and, if the pilot is sitting straight, the glider will fly straight. By contrast, once you implement a turn on a hang glider it

will continue to turn unless an equal turn is applied in the other direction.

In simple terms, for those who have never experienced hang gliders or three-axis controlled aircraft, these types of aircraft are close to impossible to control in cloud without complex and heavy instruments. In fact, hang gliders have been known to get tumbled in cloud with the pilot remaining oblivious until they find themselves lying on the sail!

Know your fluff

Assuming you are on a paraglider, and you're comfortable handling your wing with your eyes closed, the first thing you should do is assess the cloud you're considering flying in, and the day in general. Check the cloud's growth and development and satisfy yourself that there is no chance that it could become a cu-nim or even a towering cumulus that could become too strong and powerful to escape from. These kinds of judgements require you to have a sound understanding of the clouds and an up-to-date forecast of what is expected to happen that day.

Remember that one of the keys to predicting the development of the cloud you're climbing under is to look at surrounding clouds that are developing in the same airmass and on similar terrain. If the clouds are higher than 1,000m in height, or are very black and menacing, it might not be a day to go cloud flying. If the clouds are towering too high you could encounter uncontrollable lift or fail to escape the cloud when you want to. I only cloud fly when the lift is weak (up to 3m/sec).

Another factor to understanding the development of clouds is having a good picture of how a day develops, and what size of cloud you should expect to see at what time on different types of days. Studying forecasts and analysing the sky will teach you this. There is an immense difference between climbing into a rapidly expanding towering cumulus at midday with a forecast of storms in the late afternoon and going into a big cloud late in the day when the forecasters aren't predicting any overdevelopment.

Tooling up to go in

Flying with instruments, a GPS, a vario, an altimeter, and even a compass is also essential. Once upon a time GPSs didn't update fast enough to navigate you out of a cloud. However, all modern GPSs are very quick and make cloud flying far less traumatic than it used to be, provided you are gliding in a straight line. If you're circling then even a GPS will struggle to keep up, and a compass will just spin wildly. It is also possible, though difficult, to cloud fly using a magnetic compass, but you need a decent

> " **Once in the cloud your climb rate will often increase** "

equipped and under a safe cloud, then you're ready to go in.

Where to enter

Unless you are climbing under a small cloud you should make your way towards the side of the cloud that you need to exit from and try and enter there. Quite often the lift will extend right to the edge of the cloud and possibly right up the side of it if you are in the windward side. There are few pleasures greater than soaring up the side of a cumulus allowing circles to take you half in and half out of the cloud. Two other great advantages of being close to the edge of a cloud are that you can exit quickly should the air become too turbulent, and you can often also keep (unless the cloud is very thick) some visual reference on the sun each time your circle brings you around to face it. Watch out for any build up of G force that would indicate that you are actually spiralling rather than thermalling.

Deep inside

Once in the cloud your climb rate will often increase due to the release of latent energy. The sailplane textbooks quote 30% stronger as

ball compass, such as those you find on boats or microlights.

Finally, before you enter a cloud, you should be aware of the legal implications involved. In some countries cloud flying is completely illegal. In the UK gliders (including hang and paragliders) are allowed to fly in cloud even without any instrumentation as long as they are flying in unrestricted airspace. However, in France and the USA, cloud flying is illegal under any circumstances.

If you're satisfied that you're legal, suitably

a typical value. This is part of the chain reaction that makes thunderstorms dangerous and clouds get out of control. If there is a chance that your cloud could reach freezing level then the second burst of latent energy as the condensed water freezes will further boost the climb rate and increase the chance of the cloud growing dangerous. It's always worth checking the freezing point on a forecast before you go flying as a low altitude freezing point with a forecast of big development normally indicates the possibility of storms.

It can quickly become very disorientating inside clouds, and even experienced pilots can quickly find themselves lost. The trick is not to panic but instead just follow your instrument's bearing. It's best to avoid jerky movements on the controls, instead use gentle weightshift to steer, that way the instruments have enough time to keep up with any change of direction. If the air is rough and you need to use the brakes to keep the glider open, then it is inevitable that you will change direction, but just keep calm, keep glancing down at your instruments and readjusting your track. If you don't know which way is the best way being sprayed by the water running down the lines and risers. Once you get above freezing point things get pretty unpleasant as all that moisture will start to freeze. In addition to being very uncomfortable, the ice can cover your instruments and make navigation even more difficult. Pilots who have been sucked up into cu-nims and survived often report exiting soaked to the skin with their harnesses awash with icy water. If this kind of thing is happening to you it's clearly getting a bit out of hand and it's time to leave the cloud.

Look before you leap

Playing around the edges of a friendly cumulus can be fun and safe and can help you to gain that little extra bit of altitude before setting off on a glide, but anyone contemplating doing so should realise that they are entering a potentially lethal arena. Only cloud fly if you feel confident of your abilities to assess the cloud and situation, and know that if it all goes horribly wrong, you could control your wing with your eyes closed.

out, and there are no obstacles dictating which side you must leave the cloud, just pick a direction and stick with it. It's important to stick with it as it's not uncommon for pilots to fly one direction for five minutes, panic, turn the other way and spend another five minutes retracing their steps. The result is they stay in the cloud far longer than if they'd just stuck to their guns and followed the same bearing.

As you climb higher in the cloud you'll start to get wet. The longer you stay in the cloud, the wetter you and your equipment will get, and you may even find yourself

NEED TO KNOW

- Don't do it with other pilots – or mountains – around, you might collide
- Don't do it on a hang glider
- Choose your day – don't muck around with big clouds
- Know the law where you are
- Enter the cloud at the edge
- Monitor the G-force – don't spiral
- Stay calm, smooth movements, fly on your instruments
- Don't get wet – high-performance wings especially don't like it
- Only do it if you are a confident pilot

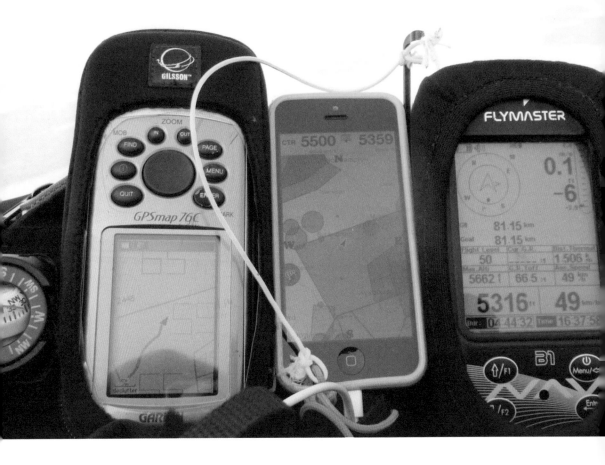

NAVIGATING AIRSPACE

By Hugh Miller

IT'S the one big untalked about subject in XC flying: avoiding controlled airspace. Yet it's one of the most critical skills. Each season, big flights get disqualified across the board, from club leagues to the Red Bull X-Alps.

"XC flying involves a huge mental workload for the pilot," says John Stevenson, the airspace co-ordinator for the UK paragliding XC League. "Pilots usually bust airspace when they're maxed-out or not fully familiar with their route – it jumps out at them amid the bustle of all the other tasks placed upon you while you're XC flying."

Thermalling and staying in the core can take up the whole of a pilot's concentration. Chuck in some turbulence and you need added effort to manage your wing. Then when gliding you're fully focused on searching for your next climb. If you're flying with others, you'll be watching out for them and spending some brainpower on radio comms too.

Navigating round airspace takes up another level of concentration. Most GPSs and flight instruments have tiny screens that you have to second-guess, and airmaps are often big and too unwieldy to read in the air. Here are some pointers to help:

66 It's easy to get freaked out by airspace 99

1. Pin up the airmap for your XC flight wishlist in a prominent place in your house. Look at it over and over again. Google Earth with airspace overlays is also good for this. You need to accumulate 'the knowledge'. In London, taxi drivers have to spend years driving around on scooters learning the different roads off by heart. Neuroscience research has shown their brains actually grow during the process. We need to do the same: memorise the maps, and visualise each route over and over again. This will drastically reduce your workload in the air.

2. On take-off, draw a line of your anticipated route, given the wind direction. See what's coming up, and make a mental note of how far from take-off each piece of airspace is, and what landmarks there are. For example, "at 40km out, watch out for drop zone," or, "keep below 3,500ft until the highway". Get together with others: more brainpower helps you become aware of areas you may not have noticed.

3. Think ahead, and start gliding crosswind early. This will get you some clear air 'in the bank' before it's too late and you're banging your head right up against the airspace. It will also mean that if you do get low, you'll have some breathing space to drift downwind in a light climb before gliding crosswind again. Getting crosswind early gives you options.

4. Work together. Fly on radio and remind each other of airspace that's coming up. This one tactic hugely lightens each pilot's individual workload.

5. For vertical ceilings, give yourself a good margin. Practise pulling big ears and gliding at full-speed through lift: you may need to do this in anger if you're pushing under a big cloud with airspace below cloudbase.

6. When you come right up close against a wall of airspace, zoom in on your instrument. Then it becomes a video game, pushing your arrow around the wall. As you come around the side of a circle of airspace, you can start to breathe more easily, knowing you have more room downwind to take a climb if you need to.

7. Don't over-compensate. It's easy to get freaked out by airspace when you've got adrenaline coursing through your system and you're pumped. Keep it in perspective.

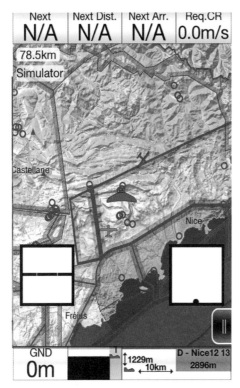

Next	Next Dist.	Next Arr.	Req.CR
N/A	N/A	N/A	0.0m/s

78.5km
Simulator

Castellane

Nice

Fréjus

GND
0m

↕1229m
↔ 10km

D - Nice12 13
2896m

▲APP FOR THAT
FreeFlight is one of many apps that display airspace on a smartphone or tablet

▲SNEAKING PAST
Tim Pentreath uses the technology to get past Dunkeswell aerodrome in Devon, England

8. Keep learning. Keep reminding yourself of what the different circles mean – airspace is complicated, and takes a lot of time to learn. Don't be disheartened if you do clip airspace – just learn from it, and learn how far back in the flight you would have needed to take action to avoid it properly.

9. Keep up to date with the latest tech. At the time of writing, the Garmin airspace systems are still the old favourite, but new airspace apps are emerging for iPhone and Android that look great. But always carry a new airmap – instruments and batteries can and do fail.

10. In the winter months, get together as a club and talk through failed and successful flights to learn from others.

NEED TO KNOW

- Airspace is complicated – learn to read the airmap
- Plan your XC routes with airspace in mind
- Anticipate the airspace – act early and you will be able to avoid it
- Work together – being on radio can help
- Don't freak out if you clip it – just move out of it safely
- Keep up-to-date with technology and airspace changes

THE MAGIC HOUR

By Bruce Goldsmith

FLYING late in the day is really something special for me. The lift is smoother, cloudbase is higher, the wind has died down and those long glides through the still air with little sink as the sun sets are real magic moments.

Not only that but they can get you into goal or add many kilometres to a distance flight. Many of my most memorable flights have included flying late into the evening and one time even after dark (naughty but nice).

Set your alarm for 6pm

Former Worlds pilot Darren Arkwright used to fly his hang glider with a large old-fashioned alarm clock strapped to an upright next to his vario. It was set for 6pm and you could often hear the alarm ringing through the evening air of the Alps during competitions. "But why?" I asked Darren.

"By six in the evening you have normally been flying for five hours and the conditions are getting weaker, you are tired and this is really when things get tough," he told me.

"My alarm clock always gives me a shock and reminds me to get ready for the most important part of the flight – getting home.

"It is too easy to give up because you are tired and the conditions are weak, but this is the stuff that sorts the men out from the boys."

Changing gear

The last hour of a flight is often the most important one. You will probably need to change flying styles as the conditions get weaker, and the sign of a really good pilot is knowing how quickly the conditions get weaker and therefore how quickly you need to change your flying style to suit the different conditions. Staying high is an important tactic later in the day. The thermals get weaker and further apart and less reliable so you need the extra height to maximize your chances of finding another thermal before the inevitable happens and you land.

There's also a big psychological element to squeezing the most out of the day. Getting home is all about extending the flight right to the limit rather than thinking the day is over. If you think the day is over you will surely go down. Often staying up is all about attitude and determination, so in the evening you need to be more determined to get up, not less!

Evening lift

Flying in the evening can mean finding different types of lift, or lift from different sources. During the day, rock is a very good thermal source, but in the evening rock gives up its heat very quickly; the sources that work well at midday will invariably only provide sink during the late hours. The reverse is also true. Trees can provide a surprising source of lift towards the end of the day. Forested areas like Bright, Australia are renowned for their incredible evening conditions. What happens is that the warm air gets trapped under the trees in the midday heat and, come late afternoon, when the rest of the land cools down, this warm air is slowly released, giving weak but consistent lift. Woods can be a real lifesaver.

"The last hour of a flight is often the most important one"

Magic lift

Another phenomenon is what's known as 'magic lift' or 'evening restitution'. Unfortunately this type of lift is difficult to search for – it either happens or it does not, and I know of no way of predicting it. There are some places where it happens more often than others, and also some conditions where it happens more often than others, but that does not really help. I know of no rule or explanation predicting this and I would be very interested to hear from any reader who has such a rule. Anyway, enough of the mystery. Magic lift is simply when you are flying and suddenly there is smooth thermal lift everywhere (not to be confused with wave lift which can also occur in the evening).

Some people say the whole valley lifts off, meaning that the warm air in the bottom of the valley that has been heated by the sun during the day all decides to lift off at one time, producing what is in effect one huge thermal. I have had this myself several times at Pandy in Wales, but as I said, there was no apparent reason.

Magic lift may be the same thing as katabatic convergence in the middle of a valley. This phenomenon occurs in mountainous regions when the up-slope anabatic wind of the day reverses and turns to down-slope katabatic wind. This down-the-mountain wind normally occurs just before dark in every mountainous area. When you have a mountain on each side of the valley the two winds can meet and cause a convergence in the middle of the valley.

I remember one particular day in the 1987 Hang Gliding World Championships in Australia when several pilots found such lift in the middle of the Kiewa Valley on the final glide home. The lift was not strong but was just strong enough for them to maintain their altitude, and some of them got into goal an hour after dark. The goal was an airfield and the pilots got their friends to shine their car headlights on the field so they could see it. It was an amazing thing to see, but such things are of course banned now in our law-abiding modern world!

NEED TO KNOW

- The last hour of a flight is often the most important one
- Thermals get weaker and further apart
- You will need to stay high and fly carefully
- If you think the day is over you will surely go down

LEARNING TO FLY THE LEE

By Bruce Goldsmith

EVERY pilot learns at school not to fly in the lee side. Flying in the lee is obviously dangerous because of lee-side turbulence and rotor. This rotor can be violent leading to collapses and accidents. In the lee side even a reserve parachute may not work if the air is too turbulent.

However, a meteorologist once told me that all thermals start in the lee side and if you fly in major competitions you'll see top pilots flying in the lee on a regular basis. And what about protected flying sites where you often fly the lee side? Why is it sometimes perfectly safe to fly in the lee and at other times extremely dangerous? And what exactly is conical hill convergence?

This article will give answers to at least some of these questions.

Thermals start in rotor

Thermals start when the sun heats the air unevenly. If the wind blows constantly and smoothly over the ground, then the ground will heat the air in a similarly smooth and constant fashion, which is not ideal for thermal formation.

What we need for thermals to form are differences in the air temperature. As soon as you introduce an obstruction into the airflow such as a house, a fence or a hill, you will get an area of turbulence behind the obstruction.

Sometimes the obstruction allows the air to remain still for a time, protected from the wind, allowing the air a chance to warm up. Then the turbulence may separate the bubble of warm air from the ground releasing it into the wind above as a thermal.

The same thing can happen on a small or large scale, so you may get thermals being kicked off behind a fence, a house or a hill. You can even get wind shadows or rotor behind a thermal itself, which can act as an obstruction to the prevailing wind.

So the lesson to be learnt is that rotor can be just as much a friend to the thermal pilot as a hazard.

Size matters

It's difficult to say when it is safe to fly in the lee side of an obstruction. The simple rule is – if in doubt, don't! That is of course the 'cover your back/limited liability' answer that you can get from any paragliding school or textbook. However, this doesn't really solve our problem, it's just the safe answer. My own personal experience says that the single most important fact is the size of the hill. The bigger the hill or mountain, the more protection it will offer.

▲ **THERMAL FROM ROTOR**
Air will warm up in protected zones. It can then be triggered to rise as a thermal.

Charlie King flying on the south-facing slopes above Gréolières where the protected area can extend higher than the hill. Note the clouds in the background being blown by the north wind. Photo: Fred Gustafsson

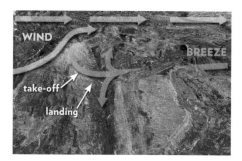

▲ **THERMAL HEATING**
How the wind works in Gréolières, southern France. The breeze comes in from the sea, allowing flying even when there is a stiff north wind.

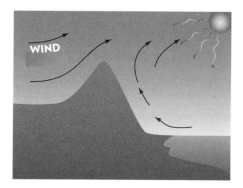

▲ **PROTECTED ZONE**
A sea breeze and solar heating can counteract the meteo wind, creating good flying conditions.

As an example, you can almost never fly in the lee side in the UK where the hills rarely reach more than 500m height. On the other hand, in Tenerife, nearly all the flying is done on the lee side of Mount Teide which towers to over 3,000m (eg the site of Taucho). You can even fly in the lee side in Tenerife when the prevailing wind is as much as 50km/h. However, you can expect strong lee-side thermals and strong winds if you stray outside the protected area.

Wind strength

The lighter the wind, the less dangerous flying in the lee side is likely to be. Wind strength is extremely important when trying to fly safely in the lee.

Flying in the lee in a 5km/h wind should pose very little problem, but if the wind is greater than 20km/h, then lee-side flying is likely to be extremely hazardous and dangerous.

Solar heating

Thermal heating of the lee side makes things a lot safer. This means that even if the air is turbulent on the lee side, it's being heated by the sun and so the air will generally have an upwards motion. This is also the case in Tenerife where the site of Taucho faces southwest and into the afternoon sun. Other sites such as Gréolières and Monaco benefit from a similar thermal-powered protection.

Sea breezes

If the heating is combined with a sea breeze or a valley wind system, then the protection from the prevailing wind is even greater. The presence of the sea tends to lead to a larger scale air movement than simple rotor, so helping to make the air less turbulent.

Conical hill convergence

When air flows around an isolated hill or

127

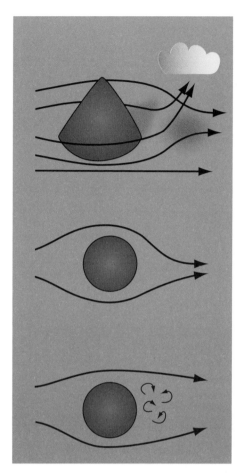

mountain, the air divides on the upwind side of the hill and then flows together again on the downwind side. The area in front of the hill is therefore an area of divergence, and the area behind the hill is an area of convergence. Therefore, where the air is converging, it can produce lift, especially if there's some thermic activity as well that helps produce some upward movement in the air when the air converges. If the air is not going up due to thermal activity, then it may be falling just as strongly as it could be rising.

Factors that influence whether or not you get lift behind a hill instead of rotor are:

- The size of the hill (bigger the better)
- Heating from the sun on the downwind side of the hill
- The stability of the air. If the air is unstable, the air may flow over the top of the hill instead of round the side, meaning that it will come crashing down in an area of sink behind the hill. A layer of stable air can help stop the air displacing vertically in front of the hill.
- The exact shape of the hill.

In summary

The main factors to consider for flying in the lee are:

- Wind strength
- Size of the obstruction
- Solar heating on the lee side
- Air stability
- Shape of the hill
- Sea breeze or valley wind considerations

▲ **CONICAL HILL CONVERGENCE**
A side and two plan views of what can happen behind a hill. The winds can meet smoothly, they can be rough and rotory, or they can converge and create usable lift.

There can be no hard and fast rule as to whether it's safe for flying in the lee. Everyone must make their own decisions based on their personal skill level and their ability to cope with any turbulence they are likely to encounter.

On the edge

It's often the edge of the lee that is the most dangerous area. If you are completely in the lee, you may be fully protected – but

> # "The bigger the hill or mountain, the more protection it will offer"

if you're at the edge of the protected area, then you may well encounter the maximum amount of turbulence. If you intend to fly in a protected area you need to go all the way into the lee. It's often more dangerous to test out the waters by feeling around the edge of the protected area than by flying all the way into it.

Flying upwind in the lee

Paragliders are generally not very fast flying machines, and when competitions set tasks upwind it is very hard to make progress. Even winds as low as 15km/h are very difficult to fly into.

One technique used a lot by competition pilots to get upwind is to fly in the lee of a mountain to use the wind-shadow effect of the obstacle to fight your way upwind. I am constantly amazed with what some pilots can get away with when it comes to flying in the lee side. In the UK you can practically never get away with flying in the lee. The wind is too strong, the mountains too small and the sun too weak. However in the Alps and other big mountains it's a different story.

Suck it and see

One final word. Lee-side flying is only for very experienced pilots, or for pilots under the instruction of a very experienced pilot. My guidelines are hardly clear rules that will help you decide, so how do you know when you can do it and when you cannot?

Experience is the first reply. Flying in sites such as Taucho in Tenerife took place with great caution at first, but as the pilots tried it they realised that it was actually relatively safe and that the wind protection of the mountain was reliable and predictable. I would have been very cautious if I had been one of the first pilots to try this.

In competitions pilots often use 'suck it and see' techniques. These are highly experienced pilots who can deal with turbulence and collapses without stress or major dangers. These pilots normally test the lee side for the fist time by flying in there and seeing what happens. If they get a kicking then they turn tailwind and fly out of there as fast as they can (normally at trim speed).

Please take all possible precautions when considering flying in the lee.

NEED TO KNOW

- We're all taught not to fly in the lee
- But sometimes we can
- Thermals start in the lee, often in the shelter of small obstacles like a house
- The lighter the prevailing wind, the safer it will be
- Sea breezes or solar heating can make some sites safe to fly in the lee
- Being on the edge of the lee is often the most dangerous place to be
- Experiences counts for a lot when deciding to fly in the lee or not
- If in doubt, don't

ADJUSTING YOUR BRAKES

By Bruce Goldsmith

WAY BACK in 1991 Ali Syrett was on final glide into goal during the Paragliding World Championships. The final glide was the classic St André race finish from the Pic de Chamatte to the main landing field. These days the glide is very easy. In 1991 it was a different story. Always turbulent, and with a headwind that varies anywhere from 10-30km/h, the final glide was always a nailbiter.

'Get off the brakes!'

Most of the British team were already in goal with our team manager, carefully checking her progress as she edged in. Suddenly the team manager spotted something through his binoculars. Ali was actually gliding with her brakes on.

"Get off the brakes!" we all hollered into the radio, "Let the wing fly! You'll never get into goal against that headwind unless you let the brakes go!" But, despite all our cries of encouragement and frustration, Ali couldn't release the brakes fully. She'd made the classic mistake of shortening her brake lines to what was comfortable for thermalling but for hands-off gliding this was a disaster.

Ali never made it into goal, but in retrospect she was lucky. It could have cost her a lot more than that.

Slack for a reason

When gliders are designed, test flown and certified, the test pilots carefully set the brake lengths to an optimum length. They are set so that the brake lines do not deflect the trailing edge of the wing when the brakes are off (hands up).

When the brakes are set up correctly there is normally between five and ten centimetres of slack in them. This slack can make the brakes feel disconnected or ineffective to some pilots, making them want to shorten the brake lines to give the glider sharper handling.

However the problem is that shortening the brakes makes them too tight, so that they permanently deflect the trailing edge. Even a small amount of deflection can mean the glider no longer recovers automatically from stalls or spins. The most common safety issue resulting from over-tightened brake lines is a failure to recover from deep stall.

Setting the right length

Setting up the brakes so they don't deflect the trailing edge isn't as simple as it first sounds. This is because the brake lines have very little load on them so the drag of the air flowing over them pulls them backwards. This drag can pull the trailing edge down and slow up the wing.

If the brakes are correctly set up there should be an arc of slack to account for this drag. This arc should also be present when the glider is flying at either trim speed (hands up) or accelerated. If it isn't the high-speed performance will be affected.

How to shorten brake lines

It is better to take a wrap than to shorten your brake lines. A lot of people fly with wraps for several reasons. The first is for feeling. Having the brake lines running over your finger gives far greater sensitivity to the feedback the glider is giving you. The second is comfort. When you take a wrap you turn the palms of your hands

towards you and in doing so you switch from your tricep muscles to your biceps. The bicep is a much stronger muscle and consequently can last longer before tiring and give you more strength for precise movements than the triceps. For this very reason, pull-ups on a bar are easier with your hands turned towards you than away. The final reason is to take up the few centimetres of slack in the brake lines and make the controls feel more precise and immediate.

Out of certification

I know that some pilots fly with the brakes shortened to give more comfortable handling. However, you must be careful not to overshorten them, too short and the glider will not recover from a deep stall. A deep stall is very serious if the glider can't recover and means an accident is inevitable. This slight adjustment also means that a glider that is certified EN A or B would not pass certification at all, or would be EN C or EN D.

Even small adjustments can make dramatic changes to the handling and security. In flight

you may pull down on the brakes and decide that there is at least 10cm of extra slack that could be removed. But you're almost certainly wrong. If you must change the designer's brake settings, do so in very small increments. Take two centimetres in and it will feel like six or even eight. Better still, don't take them in at all and learn to fly with a wrap like the designer and test pilots almost certainly do.

NEED TO KNOW

- Brakes should not deflect the trailing edge of the wing when at trim speed or when accelerated
- The most common safety issue resulting from over-tightened brake lines is a failure to recover from deep stall
- If the brakes are correctly set up there should be an arc of slack
- Take a wrap rather than shorten your lines
- If you must change them do it in small 1cm increments

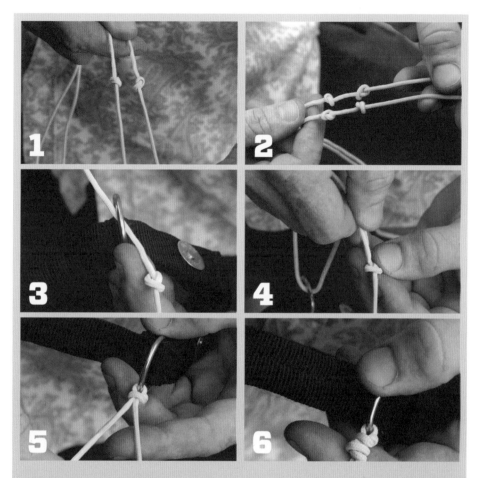

Adjusting your brakes safely

If you always follow this process you are unlikely to ever end up with uneven brakes, or forget where you are up to with your adjustments.

- Before you do anything, mark the line just above the brakes so know where you are working from.

- Pic 1: Tie an overhand knot just below the mark on both lines.

- Pic 2. Tie a second overhand knot either above or below the first knot on each side, depending on whether you want to tighten or loosen them. Check the new knots are both the same distance from the original knots and remove the original knots

- Pics 3 and 4: To re-attach the handles thread the line through the hole or ring, without pulling the overhand knot through. Then pass the end of the line through the centre of the overhand knot.

- Pics 5 and 6: Pull it tight and secure with a double fisherman's knot as shown, or any other type of stopper knot.

WINGOVER MASTERCLASS

By Russell Ogden

THE wingover forms the basis of many acro moves, yet is one of the hardest to master. As a manoeuvre it teaches you more about the dynamics of your wing than any other. It combines pitch, roll and yaw and teaches you about timing and pressure control, which form the fundamentals of paraglider control. When you implement this knowledge in your general flying, you'll find that your glider-handling skills increase significantly bringing you more comfort and security in thermic air. If you are considering getting involved in acro flying it is imperative that you master the wingover before you move on to try any of the more demanding and potentially more dangerous manoeuvres.

Pendulum and pitch

A paraglider is a pendulum and you are the weight. You control the swing by a combination of weight-shift and brake. Remember as a child how you first learnt to keep the ropes on a swing tight all the way up and all the way down? Mastering wingovers is like learning that again. You have to learn how and when to use weight-shift and brake to keep the wing loaded, your lines tight and your glider open.

For ease of visualisation in this article we'll describe our body's position during the wingover using the hours of the clock. Six o'clock is straight and level flight. Four o'clock sees the glider pitched behind you and at eight o'clock the wing is pitched well in front. At twelve o'clock you're upside-down in a full loop. First you need to master the pitch of your wing

by 'dolphining'. Flying at hands up apply both brakes deeply. The glider will pitch back behind you. The input should be assertive, progressive but only last a couple of seconds otherwise you risk stalling. Once the glider has pitched behind you let up and the glider will dive and pitch in front of you. Let it dive. Once it has stopped diving you will swing back underneath it. As you pass six o'clock, the bottom of the swing, hit both brakes again and make the glider dive again. This sets up a pendulum swing.

If your timing is correct you can make these pitch movements really big. As they grow you should find that you have to catch the dive with a short dab on the brakes to stop the wing over-pitching and collapsing. Learning this is crucial as you will need this skill again later on to control big wingovers. Now you are ready to learn about dynamic turns.

Dynamic turns

A dynamic turn is a turn initiated when the glider is pitched in front of you and you are swinging under it. Initiated properly with weight-shift and a squeeze of brake at the right moment, you'll instantly notice the extra speed, energy and height loss. In a wingover you link a series of dynamic turns together in a smooth coordinated sequence.

To start with practice wingovers using weight-shift alone. Aim to apply the weight-shift as your body is still descending, not once it has passed six o'clock. If you weight-shift after six o'clock you'll kill the wingover and find yourself running out of energy as you are climbing up past four o'clock.

It's difficult but a great way to perfect timing. Any serious flaws in your timing will come to light here and should be sorted out before you move on. If your timing is spot on you should be able to do wingovers that need brake input to stop the glider over-pitching and collapsing.

Remember at this stage you're not trying to emulate the Rodriguez brothers, instead just try and keep the wing pressured and the swing smooth throughout the manoeuvre. Once you can, you're ready for the next stage.

45-degree wingovers

To start with, keep the angle of bank to around 45 degrees. These steep S-turns should be identical in pressure, energy and body position. It's more beneficial for your training to be able to pull off 30 small but identical well-pressured wingovers than it is to do one massive one and then have it fall apart.

Enter by using right weight-shift and then applying a deep hard right brake input. Turn the glider around 90 degrees and then let your hands all the way up to make the glider dive. Remember this entry moment is critical, so put your hands up as soon as the leading edge is pointing at the ground and building up speed. Use your eyes to lead yourself into each turn, look to the exit point of your turn early and use plenty of weight-shift and as much brake as is necessary to complete the turn.

With a good powerful entry you can develop the wingover cleanly and dynamically. A poor entry results in a mistimed, sloppy wingover. As soon as you lose the rhythm (and consequently the energy), stop, and start again; it is very difficult to save a poor wingover and turn it into a good one.

As the glider dives and you swing back underneath the wing you'll have the maximum amount of energy and you need to

" In a wingover you link a series of dynamic turns together in a smooth coordinated sequence "

concentrate on the moment you're going to throw in opposite weight-shift. This weight-shift change of direction must come before six o'clock and the bigger the wingover the earlier you have to weight-shift.

When the moment arrives weight-shift positively. Push down onto your left bum cheek and lift the other at the same time, then smoothly but positively apply the left brake as you pass six o'clock and the moment of maximum force.

This braking action flicks you higher and forces the wing back around to face the ground again. As you climb higher, possibly above the wing, you may well have to apply both brakes quite hard to stop the glider unweighting and collapsing. The amount you have to use to stop it collapsing depends on the amount of energy you are carrying through the manoeuvre; the more energy you carry, the tighter your lines stay and the less you have to brake the wing.

Once you have reached the top of the pendulum you have to release both brakes to let the glider dive again. The timing of this brake release is absolutely critical. If the wing is facing the ground and you are at the very top of the pendulum you will have the maximum amount of speed and energy for the next wingover.

As the size of your wingovers develops you'll need to weight-shift earlier and as you'll be carrying more and more energy you'll need to put in very positive brake inputs to rotate the glider. A common mistake at this stage is to not use enough brake, especially at the highest point of the swing, to force the wing around to face the ground again. The timing of all inputs becomes more critical the larger the wingover is. If the timing is wrong you will lose the coordination of the wingover and will have to start again.

Building it up

Once the angle of bank exceeds 45 degrees it becomes important to start using the outside brake to keep pressure in the higher wing and stop it from collapsing. The better your timing is the more energy you carry through the manoeuvre and the less brake you'll need because the wing remains pressured and flying positively. The amount of opposite brake needed depends on the wingover. You need to use as much as is necessary to keep the wing open. Hopefully, all that is needed is a smooth application of maybe 30cm or so, but sometimes it needs a deep brake to maintain the pressure and keep it inflated. Remember, the more brake you use, the less energy the wing retains for the next wingover. Every time you touch the brakes you deny the wing the energy it needs for the manoeuvre. In a perfect wingover the brakes only flick the wing around to face the ground again; in a bad

137

"Turn your wingover into a spiral and bleed off the energy"

wingover they steal the energy from the wing.

To develop really big, complete inversion wingovers you have to really concentrate on timing so that you don't need masses of brake at the top of the swing. The objective is to fly the glider through the turn, using just as much brake as is necessary to keep the wing open and get the wing pointing at the ground again, but not so much that you take speed and energy from it.

Use this method and gradually build up the size of your wingovers. If done perfectly you should be flying a figure-of-eight pattern and have no forward drift in nil-wind; after each turn you should actually turn back on yourself slightly. With certain wings that carry a lot of energy you can even do complete inversions. If you find yourself exiting on the same heading as you entered you are doing complete inversion wingovers.

To return to normal flight you can put your hands up on the way down, let the glider dive and climb and return to normal flight on its own. However this looks messy and leaves you momentarily in a vulnerable position with the glider at a high angle of attack with little airspeed. It is better to turn your wingover into a spiral and bleed off the energy that way. It's more controllable throughout, looks better, and is great fun to do.

Using the methods I've described above you should soon be pulling off perfect wingovers. However, wingovers do not go without danger. There are several ways for them to go wrong, and they should always be treated with the utmost of respect. Learn in an appropriate environment, carry one or more rescue parachutes, and make sure you always have the height to deploy them.

Dangers and problems

Spinning the glider during a wingover is rare; deflations are the major hazard. To avoid such situations be progressive, work on the basics and build up gently. It is advisable to do your first wingovers over water. Do not practice them low. You should have at least 300m ground clearance. A badly executed wingover can lead to a dangerous cravat. The most common problem from a poorly executed wingover is a deflation from poor timing and or pressure control at the highest point of the swing. A mistimed input will kill the energy of the wingover, cause a side slip and can lead to an asymmetric deflation or even a cravat.

NEED TO KNOW

- Learning wingovers teaches you good overall glider control
- They help you fly better in thermic air
- Start by learning about pitch – practice pitching exercises
- Then start small, with weight-shift only, and build up to bigger ones slowly
- Learning can be dangerous – be high or have water for a safety net
- Work on the basics and progress gently – you are not Raul Rodriguez, yet

▲ **INFINITE TUMBLE**
Horacio Llorens setting a world record in Guatemala.
Photo: John Stapels

HOW TO GET INTO ACRO

By Pál Takáts

WHEN learning acro it is important to progress safely. This means taking advantage of the learning curve of those who have gone before. This article explains how to progress in a structured way. That doesn't mean boring – you'll have a lot of fun along the way.

Not so fast

Over-accelerated progression is the biggest danger in acro. Everybody wants to do the 'cool' stuff as fast as possible without paying enough attention to 'boring' basics.

The minimum requirements for an acro candidate are that pilots should have:

- Mastered active flying.
- Completed one or more SIV courses: big accelerated collapses, strong spiral dives, reserve deployment, etc.
- Suitable gear: a double-reserve harness, a wing in good condition, hook-knife, gloves, boots, streamlined clothing.
- Mental ability: clear judgment, fast reactions, self-confidence. If your mind is busy with your fears something is already wrong.

Once you have all that in your pocket, the safest way to learn acro is:

1 Good preparation, learning on the ground first
2 Master the very basics perfectly
3 Have a plan
4 Conscious training
5 Patience.

1 Good preparation

Before you do anything new in the air, you need to prepare and train on the ground. You must study everything about the trick you want to learn: how to enter, maintain and exit it and what can go wrong.

Visualising everything is extremely important. You won't be able to perform something nicely if you are unable to simulate it. Practice this many times, before all your flights.

Build up a good safety plan. You will face emergency situations from time to time – you just can't prevent everything. So you must have a plan, a series of different solutions according to the type of problem and the given altitude of how to escape the situation.

For example, you get a cravat: how do you react? Check your altitude? Try to yank the brake? Pull the stabilo line? Try a full stall? Throw your reserve? You have to have these kind of emergency plans and be able to react accordingly. You should never hesitate to throw your reserve when it comes to it.

2 Master the basics

These basic manoeuvres must be mastered for safe and quick progression. All the other tricks are a combination of these. To progress in acro all of this needs to be in your blood first.

Spiral dive: Be able to enter and exit quickly and exactly the way you want, controlling the movement during the entire manoeuvre. This is also a useful way to train your body to withstand the growing G-forces, because there is more to come!

Full stall: Practice this to total perfection. Once you feel absolutely confident doing it, do another 200. I'm not joking.

Wingovers: As a beginner acro pilot wingovers are quite difficult to learn. But they are really the basis of everything and will help you enormously in understanding the dynamics of the paraglider. It requires precise (but hard) brake inputs and heavy weight-shifting with perfect timing to build up this amazing three-dimensional movement. You must be able to bring out the maximum energy of your glider and make many big turns with the same height, rhythm and flow.

SAT: The easiest trick to learn. Concentrate on clean entries (without spin), as steep as possible an angle during the manoeuvre, and quick, controlled exits in not more than one complete turn.

3. Have a plan

To learn effectively you must have a training plan and goals. I recommend you follow this system. First, master all the manoeuvres as described above. When that is (really!) done the following will be a piece of cake.

Asymmetric spiral: This is the way to take speed to enter dynamic tricks and is similar to learning wingovers. In addition, next to the high, round turns you also have to be able to make really speedy, flat turns and still arrive straight down, symmetrically under the glider. This is the key point here.

Dynamic full stalls from wingover: If you really have your basic four manoeuvres nailed, with all the practice you have done this will be easy, quick and safe to learn.

Looping entered from asymmetric spiral: Again, nothing really new if you can do good wingovers although it requires a wing with

"It is like learning a language - you must have the basics right "

good dynamics. Work your way up slowly from flat (early entry) to higher turns (late entry).

Asymmetric SAT: Requires a wing with good dynamics and 'SATability'. This is already a bigger step, with some new things to learn like controlled exits and getting used to higher G-forces. Everything happens pretty fast and you must know which way is up and which way is down, where you are in the turn and when you have to pull the outer brake (pretty hard!) to exit safely. With a standard or freestyle glider this is not such a big issue but some acro gliders really need a controlled exit.

Do only two rotations with good energy and exit when the glider is set to shoot down again for the third time. It is important to go step-by-step and get the feeling of it first (believe me you won't have a clue what is going on during the first several attempts!).

Helicopter: From here on, don't expect your quick progression to continue. This is a super-sensitive manoeuvre and may be the most difficult one to master. When I was learning acro I was told that real Helicopters take a couple of years of intensive training to learn and they were pretty much right. By 'real' Helis I mean that you are not only able to enter it correctly (step one in the learning process) but you are able to correct it in all situations and make it work fine again even if everything goes bad (step two).

Most gliders require constant correction to keep them flat and stable. There are better and worse wings to do it on so pick one carefully. However, it should still work with most of today's models except the ones with low aspect ratio. Blame your skills first before you blame your glider!

Acro gliders are basically real heli-machines – but do not switch to them before you have really mastered it with a serial wing first. You can save a lot of time, nerves and maybe even some rescue openings this way. Re-learning helis on a small wing then will be a lot easier and safer.

MacTwist and Misty Flip: While you are working on your Helicopters you can mix up your training with MacTwists and Misty Flips. The MacTwist is quite easy (although not recommended with acro gliders) while the Misty Flip is like a short, controlled Helicopter turn and needs high-precision piloting. The good thing is that you can learn both step-by-step by starting with low energy entries, even just from straight flight or small swings.

Helico combos: SAT to Helico, Helico to SAT, Helico to Helico, MacTwist to Helico, Misty to Helico. From now on it is up to you. Go and have fun!

How to get really good at acro
By Horacio Llorens

1 Enjoy acro, but do it safely. The longer you fly, the more you will learn. Respect the process.

2 Learn progressively. Start with the easy manoeuvres, master them, and then progress to the harder ones. There is a learning pyramid and the first ones are the base.

3 When you train, make a plan. If you have 800m use the first 200m for dangerous or new tricks, move to easier ones as you descend. Don't try to impress with your landing – do it normally.

4 Always carry two reserve parachutes.

5 Use video to learn about your body position and the manoeuvre. This is a big help.

6 When you get stuck on a manoeuvre forget about it for a while, work on something else and then come back to it. Everyone gets blocked once in a while.

7 Try to follow your feelings. Sometimes you don't have time to think about what you're doing in a trick. A manoeuvre is in control when you don't have to think about it, you just feel it.

8 If you get to be the best acro pilot in your area, congratulations! Now move. You will progress very slowly unless you fly with better pilots.

9 When you have a big cravat or problem, first check your altitude. If you have less than 200m throw your reserve. If you have more, try to work it but keep an eye on altitude.

10 When you think you are ready, compete. It's the perfect place to meet other pilots, measure your progress and get extra motivation.

Tumbling: Do not rush into this. The best way to prepare for your first Tumbling is to perfect the Asymmetric SAT. It is the same movement, only the style of entry is a bit different. However, as it's easier to set the angle of them precisely, Asymmetric SATs are safer to perform. The higher you swing the harder it gets to exit cleanly.

Rythmic SAT, Infinite Tumbling: I left these to the very end for a reason. Not because they are the most difficult tricks to learn, not at all. Theoretically you'd only need Full Stall and SAT to be able to learn Infinite Tumbling. But Rythmic SAT is the only more-or-less safe way to learn how to Infinite Tumble. Unfortunately, some acro gliders are not suitable for learning the Rythmic SAT on because they get collapses and big cravats once the angle gets higher – even if your technique is perfect.

As a result many pilots enter the Infinite Tumble through a Spiral Dive. The concept is simple: pull a spiral as strongly as possible; release the brakes and lean outwards; wait, wait, wait; pull the brakes to enter; hands up; close the eyes and believe strongly; make some rotations and wait until it is 'finished'.

Today's gliders are good enough to complete a couple of turns without correction. Unfortunately this gives people who are learning the confidence to try it over and over again until something really bad happens. I've fallen into my canopy and I can tell you it is the worst experience ever. You really don't want to try it.

These are extremely sensitive manoeuvres and just a little mistiming or correction

failure will lead to loss of energy and a gigantic collapse while being upside down. Work your way up through all the other tricks first, then get a glider which is suitable and easy for Rythmic SAT and go step-by-step.

4 Conscious training

By now you should be getting a feel for how each manoeuvre builds on the other, and how important that is. It is like learning a language: you must have the basics right, otherwise it is a lot harder to progress and you'll make mistakes all the time. You will still be able to talk, but never really correctly.

From here it's all about training. It makes no sense to run up and down the mountain doing acrobatics. You must set your daily-, short-, and long-term goals and plan your training flights well. Find out what you want to practice according to your stage. Think about the theory and visualise your next session (you can do it in the cable car or while taking the thermal back up). Most importantly, after each manoeuvre, landing or training session ask yourself:

- What went right? / What went wrong?
- What did I do right? / What did I do wrong?
- How can I make it better? / How should I try it the next time?

Take notes immediately after landing, either on paper, your phone or into a camera. Use a camera for every training flight – it's the best way to improve. Make foot-cam onboard videos where you see your whole body and the glider. Watch it with your mentor and discover all the small mistakes. You will be surprised to see all the (sometimes unwanted) movement.

Practise everything in both directions right from the beginning. Otherwise you will quickly develop a 'strong' and a 'weak' side – later you will find it hard time to perform certain manoeuvre combinations. Don't fall into this trap.

5 Have patience

This is the last, but probably the most important point. Take your time. Don't rush from one trick to the other. Keep in mind that – like everything else in life – it takes a lot of time, regular practice and effort to master. Talent is of course good to have (to get the feeling faster) but with motivation and lots of invested time – and patience – you can compensate for everything.

If you don't have enough time to fly and train acro on a regular basis, it might not be the right discipline for you. If you still choose to do so it will be a risky path. Nothing will come easy. It will take hundreds and hundreds of flights, you will suffer failure and difficult times. At the start you will learn very fast but as you progress your learning curve will flatten out.

Think about the worst case before you do anything (and how to react if something goes wrong) and then visualise the perfect scenario and how it should all happen. And finally, remember the most important thing is to have fun. Fear is your friend and can keep you alive, but don't let it ruin your day.

NEED TO KNOW

- The days of acro being wild or wacky are long gone
- Acro is a discipline, and can be taught and learned safely
- Over-accelerated progression is a main cause of accidents – take it slowly
- You need to be a good, confident pilot before learning acro
- Learn on the ground – think things through first, watch videos, read, speak to others
- Master the basics
- Set up a training plan and goals
- Have patience and have fun

MOUNTAIN FLYING

By Bob Drury

THERE'S simply nothing like hitting a moonbeam and being fired up the side of some huge, vertical, alpine rock face with your eyes on stalks, your heart in your mouth and your brain in overdrive.

The mere presence of the terrain rushing by so close is exhilarating. Better still, the very nature of mountain-flying means you fly up and around landscapes that are otherwise either inaccessible or very difficult to reach. Take that to the extreme end of the stick and Himalayan pilots are soaring up to the summits of 7,000m peaks that have never even been climbed – or if they have it's by hardcore, multiday expeditions – and circumnavigating 8,000m mountains in just a few hours.

There is simply no greater and more privileged way to see the mountains than with cold air stinging your face and the wind rushing through your hair on a glider. But 'mountains give and mountains take' is a famous mountaineering adage that sums up exactly why the powerful and addictive elixir that is mountain flying is an intoxicating but potentially lethal potion.

Knowledge is security in our sport, so understanding how mountains work is paramount to not only your performance, but also keeping you safe in them. Ask any mountain pilot how to stay safe in the mountains and they, like Burkhard Martens the author of best selling book Thermal Flying, will tell you the same thing. "Learn about the valley winds!"

Valley winds

At first they seem like demons – blowing hard and unpredictably and turning safe places into danger spots. However, learn about them, understand them and suddenly they become predictable sources of lift and wonderful riverlike flows that can carry you effortlessly along. Valley winds can actually become your friends.

How they work

A valley wind is the air sucked towards the thermals coming off the mountains. It is an anabatic flow of air, which just means it goes uphill. This flow is formed and affected by the number of thermals, how big they are and how quickly they rise. The bigger and stronger the thermals and the higher they go, the more air they draw in and the harder the valley winds blow.

When a parcel of warmed air rises, either as a bubble or as a column, other air has to fill the space the thermal just left. It can't just leave a vacuum. Instead it draws in air from the nearest source of denser air, which is generally below it. As that air is drawn upwards, it in turn draws more air towards it and so a chain of motion forms. Because the denser air lies at the bottom of the valley, the air from there is drawn upwards towards the thermals. The air from the valley floor is replaced by air from lower down the valley, which in turn is replaced by air from the plains outside the mountains.

The massive collective convection of an entire mountain range's thermals rising at once draws in a vast amount of air from the surrounding plains. So big that, depending on the size of the range, Coriolis effect even takes place too – a very weak, low pressure system forms and starts to rotate. To get a better picture, stand near a burning fire with a burning cigarette or similar smoking object and watch how the fire draws in the air around it to replace the air being forced upwards with its heat.

Once the valley wind starts rolling, it will carry on thrusting billions of tonnes of air up high until the thermals finally stop at the end of the day. Then, all the air that has been sucked up by the big thermals on the mountains will come crashing back down again as a cold katabatic – downward flowing – wind.

This is the same process that forms a sea breeze during the day and the land breeze at night near the coast. The sunshine heats up the land more than the sea causing the air to rise from it and draw in the surrounding denser air from the sea. It forms a very regular pattern of daily winds.

Valley winds always flow upwards towards the greatest collective source of thermals, normally the main chain of mountains. The main valleys leading into the mountains act like arteries bringing vast amounts of air in to fuel the system. Hence they can get very windy, particularly if they are open and unrestricted. The higher, smaller valleys feed off the lower, main valleys, again drawing the air from the low ground to the higher. As a general rule, valley winds flow the opposite way to rivers.

They take the lines of least resistance from the bottom of the valleys, where the huge reserve of denser air is, to the very summits of the mountains that the thermals are breaking away from.

Because valley winds are made of denser air than the air they are sucked in to replace they fill the bottoms of the valleys just like water would. The similarity to water doesn't end there either. Being denser, valley winds slosh around in valleys like water does in a riverbed. They get squeezed and accelerate when the valley narrows and slow down as it widens. They slosh up the outside of corners and oscillate as they settle back down again. They also form brilliant convergences when they meet. Look around any mountainous region and trace the routes that the valley winds will take and you'll notice an abundance of places where they collide. Where they do, the two flows are forced upwards and form a reliable and often very powerful column of lift. So powerful in fact that these are generally the first places to overdevelop on unstable days. Even smaller valleys cause brilliant convergence points when their flows collide with others.

Once you start to picture the valley wind as water flowing up the valley towards the higher ground then you become able to predict where the airflow will hit the landscape to produce lift, and more importantly, where it will produce danger. Spines and faces that stick out into the flow become soarable once the valley wind kicks in. Even north-facing terrain that would never produce a thermal can have lift on it if a valley wind is bringing the warm air from the valley below and blowing it up on to it. This timeless process goes on everywhere in the world in pretty much the same way, so once you understand it you can apply the same model to any set of mountains and work out where the valley winds will be coming from and how they'll behave.

Now that you understand the process, you can start to understand the effects it has on our flying and predict where and when you'll experience a valley wind, and know how you can profit from it or be endangered by it.

Early season flying

A totally snowbound mountain face produces no lift so throwing yourself into a snowy bowl is potentially throwing yourself to the ground. However, that doesn't mean you don't find thermals where there is snow. Snow undercuts any thermals that are coming up from the valley floor causing them to release. In springtime mountain pilots find better thermals at the snowline than at the higher peaks where later in the year it will be booming. A snowy mountain face can still produce good thermals though. If there are

VALLEY WINDS

Ten things you should know about valley winds:

1. Valley winds don't go downhill. If they reach a col they release

2. Valley wind convergence forms where two valleys meet

3. Valley winds are made of denser air, so they only fill the bottom few hundred metres of the valley

4. Valley winds make spines that stick out into them soarable once they start. They also create rotor behind them at the same time

5. Valley winds generally run up the valley, the opposite direction from the way the rivers run down

6. Valley winds move like water, sloshing around corners and oscillating once the valley straightens up for a while. This sloshing motion creates patches of lift and sink along the valley sides

7. Valley winds can cancel out rotor from meteo winds as they wash it away with their horizontal motion

8. Valley winds accelerate and decelerate as the valley narrows and opens out again

9. Valley winds are often strongest on stable days as a heavy inversion will squeezes the air downwards and accelerate it as if in a venturi

10. Valley wind convergence is formed by two continuous rivers of air meeting and being forced upwards. Consequently, on days where storms are predicted, the valley wind convergence points are first to blow

▲ **VALLEY WINDS**
As rivers flow down a valley, valley winds flow up.
Imagining how water would flow up the landscape
can help. Photo: Ant Green

rocks showing through the snow then the high altitude sun will quickly warm them. With all the chilled air that the snow is producing there quickly becomes a dramatic difference in temperature between the warmth of the rocks and the frozen snow, and thermals form. With this dramatic temperature difference a remarkably small amount of rock can produce thermals from a snowy face.

Getting away in the mountains

One of the keys to successful flying anywhere is getting up and away from launch. Many mountain take-offs exist purely because of the convenience of access, not necessarily because they are in the best place to get up from. However, there's generally always a good climb reachable from launch, knowing

where that is is paramount to your success.

The first thing to consider is the take-off's aspect. When mountain flying it is important to fly on the sunny slopes, so put the landscape in your favour. It's pointless turning up at a westerly-facing take-off at 11am. It won't start producing lift till around 2pm. Fly the east faces in the morning, south throughout the middle of the day and west faces in the afternoon and evening.

Work out how the valley wind will interact with the take-off area. Some take-offs only start working once the valley wind starts blowing, others do the opposite. Some, like St André in the south of France, become too windy once the valley wind combines with the thermals of its south-west face.

The forecast meteo wind often has little or no influence on take-off choice; instead it is all

" Valley winds slosh around in valleys like water does in a riverbed "

about sunshine. Even on a northerly day you can use a southerly-facing take-off, provided the launch itself isn't actually exposed to the northerly and is slightly protected, as the thermals will bring an anabatic flow of air up onto the launch once they start.

Planning brings success

"What I love, above all in flying, is the discovery," says Ozone's Dav Dagault "And even going XC in new mountains is immensely rewarding. But, if going 'big' is the goal, then there is little room for improvisation, so it [your route] has got to be planned properly."

Taking Dav's advice further, American pilot Josh Cohn even advises you, "Get the lay of the land in Google Earth and XContest before you get there." XContest.org is an online XC league that allows you to search its archives for flights made from a site. By studying tracklogs you can see the most popular routes and exactly where pilots went to get thermals, gained height to make big crossings and surfed along ridges.

Stripping things back to basics and armed with just a decent topographical map you can still plan your routes quite accurately. Sunshine is everything in mountain flying, so it's crucial that you plan your mountain route to stay on faces that are in the sun. A perfect route starts out on east faces, moves around to the south-facing slopes then turns onto the west and even northwesterly-facing slopes at the end of the day.

If you have to cross any big chains then you need to plan the crossing to arrive at the right time of day- there's no point arriving on its west face early in the day hoping to get enough height to get over it, nor arriving on its east face late in the day. Large valleys present the same problem. Big crossings need to be timed so that you leave from a high point and glide to a good place to climb.

Getting up from low down

One way that mountains win fans over flatlands is that you can regularly get up from very low down. In the plains you'd just be landing, but find a slope in the mountains that faces a decent valley wind and extends upward for a few hundred metres and using basic soaring techniques you can get back up from just a few metres from the valley floor. This is where your knowledge of the valley winds really comes in.

A steep face that sticks out into a valley wind will allow you to get back up, or at least wait at the same altitude until a thermal comes along. If the terrain below is producing thermals and the valley wind bringing them onto the face then eventually you will get up. However, it may be a stage-by-stage process as you gain little bits of altitude in each bubble and gust until you are high enough to catch a proper climb. As you fly along your route be aware of where you could run to if you got caught out and sunk low.

Spines versus gullies

Spines collect climbs. Gullies collect wind. Because thermals have buoyancy they always want to rise upwards, and climb out of a gully and on to a spine. They try to take the most direct line upwards, until they reach a spine. Once there they become quite tenacious and hang on hard to the terrain. A thermal will roll up a spine until it reaches its summit or the spine changes angle, where the extra effort of hanging on to the terrain becomes too much and it releases. Anytime you can get yourself over the top of a spine, or a point on a ridge where its angle lessens, there is a higher chance of finding a climb.

When you study a long mountain chain with peaks on it you will notice the cumuli are better – bigger and more defined – above the peaks than they are along the main sections of the ridge. That's because the peaks have the most air streaming up them because a peak on a ridge by definition is a point where several spines meet. If you can get yourself to one of these peaks, or even one of the spines leading to it, you stand a better chance of catching a climb.

Gullies on the other hand mainly collect wind. If you are low you might be able to soar up or at least maintain altitude, but you're unlikely to find a moonbeam in the back of a gulley. However, if the gulley is steep enough to produce dynamic lift you may be able to gain enough altitude to reach a position to catch a thermal and get back up again and head out to the spine to catch a climb.

Do I stay or do I go?

A common mistake new mountain pilots make is to keep moving along their route, getting lower and lower, unluckily never finding a thermal, until they land. They may have passed over some really reliable thermal sources, but just missed the cycles. Had they only stopped and waited above the best sources, they wouldn't be hitch-hiking home, they'd be flying there. If you are getting low then you have to make the decision to stop moving along your route and wait.

Luckily, because of the valley winds, the mountains are full of places where you can soar and wait for a thermal. A simple rule when you are getting low and need to find a climb to get back up again, is to only keep going if you can reach a better place than where you are, if you can't then wait where you are until you have enough height to get to a better place.

Obviously your ability to judge how good the next place is is paramount to your success. This judgement will grow with experience, but to help you assess the terrain try grading it using the 'Five Star System'. That is, award

your destination one star for each: the Sun, wind, landscape, clouds, birds and gliders.

Afternoon cruising

If you want to get the most from flying in the mountains then make sure you don't miss the best and easiest part of the day, mid to late afternoon. By 3pm vast tracts of the landscape have been heated and the thermals are abundant, large and high reaching. If you can find long, continuous west-facing ridges you'll find a pretty continuous stream of thermic air rising from it that will allow you to surf along effortlessly. This is how the really big alpine flights have been done, by connecting one motorway to another and making sure that when the easy part of the day arrives you're positioned on the best landscape to profit from it. The important message to take away is: follow the sun and understand and make use of the valley winds and you'll not go far wrong in mountains anywhere in the world.

NEED TO KNOW

- Stay in the sunshine
- Stay out of the lee of the valley wind
- Watch out for local acceleration of wind as it passes over cols and ridges and through restrictions in valleys
- Make sure you always have a reachable landing in sight
- Wind, wind and wind! Understand it, fear it, use it and hide from it
- Be careful thermalling in strong winds. Don't let your circles drift you into the lee and the rotor
- Take note of the altitude of the inversion. It can be unexpectedly rough there so be careful especially when gliding at speed at that level
- Listen to your gut. Only go big when you're feeling great and ready for it. Don't try and force every flight into an epic one
- Fly the day not your desires

PICKING YOUR LINE IN THE MOUNTAINS

By Kelly Farina

CHOOSING good lines when gliding is such an important skill, and one that is often overlooked. Paragliders are inefficient at the best of times, and we have to take real care what air we fly in if we're to avoid sinking like stones. A good line on an intermediate glider will beat a poor line on a competition wing every time.

Good lines enable us to arrive higher over the next hot spot or trigger. Thermals are generally easier to fly the higher you find them, when they're well clear of the terrain

◄ CLASSIC CONDITIONS
Acres of rock heated by the sun will provide a booming day in the Alps. Note the biggest clouds are above the biggest peaks. Photo: Bruce Goldsmith

increase massively, whereas long glides along cool north faces or fighting into a headwind will usually result in you sliding off down the hillside into the bowels of the valley.

As much as you can, avoid gliding on the lee side of a strong meteorological wind – this could really punish your glide angle. Strong meteo winds make flying hard work: the lee side is awash with turbulence and large volumes of sink. If possible always stay windward, especially with winds over 15km/h.

Snow and shadow lines

In spring in the mountains we usually have a defined snow line running along the ridges, separating the remaining snowfields up high from the warmer slopes lower down. This acts as a trigger, and is often the very line we need to follow to take advantage of the most lifty air. What happens is warm buoyant air from the valley gets pulled up towards the sunny southerly faces, as if they're giant air-magnets. The hot cliff faces warm the air even more, and as that happens air feeds in from the valley floor below. The air travels up, sticking to the forested slopes with their great conductivity capacity, until it meets something that forces it to leave the terrain. In this case, it's a wedge of cold air rolling downwards from the snowy peaks in the form of a katabatic flow.

It is not uncommon to see clouds form well down and across from the peaks when there are still snowfields up high. Even on blue days, the snow line will trigger huge amounts of warm air, so following it will lead you to strong thermals and lifty lines.

below. Arriving high increases the chance of a reliable and safe climb out and allows us the luxury of spending more time gliding onwards again, rather than panicking down low trying to climb up high again.

Traditional good lines

With good cloud development, lines are easier to spot, but remember that what makes a good line with clouds also works on drier, blue thermal days.

Gliding along warm faces and working with valley flows will see your glide angle

▲ SNOW LINE TRIGGER
Warm air rolls up the slopes and meets cold air coming
down, triggering thermals which form clouds off-centre
from the peaks. Photo: Kelly Farina

If you see cloud shadow on the top of a ridge, this can create the same katabatic flow as a snowfield. However, the shadow has to be there for a long time for it to cool the air sufficiently for the process to get going – usually an hour or longer.

Simply joining the dots between potentially reliable trigger points is half the battle. But it's also important to take note of the viscosity of the air you are playing in, as this makes a huge difference in the lines you'll want to take.

Low pressure 'fizzy' days

On low pressure days, thermals release from the terrain at the slightest change in topography. The air just wants to bubble and fizz upwards, like bubbles in a glass of Coke. Cloudbase will usually be lower than high pressure days, and the thermals will be closer to each other. The climbs may be softer edged and pulsing more often. The climbs roll up the slope under their own steam, the temperature they need to rise is lower and their rise is unimpeded by inversions.

Expect good lines to be further out from the ridge in these conditions. You will nearly always get clouds and it is easy to spot good lines, especially when you start to know an area – you can begin to see why ridges work the way they do.

A heaped cloud in a continuous street usually means there's a stronger source in that area. However shade down below can quickly kill the day. As cooler air is dragged into the system it turns once lifty lines into sink patches as climbs fall apart.

High pressure 'sticky' days

On high pressure days, the air has to reach a much higher temperature before it starts to rise. These fingers of hot air stick to the terrain, heated all the way to the top before being wrenched from the mountain at its peak. Imagine a three-dimensional topographic map drenched in honey and turned upside down: this is how the air will flow, dripping along the ridges and off at the highest summits.

Hot air can't travel downslope, so it is forced to leave at the very top of the ridge. Air from several different sources may find its way to one break-away point, making the thermal long-lasting, strong, hard-edged and potentially turbulent.

On higher pressure days you're best off flying right over the peaks themselves. Base is generally much higher on these days, but a persistent high pressure system induces warm layers of stability. When the air mass becomes inverted, conditions get less predictable, less textbook and more challenging in more ways than one. There are fewer clouds, the climbs are slower and more stunted, but they're still rough! Not so nice.

The perfect days

The perfect days are somewhere between the overly 'fizzy' and the too 'sticky'. Pressure and humidity levels ensure the day is long-lasting with no chance of overdevelopment. The climbs are consistently strong and long-lasting with manageable turbulence, and friendly clouds form in obvious places. We all flow over terrain like we were born to fly. When all these elements line up the conditions are textbook.

Inversions

Inversions can make flying really unpleasant. Super-heated air will always be aggressive compared to air that's left the ground on its own terms. In these conditions, lines become even more important. The simple answer is to stay in the higher terrain. Avoid gliding to low trigger points and make short glides from peak to peak. Don't allow yourself to sink below the low inversion and into the warm stagnant air of the valley, especially in summer.

Climbing out on inverted days is something of a 'black art' too. It requires second-to-none mapping skills and the precision of a surgeon in the associated

▲ FIZZY FLATS
On low pressure days cloudbase will be lower, thermals will be closer together and the air just wants to bubble and fizz upwards. Photo: Kelly Farina

▲ STICKY FLATS
On high pressure days cloudbase will be higher. Thermals stick to the terrain and will release at the peaks or when the day heats up. Photo: Kelly Farina

Valley wind depth

▲ CROSSING A VALLEY FLOW
Valley wind is left to right. To cross, first tack 'upstream' and then turn and use the downwind flow to get you where you want to be. Photo: Kelly Farina

turbulence surrounding the climb, which feels similar to the lee side. It can be slow and stressful but it's so rewarding when it works. Once the climb has been halted by the inversion, track back to the higher terrain. The thermals rolling up the side of the mountain will not have lost heat as their triggered-lower counterparts have, and may be your only ticket up.

Crossing passes

Great care should be taken when attempting to cross steep mountain passes. This is mainly due to deep, fast flowing-valley winds that can be spilling over the tops of them. This flow tumbles down, creating a relative low pressure or huge lee down low and this drags air from altitude down to fill it.

Only cross these areas either early in the day when the valley flows are light or if you are sure they are areas of known convergence. Otherwise expect to be tractor beamed out of the sky. A fix in this situation can be to run with the offensive flow onto a windward face nearby, usually the other side of the valley.

Crossing valley flows

When embarking on a long valley crossing, in orbit under a high base for example, it is possible to just take a straight line to a reliable source.

If you do suspect some potential lee side activity after the crossing due to the valley flow, it pays to glide further in, especially if you are arriving in the influence of the valley flow. The protected thermal will usually deliver a smoother time on the next climb out. Better still, use an into-wind area if the flow is strong.

The small things add up

One thing that is not widely spoken about is 'active gliding', using the speed bar to trim the wing and keep the risers level. When the air is rough and a pilot feels the risers moving up and down, what is happening is a repeated series of small oscillations. The earlier a pilot reacts to these pitch and roll oscillations the less the pilot has to react. This is corrected with balance and subtly rolling hips to maintain direction and canopy pressure. Brakes control pitch, or rear risers if you are

in a hurry. You may be surprised what a little effort will bring over a 10km crossing – after all, we have nothing else to do for those 15 minutes.

Crossing the valley: The low line

Ensure you have chosen a good place to aim for on the opposite side of the valley before starting your transition. If you expect a strong valley flow, make sure that you are not blindly gliding into a turbulent super-heated lee side.

A very simple tip for arriving higher when you are only a few hundred metres above the valley flow is to glide at an angle into wind (up flow) first, so that when you sink into the flow you can have a freer ride more cross- or

▼ **THE 45-DEGREE RULE**
It is usual to feel nervous around strong clouds. If you keep the edge of the cloud with 45-degrees you will always be able to escape. Photo: Kelly Farina

downwind towards your goal. The amount varies with your altitude and expected valley flow strength.

However, usually whatever angle you choose is better than going downwind or just straight towards your target, as these will result in a cross-wind or into-wind glide, which is really inefficient.

Often in the main Alps, above the strong valley flow, there is little or no wind as the mountains tend to block any meteo flow, creating a neutral area. Use this to your advantage. Just this subtle hint can mean the difference between staying in the air or sinking out.

The corkscrew line

It's usual to feel a little nervous of strong climbs when you're gliding under a cloud street – the last thing we want is to be sucked up high into cloud. But there's an easy way of gliding safely – I call it the corkscrew line. Basically, logic states that if we're flying at 10m/s forward speed (which we do) and we're getting sucked up at 10m/s (scary, but it can happen), then we're flying upwards at 45 degrees. So, we just have to make sure we always have the edge of the cloud within 45 degrees of our left or right shoulder. That way, if we feel endangered, we simply head out for the edge. Choose either the windward side or the valley side of the cloud – this is the side where you can escape to safely!

This rule can be used for clouds of all shapes and sizes, as the angle is the constant. You just adjust your position to ensure you're never less than 45 degrees off the edge.

If we understand the 45-degree rule, we can use it to great effect under continuous lines of lift. Gliding slightly out from the centre of the cloud should lead you to neutral or sinking air. Once happy you are safe from going in, move back to the 45 position again and just repeat until either the cloud street finishes or you need to make a transition.

Plan, but adapt

Finding good lines is high-end stuff. Generally, keeping out of the valley wind influence will see an increase in average speed, and you can plan for that way in advance of your flight. Having a solid plan on the ground, and understanding what made it a solid plan so it can be adapted in the air, is really important. Then, when you're up there, you need to keep watchful and flexible. There is no 'one-size-fits-all' method for choosing a line, but hopefully these concepts will help a little.

NEED TO KNOW

- Choosing your line is an important skill to nurture
- It can mean the difference between flying far or landing
- Lines can be obvious when there are good clouds present
- But on blue days you need to choose wisely
- Follow the sunny side of slopes
- Follow the snow line, thermals kick off here
- Cloud shadow-lines also trigger thermals
- Understand the air on the day you are flying, it will give you an idea of what to expect and where to find lift
- Be careful crossing passes, watch for 'waterfalls' of valley wind spilling over from the other side and down
- Glide actively, controlling your pitch
- When crossing valleys glide upwind first, then drop onto the windward face
- At base, use the 45-degree rule to stay clear of cloud
- Have a plan, but stay flexible and adapt

FLYING 100KM IN THE MOUNTAINS

By Bob Drury

IT'S one thing flying 100km across the flatlands on a perfect day with a 20km/h tailwind and a barrelling cloud street, it's another to weave your way through complex mountain terrain, jumping deep valleys, high cols and skirting rocky peaks to clock up the elusive three figures! However, you can stack the odds in your favour by applying a few simple strategies.

Casing the joint

First you need to work out your route. Study tracklogs online, Google Earth and maps and look for the lines of the least resistance; any long continuous chain of mountains facing the sun will almost certainly provide you with a consistent line of lift and once you get established above one of these 'motorways' you can devour the kilometres. Look particularly for any continuous line of terrain that faces west. If you find one then you should incorporate it into the latter half of your route, as later in the day when the thermic activity is truly established, you can expect to get an easy ride along it. Likewise, you should build any east-facing terrain into the early stages of the day.

Next, work out where the cruxes or difficult sections are. If you are going to have to cross a high chain of mountains from east to west then do so early on. Equally you don't want to be gliding on to a west-facing chain early in the day as you could end up waiting until 3pm to get a ride out.

Some valley crossings can become easier late in the day if there's a spine or bowl you can soar up in the valley flow, others might become much harder; gliding onto a southeast face that's crosswind to the valley flow at 3pm is probably going to put you on the ground!

If crossing over a high plateau or range of hills is going to be a problem then tackle it later when the base is higher and try to put any meteo winds in your favour. It's sometimes better to fly slightly off route in order to climb high and glide downwind over your obstacle rather than to attempt a crosswind glide from lower and earlier in your flight.

Use the valley winds to your advantage and identify any sections you can dynamically soar along without bothering to get high. I was once told by a top pilot that you never ridge soar in the mountains, you only ever thermal! It turned out to be far from true, as in fact to fly a long way in the mountains you mainly ridge soar. Climbing wastes precious time so you only really want to climb high when you need the extra height to make a big valley crossing or to clear a high ridge. Knowing when to be low and when to be high is a crucial skill all good mountain pilots need to understand.

You should look at the relationship between the meteo wind and the valley flow, particularly if your route is an out-and-return. Sometimes you can avoid flying into a meteo wind by staying low and riding the valley flow upstream. At other times it might be better

" Don't follow a plan blindly – flying is a complex art "

to stay high to use the downwind component of the meteo wind to avoid getting pinned in the valley flow. Sometimes an out and return will be best flown high on the way out and low on the way back, allowing you to stay on the downwind leg all day long.

Your ideal route should incorporate as many motorways as possible – in the right order to take advantage of the sunshine, at the right altitude to avoid headwinds, and make best use of the valley flows. You should know exactly where the tricky bits are, where you need height and where you don't, where you're going to cross any big valleys and where you're just going to cruise along high peaks, and you should have a good idea where you're going to find the best climbs – generally sunny faces that face directly into a strong valley flow or convergence points. Once you've staked out your route like this you've already won half the battle. Now all you have to do is pull it off.

Sharpening your tools

If you're going to fly a long way then you're going to be in the air for a long time, so you need to be both physically and mentally prepared. On average a 100km route in the mountains is going to take you 5-6 hours flying at an average of around 20km/h, which is a suitable pace to allow you to enjoy the scenery en route and even get stuck a couple of times.

Make sure you're dressed for the occasion as getting cold is incredibly debilitating – it will destroy your psyche and can totally ruin your day. I once set off on an XC with a friend who, having put on all his thermal underwear before

he left the house arrived at launch sweating. This lured him into thinking he'd be too hot in the air if he wore all his clothes, despite the snow on the ground and it being the beginning of April. An hour later, he was forced, shivering, to the ground after only 30km which didn't bother him too much until I phoned him from 110km further on and five hours later!

Many layers is the answer to staying warm, and little items like a neck scarf or a balaclava can really make a difference to your day. Good gloves are essential on a big day out. I wear three pairs on cold days but more importantly I spend ages tucking them all in perfectly. It's better to spend five minutes on the ground sealing every possible gap that the cold might seep through than to struggle in the air to re-seal them later.

Next choose your take-off. If it's a classic day, the last place you want to be is a low level site that's tricky to get up from. You might easily waste half the day trying to get up, so instead take yourself to the highest, easiest and most consistent take-off that puts you in a good position in the sky to get on with your planned route. If this means walking then do so – you won't regret it half as much as you might regret not having done it if there are gliders cruising over your head at 11am while you're still grovelling around low or down.

Once you're on take-off, wait till you know you'll definitely go up before you launch. The big days don't happen every day, so it's better to launch half an hour later and definitely get away than to sink back down again and give yourself an infuriating hike back to launch.

161

Pulling off the heist

Once airborne, you should take a little time to settle into the flight rather than blasting straight off. I normally take the first climb all the way to the top regardless of whether I need the height or not. It's my way of settling in, assessing the day, getting the chance to look down at my route from up high to see if the sky and clouds indicate whether the day is working as I anticipated it would. It also helps calm down all the tension and excitement that's been building up ever since I saw the forecast the night before.

Fly slowly and conservatively at first – at the start of the day there are generally fewer climbs about and they'll be smaller and weaker than later in the day. Really avoid getting low before 1pm or until the day gets going properly and the valley flows start to blow well. Once they do, you can often soar up in the flow from very low down and can therefore afford to take more risks and go on longer glides. Until then take it easy – it's far better to do only 10km over the first two hours and then knock off 90km through the heat of the afternoon than it is to race 30km straight from launch and be on the deck by 1pm just when the flying starts getting easy.

Try to follow your planned route and believe in the decisions that led you to plan that route. It's easy when falling out of the sky in endless sink to get negative and pessimistic. If you do you'll start flying badly and you'll be hitching home in no time at all. Instead, believe in yourself, turn your sink alarm off and smile inwardly in anticipation of the ripping climb you're about to hit.

Nevertheless, don't follow a plan blindly! Paragliding is a complex art. Conditions

"Use the valley winds to your advantage"

change, skies cloud over, blue holes appear from nowhere, the normal route that everyone takes becomes impossible and routes you've never imagined might work suddenly become the only way through, so be prepared for change. On a day with lots of cumulus about you have to be pretty unobservant to throw yourself into a blue hole, or pretty sure that it's formed by very dry thermals and not very sinky air! Opportunities will arise though, and an observant pilot will notice the change and be planning his new route to avoid the new obstacle and get himself back on his route as soon as possible.

As the day heats up and the sun swings around to the west faces, you'll find that you can fly faster and faster as the thermals get bigger, stronger and more abundant. Between 2pm and 4pm almost everything in sun will be thermic unless it's flushed clear by a fast valley flow, and between 3pm and 6pm you'll often find such a long continuous line of lift above west faces that it really is a waste of time thermalling. This is the time of day to really boot it. Climb only when you really have to, and then only under the best-looking clouds around.

After 5pm you have to start paying attention to your height again because as the heat of the day dies away the thermals will begin to get weaker and less abundant and the valley flows will get weaker, making it trickier and slower to get up from low down. If you are high and able to stay above west to northwest faces you should be able to take your foot off the gas, slow down and milk the last few kilometres out of the day.

If all's gone according to plan, you should now be circling above your pre-selected goal field looking for the retrieve vehicle that your mate who went down early is driving.

Stashing the goods

Congratulations! You just cracked your first 'Mountain 100', a landmark in every pilot's career. But don't just sit on your laurels – go back over the flight in your mind inch by inch and look for any mistakes you made or things you did that nearly ended your day, and learn from them. Lastly, don't forget to pat yourself on the back for all the good moves you made that kept you in the air, If you can tick 100km in the mountains then you're obviously flying well.

NEED TO KNOW

- Plan ahead: study maps and tracklogs online and elsewhere
- Look for 'motorways' where you can fly far fast
- Work out what faces will be in sun and when
- Work out where the hardest parts will be and how to get through them
- Use the valley wind to your advantage
- Be physically and mentally prepared, fit and in warm clothing
- In the air, believe in your plan and decision-making, but be prepared to change route and gear if conditions dictate

◄ ABODE OF THE SNOWS
Flying in the Himalaya is an amazing experience but
needs proper preparation. Photo: Fred Gustafson

GOING OVER THE BACK IN THE BIG STUFF

By Antoine Laurens

ADVENTURE flying in remote locations appeals to many, but to take part you need to be properly prepared. Bir in India is an amazing site, which allows pilots to fly long flights in close proximity to the Himalaya. But increasingly, pilots often want a taste of the high mountain flying possible in the mountains behind the main ridge.

The result is that jumping into 'The Back' (the area behind the main mountain range which is great to fly but can be quite ferocious territory on the ground) is now something quite current. Some very good days with high cloudbase will give you the choice to challenge yourself with a flight close to the 5,000m-6,000m peaks and cliffs.

Unfortunately a lot of these pilots, who are often inexperienced in mountaineering, find themselves stuck. They land out and find they are without any system of communication, don't have adequate equipment, are far from the Indian telephone network and have bears and snow leopards as neighbours. Over the years several pilots have disappeared and never come back.

In wild places it is important to be prepared and to be self-sufficient. Your normal daily paragliding equipment is not enough. You need to be equipped with food, water and gear to spend the night out, maybe two or three, and to let your buddies know that you are ok while doing it. There is no excuse nowadays for causing an unnecessary panic: tracking systems, the right type of phone and radios make communication almost anywhere possible.

The terrain

It is important to appreciate the scale of the environment you are in. You might think you are doing well flying at 4,000m, but the pass at the head of the valley might be 4,500m high. Even the valley bottoms in the mountains behind Bir are at 3,000m.

Warm hands

The cold weather is the primary element you will have to fight. Very efficient gloves and/or hand warmers are essential. Hand warmers stay warm for around four hours. These are essential as it is important to be comfortable and not cold if you want to be aware, alert and confident that the decisions you make are clear.

Water

You need enough to drink during the flight and if you land somewhere that has no snow. Take at least a spare litre of water to heat up and either drink or cook with. To be very safe three litres is a good amount to carry.

Food

Something that is easy to carry and prepare and is also highly nutritious: nuts, almond paste, nougat, dried fruit, soup mixture, tea. There is nothing better than warm food.

66 The most important part of this kit concerns communication 99

A first aid kit

All of the basics included in a standard kit. Personally I pack this into my cooking pot.

Sleeping gear

A sleeping bag and inflatable mattress are essential. They easily replace the back protection in the harness and will give you a comfortable night if you wrap your canopy around you like a tent.

Communications

The most important part of this kit concerns the geo-localisation and/or communication. Examples include the satellite phone, which is the best option (although unfortunately not allowed in India). The second option is to carry a GPS tracking device. This device will not only give your friends the ability to know exactly what your position is but it will also allow you, via satellite, to send an SMS or an email with a message of 'OK' or 'Help' to your chosen friend.

Multi-tool and rope

I once experienced an incident with a student who had thrown his reserve and ended up hanging between two trees at over 2,500m. Everyone knows the technique of being able to use your reserve to climb down if hanging in a tree, however, this option was not available to him. After locating him and landing quite nearby I was able to bring him down after working to assist him for over an hour. Two things became very clear to me after this incident. You need a good multi-tool (a Leatherman is a good example) as this will help you to cut lines and unscrew karabiners. The second thing you need is a 10m length of 8mm static rope. Worth thinking about if you are flying over tree-covered mountainsides.

NEED TO KNOW

- Cold is your enemy: warm hands are essential
- Take water and food
- Take a sleeping bag and first-aid kit
- Carry phone / radio / tracker / and emergency locator
- Take a multi-tool and tree rescue kit

FLYING THE FLATLANDS

With Will Gadd, Steve Ham, Dustin Martin, Hugh Miller,
Karel Vejchodsky and Godfrey Wenness

WHILE mountains may be the theatre of circuit flights and high altitude dreams, it's the flatlands where the really big distances get flown. But as easy as chewing up miles in the plains might be, to many getting anywhere further than the first glide is an enigma. Talk of cloud streets that stretch to the horizon, lines of unending lift that carry you effortlessly along and thermals that start at 20m and blast you to base remain nothing more than fishermen's tales.

Mountains and the flats

In the mountains, your options are pretty much limited to following the ranges, but they're wide open in the flats – there is always the potential to etch a new path, limited only by daylight.

And low saves in the flats are special in a way you don't experience in mountains. As Karel Vejchodsky explains, "In the mountains your route is marked by ridges and valleys; in the flats it's mainly determined by the conditions along your planned route. You need to be patient, stay high, and often there's no need to fly really fast – subtlety and changing tactics according to conditions is the name of the game."

All in all, it's a very, very different arena. In the mountains specific spots work in certain conditions because of the valley breezes and the sun's action as it moves across the sky. In gently rolling countryside these forces are more easily diverted by meteo winds, uneven shading and different surfaces. Essentially this makes decision-making in the flatlands more speculative and 'on the hoof', though local knowledge and some understanding of how thermals form, flow and trigger will improve your odds.

Will Gadd puts it this way: "The flats are much more technical to read and understand. I very rarely sink out on a good day in the mountains. I still rarely, but regularly, lawn dart on good days on the flats!"

Sources and triggers

With the flatlands, it's all about the subtleties, reckon regular flatland flyers like Godfrey Wenness: "The sun angles, shadows, slight slopes, trigger lines, ground types and wind."

"A thermal source is a breeding ground for heated air: an area that receives more ground heating than another, determined by the amount and strength of sunshine it receives and the landscape's potential heating contrast. Time of day and sun angle on slopes, even subtle ones, is important to observe as this affects the heating potential of the surface," he says.

The trigger is where the heated air is assisted to release or trigger and shoot up in the sky as your friendly thermal. The landscape has triggers everywhere but thermal sources are less common. The trick is to find a thermal source that is lined up with a trigger especially when the wind is blowing.

A trigger can be an into-wind slope. Even a shallow one or a bump will help a bubble to release its earthly bond. A common

mistake is to not recognise a slight down slope/downwind on what looks like a perfect source paddock – they never trigger! A tree line works like a slope works, although more abruptly, and is always a good last-ditch option when low.

On a light or nil-wind day triggers are more difficult to find. You need to find a 'hot spot' in the fields – maybe more bare ground or a change in the colour of the landscape where the superheated air might unstick and draw the rest of the less heated air up with it.

"There is a story from the 1990s about the Moyes World Record tow crew who would drive madly around a paddock to trigger it for the pilot above," says Godfrey. "I've had success yelling at a large flock of sheep to get them moving and trigger a thermal – a mutton smelling one at that!"

A trigger can also be an area of cooler air that creates a higher temperature difference as the bubble comes in contact with it. Shaded areas like forests and cloud shadows work well, as do rivers and bodies of water. Wind speed is critical, as smaller sources may not have enough heating potential. If it's windy then potential thermals just get blown away in small scraps. The rule is the windier it is, the larger the source you need to find.

Steve Ham agrees. "Few flying areas are really flat," he says, "there are always gentle contours." He adds: "There may be gentle hills and ridges but we have to assume that none will be dynamically soarable in the flats. I always try to avoid reaching any ridge at a height that would put me low on its windward face. It's likely that the thermal will be triggering off its peak or lee side so you must be able to over-fly

"If you want to take control of your flying, you have to fly deliberately"

it on your last ditch attempt to get up."

In a completely flat landscape with no lee-side protection from the wind then even a crop of tall, dry wheat can give good enough protection from the wind to allow higher temperatures to be reached amongst the stalks. Early in the day this can be more effective than a dark, ploughed field. However, later in the day naked earth or rock will maintain a higher surface temperature allowing quick heating of the air above it and possibly provide a near constant column thermal. The field of wheat, having once released its thermal, will take longer to re-heat and re-release.

Apart from the usual physical triggers like irregularities in the landscape, small hills, tree lines, conurbations, buildings and bodies of water, you'll also find certain airflows trigger thermals too. A small hill can split the wind and when it converges again behind it it may draw air from your source.

Cold air will undercut and release warm air at the source too – for example air blowing off water or coming from a shaded area – so it's a good idea to fly the shadow line of a cloud as you fly downwind.

Sometimes you can get a source and trigger combination to fly along. In very dry flatland environments like Manilla and central Spain river courses work well. They are slightly lower than the surrounding land, allowing some protection from the wind for better heating and the surrounding air will have a slightly greater relative humidity. Vegetation along the banks gives contrast and protection from the cooling wind, and trees lining the banks act as useful triggers.

Flatland cloud development

Cloud development is an incredibly important thing to learn about. "Whenever I have time I watch the sky and how the clouds form," says Karel.

"I think it's impossible to say exactly when a cloud stops working. Each cloud is different and only years of experience in the air and watching from the ground can teach you about them. Check the sky constantly when you are flying and visualise which clouds are forming and which not. One good rule is to look at cloud shadows on the ground beneath you. If the shadow has no holes then it could be active. If there are holes in the shadow it's probably dying."

Although there are no big mountains to observe, there's an infinite amount to learn about clouds. When you're flying, you don't have so much time, so a good trick is to take a mental snapshot of the clouds ahead when you're halfway to base, and another couple before reaching base. Comparing these mental snapshots can tell you if the cloud's building, stabilising or decaying over time.

Dustin says its good to be skeptical early in your flight, and slowly build up trust in the clouds that work – a few clouds each day prove to be reliable and predictable, while some are duff. "Whatever the nature of the clouds," he says, "at least they seem to follow the same pattern for the rest of the day."

"You have to think ahead if you're flying crosswind "

"If you're getting all your climbs on the downwind, shady side of the clouds, then there's probably not much reason to waste time and altitude detouring to the upwind, sunny, crisp side of each cloud because wishing doesn't seem to change things very often."

Blue days

The great thing about blue days is that there is more sunshine on the ground and no chance of scary moments below or inside big clouds.

"In the dry areas I fly in central Spain," says Steve, "in summer thermals often go to over 4,000m without condensing. On these days I just point the glider in the direction I want to go, it is rare not to find something on the glide path. I am sure that if you compare tracklogs of pilots on good blue days against cu filled days, the former tracks would be much straighter."

If the blue day is due to inversions preventing thermals reaching the condensation point, then you'll often still see the occasional cloud forming where thermals are strong enough to break through the inversions – on distant mountain peaks for instance. If you see cu's regularly forming in a specific place on an otherwise blue day in the flats it's worth noting where as it will also be the place that will boom on a less stable day, and possibly the place where cumulonimbus clouds are likely to form on a very unstable day.

When climbing, listen to your intuition more than your vario. A blue day implies stability, which means the thermals are squeezing up through warm layers, and can act quite chaotically. Follow the energy of the climbs, really feel through your harness and brake pressure for the cores, and use them – they will be a much better guide to help you catch a core to carry you through the inversion layers. Your vario might be squealing just because you've just hit some wind shear. Also, on blue days you often get large patches of weak lift. Keep surfing through these till you hit the core. Experience in blue days counts for heaps.

Cloud streets

Cloud streets are the nirvana of XC flying everywhere, but they need wind – and paraglider pilots rarely fly in strong enough winds for long streets to form. But whatever the length, a few rules will help you get the most out of them.

"One thing I have learned the hard way is not to leave the climb before base," says Dustin Martin. "I've wasted many great cloud street runs by leaving the first climb in the street too early and not getting any more lift for the entire length of the street. So get established at base and then start cruising."

Cloud streets set up in the flats less often

than on mountain ranges though the same reasons apply: a line of sources and triggers; a mid-level unstable layer; or a convergence zone can produce cloudstreets or useable lines of lift.

Cloud shadows can create conditions for sources and triggers to line up in a domino effect. A river course or long highway lined up with the wind can have a similar effect in providing a line of triggers.

Whatever you do, you need to fly fast to make the most of them. "I've only flown real cloudstreets over 50km twice, says Karel; "I think we are too slow to use them as they die before we can get that far along them. The other problem is that really long cloudstreets usually form on days with very strong wind."

Cloud streets tend to work best late in the afternoon and evening, when cloud cycles have slowed right down and the clouds produce lift for much longer. The trick is to get up in the sucky air just below base and boot it. The clouds may look solid ahead, but chances are they're already on the turn, so get gliding and surf the energy while its still there. But, if it's a really active street – like the ones that set up with convergence in central Spain, you can easily be hoovered up so it's best to surf the edge.

The thirds rule

There's a common rule in flatland flying, where you divide the sky up into vertical thirds and make your decisions based on the terrain when in the bottom third, on clouds in

the top third and both in the middle section. However, most experienced pilots are a lot more fluid in their decision making than that, looking much further ahead down route to suss out the best moves.

"I never just look for the obvious next cloud, but how the pattern continues beyond," says Steve. "This is particularly relevant in central Spain where long chains of cumlus can set up with little cumuli either side of it. Some of these streets are better formed than others, so it makes sense to set yourself up to run the best street well ahead of time."

There's a psychological bonus here too – thinking of how easy it is going to be 40km down the line when you hit that cloud street is a positive thing to think about on a glide rather than stressing about not connecting with the next cloud en route.

Dustin Martin is dogmatic about clouds: "If it's a cloud day, I'll defer to a cloud all the way to the dirt," he says. "If I'm low and can't reach any clouds then I'll go for the most productive terrain. But even then, I'll be much more interested in real-time signs of lift like dusties and birds."

Meanwhile, it's useful to have a virtual 'floor' to your flying in mind, to save yourself from having to catch too many low saves. It's a minimum XC height – the height below which you have no options left but to desperately find ground sources.

"This is an important concept, as once below it you are destined to deck it if you don't have some good ground sources laid out in a row. Godfrey Wennes explains that, "It's best to have two or three options within glide and 100m to spare to work if below minimum XC height.""

Blue holes and the chequerboard theory

It can't go up everywhere, and blue holes are caused by a big localised lack of lift. They are a big cause of bomb-outs – often they're just too wide to cross, and you're better off gliding gingerly around their sides.

Blue holes are caused by a higher ground moisture content delaying heating – for instance rain from a local storm cell the day before leaving the ground wet – or a lack of a trigger, downslope terrain and all the usual reasons why one area has better thermals than others. In combination these can create a severe blue hole with a doughnut of cumulus clouds surrounding it. In Florida, for example, the lakes and the wind blowing across them cause big blue holes. If you know this as fact, then on blue days it definitely pays to know what not to fly downwind of. In stronger winds, the downwind end of a cloudstreet will result in a blue hole as a line of sink flows beyond sometimes for 10km or more.

It's sometimes useful to think about the sky as a chequerboard, where the white squares have lift within them, the black squares have sink. The higher the cloudbase, the bigger the squares – on a good day here with a 1,500m base, the squares will be around 5km wide. "Your job as a pilot is to keep to the white squares as much as you can," says Hugh.

Blue holes and shaded-out areas are typical 'black squares'. "There's little point gliding for a tractor ploughing a field if it's in the middle of a black square, as all the air above it is sinking", he says.

Sunny areas with cumulus just downwind are the obvious white squares. We know this principle is true, because when you set off on a glide from a high base in the UK, you typically glide for 3-5km or so before hitting your next climb.

The siesta

Many flatland places have a 'siesta'. The day starts to get going, but then it pauses for a while before it really gets going. Dustin writes, "Almost everywhere I've flown has a pause between the earliest climbs and stronger climbs. In distance flying it's wise to be critical of any change in conditions and save the drag racing for the afternoon hours."

The effect can be caused by an inversion breaking. In Piedrahita, for example, it's common to be able to launch with very light or nil-wind at around 11am and stay up on thermals way out in front when the launch isn't soarable. Then, the thermodynamic breeze on launch starts and the thermals close to the hill become more consistent, but those further out weaker and scarcer.

This is probably due to the newly started anabatic flow ventilating the hill and stopping the ground heating the air above it as effectively. Also, initially the thermals are stopped by a low inversion, but the inter-thermal distance is small, so the pilot has a greater chance of finding one. Once the early morning inversion breaks, the thermals rise higher and are stronger, but the inter-thermal spacing is greater, so they are harder to find.

"I used the term 'siesta' in the mid-90s to describe the effect here in Manilla," says Godfrey. "It happens just after the mid-morning burst phase. The ground air temperature is still quite low and the sun quite hot creating tight, strong climbs initially. The ground inversion also stops the upper air mixing down to lower levels until later."

"Once the burst phase is over, the ground temperature shoots up over the space of an hour or so to then build steadily to its peak in mid-afternoon. When the ground inversion breaks the cooler upper air mixes down low and previously good sources need time to re-charge. The process takes an hour or so and if you are on an XC then you really need to be high and look for good clouds."

In more temperate climes, the 'siesta' happens later in the day. "In the UK a lot of pilots seem to land at around 2-3pm. I'm one of them!" says Hugh. "Recently I've just had it as a mission to stay in the air after 3pm. You can often see the clouds start to look a bit ragged around this time. You have to change down gears and just hang out, wait for the sky to reactivate, and when it does, it is much, much better than before with more 'gloopy' consistent climbs."

It even happens at world record destinations, says Will. "It's a transition period from the relatively low morning lift to the strong afternoon lift," he writes. "In Zapata and Hobbs we call this the 'witching hour'. You just have to survive!"

The long glides

The real beauty of flatland flying comes late in the day. Thermal life cycles are much longer, and clouds stay and just keep sucking up the air – sometimes until after dusk. The sky is much more predictable, and it's the time when all your hard work earlier in the day can pay off. Stay high, take each climb to the top and revel in the long, floaty late afternoon and evening glides: this is the time when the big distances really get clocked up. Sometimes you'll be amazed just how long the day lasts, and just how far you can go. And remember – if you give up, you go down!

Working as a team

One final piece of advice is that flatland flying is so much easier with a gaggle. Often, the gaggle takes a while to 'get going', with pilots a little hesitant in their decision making early on in the flight. On glide, it's important to fan out. You notice dramatic differences in glide performance even when pilots are less than 50m to your side. You want to be far enough apart to 'taste' the air on different lines, but close enough to get over to each other if you need to. It's particularly important down low.

Will remarks, "It's amazing how seldom the whole gaggle sinks out in flatland comps."

NEED TO KNOW

- Go where the sky leads you, there's nothing to hit
- Stay high, turn in everything, and the flight ends when you touch the ground. Low saves are part of flying in flatlands
- It's never over until you're on the ground in the flats
- The skill in the flats is to avoid bombing out when low by being able to successfully track weak drifting climbs
- If there is any wind then drift like a leaf and be sure to re-set into the headwind by extending the headwind part of the 360 until hitting the peak lift point
- Look at paddocks as if they were small hills where the high point is at the downwind end of the paddock. Then imagine the wind blowing over it and where you would want to be positioned to find or wait for a climb
- Think way, way ahead. Unless you're in a gaggle of great pilots, or the clouds are just insane, simply stumbling into your next climb just won't work every time
- Learn to shift your aggression level based on conditions ahead. If you're not thinking a couple of moves ahead, this part is learned the hard way, which is very effective
- Book a block of time, say a couple of weeks, to get good at flatland flying. It takes time
- Avoid reaching any ridge at a height that puts you low on its windward face. It's most likely that the thermal will be triggering off its peak or lee side so you must be able to over-fly it on your last ditch attempt to get up

EMERGENCY PLANNING

By Ian Blackmore

WITH luck we will launch safely, spend a day soaring high above the peaks and plateaus and return safely to watch the sunset while sharing a beer with friends. But it doesn't always work out that way. We need to plan for the unthinkable: anything from a few hours spent hanging in a tree to lying alone and injured somewhere deep in the mountains.

Mobile phone

Vital. Coverage, however, can be sketchy, so they are not to be relied upon. As well as the obvious safety function, if you go missing it is possible for 'the authorities' to get an estimate of your position depending on where your phone was last in range. Remember to use it: if you're going flying tell someone before you go and check in with them when you land. There's nothing worse than worrying about a pilot who is later found safe and sound in a Spanish tapas bar, mobile phone switched off.

Satellite phone

A satellite phone has far greater worldwide coverage than a regular mobile phone. They're expensive, but if you're going off the beaten track then they can be worth their weight.

Trackers

Tracking devices are either standalone, can run through your smartphone or, increasingly, are incorporated into flying instruments. They work on the satellite or mobile phone network and often allow you to be tracked in real time online. This is great for competition retrieve and spectators. It's also good for those back home who might wonder how your day is going.

Radio

The other most common communication devices in use by free flyers are two-metre or airband radios. To be completely legal you need the appropriate licence, but whether used legally or not, they have saved many lives over the years. Range is fantastic air to air, usually 40km or more, but only line of sight or less when on the ground. It is generally more useful for co-ordinating rescues than actually calling for help as an individual. Annoyingly, neither phones nor radios work with flat batteries – always carry spare ones.

GPS

The ultimate navigation device and ideal for communicating a precise location to your rescuers. Make sure you use the same map datum and position format as your retrieve crew or they may not find you.

Map

A detailed terrain and road map is vital for finding the best route out of an area following an outlanding, and also for describing your location to rescuers. Airspace maps are fine for airborne navigation but generally lack sufficient detail to find the nearest track – or the bar. Works well without batteries.

Compass

A decent compass is another essential for navigation both in the air and on the ground.

It doesn't have to be big or expensive, just sufficient to take some vague bearings out of cloud or on the ground. It too has the added advantage of never having a battery threatening to go flat.

Torch/strobe

Sooner or later everyone who flies XC ends up with a long walk that takes them into the hours of darkness. Walking over rough terrain with a 20kg pack on your back in total darkness is as likely to injure you as the flight itself. A lightweight torch or headtorch can be a godsend, for avoiding injury, reading maps and compasses and also for signalling to your retrieve exactly where you are.

Multi-tool

A small multi-tool is one of the most useful pieces of kit you can carry whether injured, lost or simply ready to launch and needing to unscrew the battery compartment on your vario. Look for one with pliers (for karabiners), knife, wood saw and screwdrivers.

Cigarette lighter

Useful on the hill for heat-sealing frayed line, thread or webbing the humble cigarette lighter is also by far the simplest way to light a fire to avoid hypothermia should you ever have to spend a night on a mountain.

Water

The single most essential part of your flying kit. Dehydration can kill a healthy individual in a matter of days and will seriously impair your judgement within hours especially considering the loads we carry and the arid environments we sometimes encounter. Since it's impossible to guarantee exactly which side of your harness you will crash or fall on it makes sense to store your water in several different smaller containers rather than one large one. If you fly with ballast, think carefully before dumping it before starting on a long walkout in the afternoon sun.

Food

It takes a long time to actually die of starvation, but when it gets to midnight and you're still walking, that large bar of chocolate lurking in the back of your harness develops a distinct appeal, even if it has been there all summer!

Dental floss

Clean teeth may not seem a priority when you're stuck up a tree but this tiny, lightweight reel of thread combined with a karabiner makes it far easier for your rescuers to pass a rope up to you. Floss is also very useful for tying things together in an emergency.

Space blanket or bivi bag

Usually made of an aluminised reflective foil, these pack small and can be used for everything from keeping warm to a signal marker. Not absolutely essential as either your paraglider or reserve make a perfectly acceptable sleeping bag in an emergency.

Sticky tape

Useful, cheap and versatile. Pack normal electrician's tape or heavier gaffer tape. Can be used to tape a damaged radio, GPS, torch or even to tape bandages in place.

First aid kit

A simple first aid kit is a must – you will invariably end up using it at some point. Be sure to choose one with sterile bandages and the essentials to help stem bleeding.

Drugs

Unskilled use of drugs on an accident victim can have more serious consequences than the injury itself. Unless medically qualified it's probably best just to carry First aid essentials like anti-diarrhoea tablets like Imodium, and antihistamines – useful for anaphylactic shock as well as hay fever.

DEALING WITH A GUST FRONT

By Bruce Goldsmith

DURING one of the practice days at a World Championships in Brazil, myself, Xevi Bonet from Spain, and Americo de Souza from Portugal had to outrun a thunderstorm. It was a pretty exciting experience – almost a bit too exciting for comfort to be honest – but it got me thinking that an analysis of how I was assessing my situation that day could make a useful insight into 'how to' or even 'how not to' fly in thunderstorms.

Thunderstorm threats

There are two main threats to pilots from thunderstorms.

Number one is gust fronts. These are downdraughts of cold air that are pushed out in front of the thunderstorm. Normally they are quite visible. Gust fronts are only really dangerous when you are on or near the ground, where sudden high winds could cause you to crash or be blown into obstacles. Gust fronts can't really hurt you in the air, so the most important thing to remember is to avoid landing as a gust front comes through.

Number two is strong lift. Thunderstorms can produce very strong lift that can suck you up to such high altitudes that you could pass out or even freeze to death. There can also be extreme turbulence inside a thunderstorm; gusts of up to 300km/h have been recorded within powerful cu-nims. Even 747s avoid flying into thunderstorm heads as the forces within have allegedly broken the wings off aeroplanes in the past, so they're pretty powerful things.

Planning

If in doubt, don't fly. This almost goes without saying of course, but on the day in question I nearly got caught out as things developed faster than I'd expected. The forecast gave a possibility of thunderstorms, but this was nothing new – most days in Governador Valadares we had a forecast for thunderstorms and we all flew, cautiously, and the storms never arrived.

But on this day, even before launching, I could see an area of strong rain clouds 10km northwest from launch. The cloud showed a lot of strong vertical development and rain beneath it, but there had been no thunder; there was no anvil towering above and still no gust fronts. Over the previous days we'd seen lots of similar clouds, and they nearly always developed into large clouds whose own shadow cut off the sunlight and hence the convection to them; these cloud normally died out in half an hour or so. However, this cloud had other ideas.

Monitoring

I decided to launch, and headed south down the road from Alpercata while keeping a close eye on the cloud. I was looking out for any signs of a change in the size of the storm, so I studied how high it was towering, and whether there were any gust fronts forming. I also took note of the position of the storm by watching its progress relative to a ground feature every five minutes. By noting the times I could calculate the exact

▲ **SAFE LANDING**
Rapid development leading to a cu-nim and downburst
in the hot, dry air of Namibia.
Photo: Vianney Tisseau

speed and direction that the storm was moving.

At first the storm was growing bigger but not really moving towards us; it was fairly stationary staying just north of Valadares. Then it moved into town, crossed the river and finally moved onto the take-off mountain.

I noticed a gust front developing in front of the storm. In many situations you should be extremely worried about the presence of any gust front but in flat open terrain like Valadares gust fronts are less of a threat than in mountains.

In mountainous areas gust fronts can be funnelled and accelerated through valley systems and the terrain itself can cause severe rotor turbulence. Added to that your escape options can be severely limited by the mountains themselves. In the flatlands you can escape from an isolated storm in any direction you choose and you can study the development of the storm better, as changes are often easier to observe.

Our storm had been pretty stationary for about 30 minutes when I suddenly realised that the gust front was now moving southwards at what looked to be around 20km/h. It was time to get out of there.

Escaping

The gust front was clearly visible with the rain behind it forming a wedge shape that was moving towards us. The winds were 30-40km/h within the gust front. In a situation like this the worst thing you can do is try to big ears or spiral down because you'll be in lift – it will probably take longer than you expect to get down. Therefore, as you can't be sure you'll get down before the gust front hits you, you risk landing at the worst possible time.

So instead the three of us decided to turn south and run for it. There was plenty of lift around as the gust front was undermining all the air ahead of it and pushing it up and the storm was growing bigger at the same time. We needed to fly fast.

We soon found that the storm was moving at about the same speed as our trim speed, we could only get ahead of it by accelerating; it would catch us if we slowed up. Getting sucked into cloud was also a real danger as cloudbase was lower when the gust front arrived and there was heaps of lift everywhere.

We found there was smooth lift everywhere to the right and behind us but sink in front and to the left of us. By understanding this and staying away from the strong lift we were all able to fly safely away from the storm and control our height well enough so we could reach a suitable place to land that was also far enough from the storm and its gust front.

We flew 25km in a straight line at over 50km/h before landing next to the main road. Just five minutes after we landed, the gust front hit us. But as we'd flown so far from the centre of the storm it had almost completely dissipated. When it arrived it was just a 10km/h breeze of cold air from the north.

NEED TO KNOW

- Gust fronts are downdraughts of cold air that push out from thunderstorms
- They are most dangerous when landing as the wind can be very strong
- They are usually visible as they approach, and will have an area of extensive lift in front of them
- Don't try to spiral down – you'll be in strong lift, it will take a long time, and the storm could catch you
- Instead, avoid them or fly quickly away from the associated cu-nim

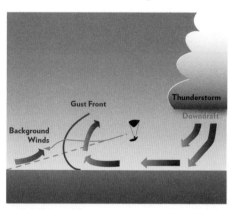

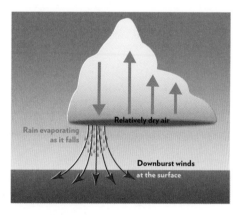

▲ GUST FRONT

A gust front is the leading-edge of cool air rushing down and out from a thunderstorm. Since cool air sinks this causes a down-rush of air that spreads out at the ground. The edge of this rapidly spreading pool of cool air is the gust front. If the wind following the gust front is intense and damaging, the windstorm is known as a downburst. Being 'gust-fronted' is no joke. There will be lift all around and it will be hard to get down. Out-running it is your best option. A better one is to avoid getting in the situation in the first place.

▲ DOWNBURST

A downburst is a localised area of damaging winds caused by air rapidly flowing down and out of a thunderstorm. They can occur when rain falls through relatively dry air. Damage from downbursts can be as severe as tornado damage. The damage pattern from a downburst however will be straight-line or diverging, indicating the winds were flowing outward, rather than circular like a tornado. Downburst damage can cover hundreds of square miles, or be limited to a single field – the smallest ones are called microbursts.

FLYING NEAR BIG CLOUDS

With Josh Cohn, Bob Drury, Jonny Durand, Will Gadd and Alex Hofer

WHEN is a cloud simply too big? And what do you do if you find yourself out of control and being sucked up? It's not an irrational fear. Lots of pilots have been sucked up, none more famously than Ewa Wisnierska. In 2007 in Australia she reached 9,947m in a supercell and was extremely lucky to survive. She puts it down to losing consciousness and her heart rate slowing in the extreme cold. Fellow pilot He Zhongpin (CN) was in the same cloud and wasn't so lucky. He was found dead 75km from his launch site having been struck by lightning at 5,900m inside the cloud.

So what's the best way to avoid a big cloud when flying XC? Alex Hofer, twice-winner of the Red Bull X-Alps, says, "Make sure you're far enough from the cloud, with an escape route to the wide-open blue sky. A little area of blue sky is not enough."

He adds: "The cloud can grow quickly and close you out. It can be tricky to fly in those conditions, and it's best to land unless you are really sure about what you are doing. Big clouds aren't inherently threatening, as you can see them. They only get dangerous when you try to play with them."

Will Gadd, who has held the paragliding open distance world record twice, questions why you even need to be there. "Why exactly do you need to go by it? The biggest error I, and most other people, seem to make is to confuse a momentary 'want' with a 'need'. If the cloud is really a concern then you don't need, and shouldn't want, to be anywhere near it. So the best way to pass it safely is to not fly near it."

Sounds basic, but it works. "If the sky is getting crazy enough in one area to produce a nasty cloud, then I probably don't want to be in the air, anyhow. I'll go land."

Dangers of clouds

Strong clouds can be used, however, says US competition pilot Josh Cohn, if you know what you're doing and you are careful. "There are two main dangers from large clouds," he says, "gust fronts and cloud suck."

"Dangerous gust fronts are caused by a large volume of air sinking quickly, hitting the ground and spreading out. Factors to consider are the area of the zone of descending air marked by rain, virga or hail, as well as the height from the cloud top to the ground. If the gust front is funnelled through a constricted valley it will accelerate further.

"Cloud suck is caused by the latent heat of condensation. The formation of cloud releases heat and accelerates the rising air near cloudbase. It is usually felt within a few hundred feet of cloudbase, and can provide a fast line on XC if used carefully. It's best to keep near the edge of the cloud, keeping an eye on the vertical development of other clouds, as it is very hard to see how high the cloud you are underneath is going. By using the speedbar and changing direction to go further from the centre of the cloud, it is usually possible to keep a margin of safety below cloudbase."

181

To do that it helps if you know the area where you are flying. "Understanding the local weather in the place you are flying is important," says top comp hang glider pilot Jonny Durand. "In Australia the storms move from southwest to northeast, so I would attempt to pass by the big cloud on the southwest side, knowing that if I encounter any trouble, I will be on the edge of the cloud, and most likely on the sink side of the cloud. Also, if I land, the likelihood of a gust front is much less on this side of the cloud."

Another point is to plan ahead. "Watch the cloud development throughout the day to get a picture of how big they're growing, and how quickly," says Himalayan pilot Bob Drury.

"If you want to pass a worrying cloud on an XC, you should be low enough to glide right under it in strong lift and still glide clear without going in. Take a route that keeps you close to the edge or a blue hole. If you hit lift that will take you in if it continues at that rate, turn out towards the blue immediately. You can always move back in if it dies off."

Sucked in

What happens if the worst happens though and you find yourself being sucked in? "If the climb rate is less than 10m/s, then spiral down," says Alex Hofer. "But make sure you don't hit other pilots! However, if big ears combined with speedbar are effective enough to help you reach the blue sky, then this is your choice."

Will Gadd again says don't put yourself in the situation in the first place. "I've had to take extreme evasive action with clouds all of about five times in over 10 years of flying some of the most dynamic air around, from Texas to the Owens Valley." Getting dramatically sucked into a serious cloud is a "really, really rare event" he says. He was in the same sky as Ewa Wisnierska in 2007 and did a "hard spiral" to escape. "The cells behind me were starting to grow faster than I could fly, so I pointed the glider at the ground and landed after some hard spirals. I simply didn't like the sky enough, anymore.

"Worrying about what to do once you're under a cu-nim and getting yanked into the sky ignores the whole chain of errors that put the pilots there. More than half the field made

a decision that day not to go anywhere near the cloud. No disrespect to Ewa or Mr Zhongpin, but flying under that cloud and then continuing as it built was a stupid decision.

"By the time you're in the situation where you're getting sucked up you've already made a half-dozen errors. Asking what to do when getting sucked into a cloud is kind of like asking what to do once your car is sliding backwards toward the ditch on an icy road."

However, if you are climbing and you are concerned, "centre the thermal, then fly toward the edge of the cloud until the lift turns to sink. Now, fly back into the lift until you're closer to the cloud and getting concerned again, then fly toward the edge. If you suddenly find yourself closer to a cloud than you want to be then fly toward the closest edge. Use as much bar as you can and still keep the glider comfortably open – the idea is to get out of the lift by flying toward the edge of the cloud with good glider control."

Bob Drury agrees: "Turn and fly towards the blue. I don't use big ears and speed bar as I don't like giving up the control of my wing." He adds: "You're better off boxing clever from the outset and being able to glide clear without needing the ears in. The only time I've used B-lines to escape was in the Himalaya when I wanted to land directly below, as I didn't know if pushing on would lead to a worse position."

Jonny Durand agrees on cloud avoidance: "When you are within 500m of cloudbase evaluate the strength of the thermal, the size of the cloud and how far from the edge of the cloud you are. If you notice that there is a big area of lift you should immediately head for the closest edge of the cloud. If you find that you start sinking, then turn back to where the lift is, but make sure you know where to escape if it becomes necessary."

Spat out

If the worst happens and you get sucked in and can't see anything then what do you do?

"First off, relax and fly the glider," says Will. "As Ewa's story proves, even tweaked competition paragliders fly just fine in clouds, even really nasty ones where the pilot is unconscious.

"A lot of the fear factor about clouds comes from hang gliders and fixed-wing planes, which are much, much harder to fly than a paraglider with no horizon line. Paragliders always tend to fly with the pilot dangling below as per normal. You're likely going to be just fine unless you've made a massive error and flown under the cu-nim from hell.

"You also already have a bearing in your mind, so get on that bearing and trust it. Relax and let the glider fly until you pop out the side. Big ears, B-line or full stalls to get out of a cloud are more likely to be dangerous than the cloud. They don't produce a high enough descent rate to be meaningful, and they put the pilot directly below where he just was: back in the lift."

He concludes: "The best solution is to just fly through the white room, this takes the pilot laterally out of the lift.

Josh Cohn agrees: "Fly toward the closest edge of the cloud, using your GPS or compass. Keep in mind that clouds can grow horizontally, and that very wet clouds can block the signals that GPSs use."

He adds: "If you have no idea which way to fly, or are not close to the edge, a hard spiral may be the best option, keeping in mind that it carries the danger of you blacking out or it locking in."

Jonny Durand is unequivocal. If you're in, "You've messed up!" He says: "When you arrive at cloudbase and don't know where the closest exit is you will for sure get lost and have no idea which way is out. Always look at the GPS when you're climbing and know which direction on the GPS you'll need to follow for your closest exit. This is the only instrument that will help you once you enter a cloud as it will only take a matter of seconds before you are totally lost and scared. You should then look at your instruments and try to maintain the direction it might be to the edge of the cloud. If you try to fly too fast on a hang glider it is easy to get turned."

At the end of the day, "the safest thing is to get out or stay out of the sky when big clouds develop," says Josh. "Studying the day's weather can give a heads-up to the likelihood of cu-nims in the area. Always leave yourself a plan B and a plan C."

NEED TO KNOW

- Playing with big clouds can be dangerous – avoid them
- Watch your approach as you climb to base – leave before base if it's strong
- Use big ears and speedbar on a PG, pull on speed on an HG, and fly away
- If you get lost maintain direction (GPS) and fly through the cloud until you can core sink

LANDING IN STRONG WINDS

By Honza Rejmanek

IN strong winds the best place to land is at the downwind end of a large open field. Ideally you want a series of such fields slap-bang in the centre of the valley. You want the valley to be wide, not narrow. This will give you the best chance of avoiding any choppy air.

Lee turbulence

Given enough wind any sharp terrain feature or large obstacle on the valley floor can create significant shear and create turbulence in its lee. This is why the immediate lee of such features is best avoided, if there is a choice.

Some features, like a row of trees for example, will create wind shadows or areas of lighter surface wind. At first glance this might look like a welcome place to land, because the wind would be lighter and you'd have less chance of being dragged.

The problem, however, is that landing in such a wind shadow could well require a final approach through a region of strong wind shear. Which means you could take a collapse, or experience loss of control low down. Not good.

Upwind turbulence

Less obvious are regions immediately upwind of features that rise abruptly from the valley floor and lie perpendicular to the wind, for example a building. These also present the danger of turbulence on the upwind edge on the valley floor and are known as upwind bolster eddies. Think of what happens when

water in a river hits a rock in the stream.

Depending on the shape of the feature the bolster eddy can lie as a semi-permanent feature, a sort of roller bearing. In other cases it can be a region of chaos – of constantly forming and shedding bolster eddies.

One tip is that if crops or tall grasses are present you can often see random gusts from all directions. These are a sign that bolster eddies are present.

Mapping the air

If you are coming down into large fields it is best to be ready to back into them. Don't line up a landing approach right at the back of the field – you might not make it in. Instead, line up at the front or above, or even a little past it, and aim to land in the first downwind third of the field. You'll always be able to reach it with a quick downwind dash.

Once you have committed to a landing, and if you have a large enough field to land in, then circling down in a sinking batch of air can be a wise move. It is as if you are reverse thermaling. Keeping a moderate bank angle gives you better wing loading and more control. Circling also helps assure you that you are maintaining your presence in, and are mapping out, a particular zone of air.

Visualising a sinking zone of air striking the valley floor in a windy situation can be difficult though. The upwind edge will counter the wind while the downwind edge will accelerate it. If you are lucky you can land just upwind

►**WINDY**
Narrow valleys will constrict the wind, making it faster. Above
Zermatt during the Red Bull X-Alps 2011.
Photo: Olivier Laugero/Red Bull Content Pool

66 Get your wing under control on the ground 99

of the centre of your sinking batch so the net wind you land in is slower than average and you get enough time to get your wing under control on the ground.

The best of a bad situation

Even a dire strong-wind landing situation that puts you well beyond your comfort level needs to be approached cool headedly. Remember that even strong and fast windflows are not completely random. There will always be preferable areas and preferable moments for landing. As you descend and the strong-wind landing becomes inevitable watch the trees, bushes, smoke, flags and grass for intensity and regularity of movement. Then make a plan and execute it. This means:

1 Choose the most open spot
2 Back into it
3 Circle a batch of sink down into a landing
4 Fly actively to landing
5 Control your wing immediately after touchdown
6 Pack up
7 Kiss the ground
8 Reflect on why it was so windy in that particular valley.

NEED TO KNOW

- Pick a big open field
- Watch for rotor in the lee of objects
- Watch for bolster eddies in front of objects
- Circle down at moderate bank, keeping the wing loaded
- Be ready to back into the field – line up at the middle to front end of the field, not the downwind side
- Watch everything for signs of what the wind is doing
- Stay cool and land normally – it often feels much windier than it is
- Control your glider on the ground, don't get dragged

THROWING YOUR RESERVE

With Mike Steen, Carson Klein and Jocky Sanderson

MIKE Steen and Carson Klein are two US pilots who, as well as flying paragliders in Utah, spend a lot of time wingsuit flying, BASE jumping, and jumping off anything higher than a Big Mac. So, how do you throw a reserve?

Carson: "Very deliberately and hard."

Mike agrees: "Quickly! Always mentally be prepared. After you take off, reach down and touch the handle. So when you need to throw it it's not just a question of 'Where's the handle?'

"By the time you're thinking about it, the reserve should already be gone. Throw it fast, and don't throw it under your wing."

Carson chips in, "Throw it down and away." He has thrown his once in anger. "It came out, and hit my wing a little bit. So pay attention to what your reserve is doing as it comes out. I had to grab my bridle, yank on it a couple of times to make it come out and open all the way and then I landed in a tree."

Mike has also thrown his, "a couple of times". How was it? "Scary," he says. "Typically, as a beginner pilot or an experienced pilot, the situations you are going to be in are going to be scary.

◄ **TUG OF ANGELS**
Reserves come in many shapes and sizes. This is a
Rogallo-shaped steerable reserve. Most are round.
Photo: Sky Paragliders

" Look at it, then grab, pull, throw and deploy "

"You're not in a simulator sitting flat, you're being twisted, being thrown around, your glider's doing things you've never seen it do before. It's just important to get it out there."

Someone who has spent a lifetime teaching people how to get out of scary situations, and also how to throw a reserve, is British SIV instructor Jocky Sanderson. "The most important advice is look at the handle, grab the handle, don't feel it, and pull it out the way it goes in. So if it goes in the side, pull it outwards – don't pull it out over your lap, because it will create friction and get caught on the gates. So pull it out the way it slides in, and then a big swing and throw."

Bob Drury, former editor of Cross Country magazine says, "That's what nearly killed me." Flying with a back-mounted reserve with the handle on the shoulder, when he went to throw his reserve the friction of trying to pull it over his shoulder meant the handle came off. "With those harnesses you need to punch up the way," he now says.

Once the reserve is out, the advice is the same: "Get your main in as soon as you can," says Jocky.

Jocky has thrown his reserve four times. How was that? "Fantastic!" he laughs. "It was like the reassuring tug of angels!"

The first time he threw it he was low and he "made a mistake". "I didn't throw it hard enough, and it went into the sail and the lines, and then I had to pull it back out and throw it again, and I only had time for it to open up and I swung under and landed on a bush."

How is it possible to have the presence of mind and split-second reactions to act like that? Isn't it all going haywire at the time?

"No, because when you're under stress, your heart rate increases and everything slows down slightly. So you can actually focus, and it goes into speed-frame mode and you can look, locate, grasp, pull, punch, is what the parachutists would say.

"So you look at it, grab it, pull it, throw it and deploy it." Then get the main in and prepare to land.

NEED TO KNOW

- Keep your reserve well maintained, pack it properly and every season
- In day-to-day flight, check out where it is, occasionally reach down and touch it
- When you need to throw it, throw it
- Look at the handle
- Grab the handle – don't simply feel it
- Pull it out
- Throw it into clear air
- Let go
- Get your main in
- Land. Breath.

DEALING WITH DEMONS

By Greg Hamerton

FEAR can bind you in a web of limitations which will leach the joy out of the sport you once loved. Often you don't even know you're afraid, your only sign is that the fun has evaporated like a once-promising cloud.

Don't be too hasty to scoff at the idea – "What, me? Afraid? I'm a daredevil, I'm beyond weakness!" For if you find just one of the points below to be cause for thought, then you've touched first base – the acknowledging of the fear.

Second base is striving to understand the fear, third to master it, and finally, in the last step, to let it go, and you're home free.

My glider might collapse

All modern paragliders undergo rigorous safety testing, which is focused more on stability than performance. Match your glider to your experience level: an A for training, an A or B for recreational flying (or below 50 hours airtime), a high B or C for regular experienced pilots and cross country flying, and a high C or D for advanced and competition pilots only.

Added to this, you can practise instability manoeuvres in a structured training programme such as an SIV course or safety course. You'll learn how to get your glider back into proper flying order from every possible collapse.

If your glider isn't rated, then check out the next question, for there is a strong possibility of the glider not recovering properly from some situations.

I don't trust my gear

Load tests are very severe. For a glider to have achieved certification it must be practically indestructible under loads the pilot can induce during flight. So equipment failure is likely to have been due to negligence.

It is your job to ensure:

Regular factory checks: at least once a year, send your entire kit to your agent or school.

Daily equipment inspection: before you fly, methodically check each element of your aircraft.

Pre-flight checks: before every take-off, methodically check the vitals (protection, harness, suspension, wing, weather and air traffic).

Reserve parachutes provide immense psychological comfort, and will catch you if all else fails.

What if I get sucked up?

It is fairly easy to make a paraglider descend, using big ears and speedbar or in a spiral dive. Only in severe cumulus development or extremely strong winds will you find lift strong enough to overwhelm your attempts at descent.

So the danger of disappearing into the heavens becomes more a danger of not seeing the developing cumulonimbus cloud – they do not appear instantly. Remain vigilant. A simple rule is don't fly when there are 'cumulonastiness' clouds developing within 30km of where you are flying, or the weather forecast warns of embedded cu-nims (thunder-cells hidden in an overcast sky of stratus).

What if I have a mid-air?

It requires two pilots to have a collision. You are one of them. The principle is defensive flying. All paragliders travel at very similar speeds. By varying the amount of brake you use you can synchronise your speed with pilots around you. The easiest way to avoid traffic problems is to follow the glider in front of you at a safe distance, just like driving on the road. This creates space around you, a safe space within which to fly.

Indicate your intention to turn. Check around you before you do anything to alter your course. This helps to maintain your space. If someone insists on driving like a drunkard, and collision is unavoidable (ie you could not fly away or land), a reserve parachute is vital. Throw it.

What if I panic?

Panic is caused by overwhelming lack of experience in an extreme situation. Doing the wrong thing in an emergency can just worsen the problem. Fly the glider, whatever is there. You are the pilot, no-one else is. By practising instability manoeuvres on your glider, you increase your experience of extreme situations, little by little. Do an SIV course. They are designed to improve your safety and should help familiarise you with extreme flying dilemmas.

What if I crash?

Accidents on take-off are invariably caused by poor ground-handling skills. The glider begins to fly you, instead of the other way around. Open, clean strips of ground can be found in any town if you look hard enough. All you need is a wing and a wind. Go and practise your ground-handling. Pull up with one riser only. Pull up skew. Pull up blindfolded. Pull up with twisted risers. Then keep the glider there, never let it drop back to the ground. Walk it around obstacles. Let go of the brakes: use only your running to balance and steer.

Go play in turbulent air (behind some trees). Then do it all again on a friend's wing.

Accidents on landing can be softened by using the PLF (Parachute Landing Fall). It is a fantastic method for absorbing the impact of a crash. Practise this at home, first on a mattress, then on the grass. It is not a natural body response, so regular practise is essential.

The other kind of skill you can cultivate is your landing approach. Pick a stone or marker on your landing field every time you land. Reward yourself if you land within a metre from it! This skill may be invaluable when you only have one clear patch in the forest in which to touch down.

What if it's remote?

Every pilot's nightmare: crashing in some remote gully, out of sight. First, carry a radio, so that you can contact other pilots. Second, fly with a mobile phone as emergency services are just a call away. Thirdly, pack some flares and a personal locator beacon or tracker. And always fly with friends; they'll know you're missing, especially if you make your intention clear by discussing your flight plan before you launch.

What about the walk-out?

Always carry some food (biscuits, dates, energy bars, glucose) and lots of water when you fly. Today might just be the day when you hit that boomer and whistle over the back, landing 50km distant, lost and far from civilisation. With a bit of sustenance, immense walkouts are possible. They may be uncomfortable, but you've nothing to fear – you'll live.

I feel really rusty

Humility is your greatest friend here. Adopt the mantra "there is a lot to learn". If you haven't had more than one flight every month, then you are certainly rusty. Pretend your licence has been downgraded – if you're a cross-

" It hasn't gone away, but it doesn't contain you any more "

country pilot, you're now an intermediate, if you were a newly licensed pilot you are a student again. Find the appropriate guidance, let a more current pilot offer assistance. And just get some airtime in mellow conditions. Keep it simple.

I might just get clobbered

The risk of getting clobbered by a freak gust is assumed in return for the reward of freedom. We all have this fear, in greater or lesser extent. But very seldom is the gust a freak – bad air is normally caused by something. Either by obstructions to the airflow, by shear turbulence or thermal turbulence. Increase your knowledge of meteorology by reading so that you don't put yourself in bad air. There are very few freak situations that will overwhelm all pilots.

Acknowledgement helps

I hope the above helps you. In each case, you are not ignoring the fear, you are acknowledging that you have it, that it is a legitimate concern. Then to understand it you need to explore all the angles of where it comes from, and all the information you have on the subject. If you lack information, ask

an experienced pilot. If the answer you get doesn't satisfy, ask another.

To master the fear means you have contained it, answered all of its questions. It hasn't gone away, but it doesn't contain you any more.

You are now ready to let it go – pass beyond the fear, having made all the protection that is within your power to make, you can assess its risk to you, and have a solid parameter to work with. It has moved from a fear into a risk, you have transformed the metaphysical cloud of dread into a solid black rock, which you can choose to jump over or kick aside, or use as the boundary to your flying envelope. But now you have the choice to be free, to be the juggler of those pebbles of doubt.

NEED TO KNOW

- Don't worry, everyone gets nervous sometimes
- If you get scared, acknowledge it
- Understand it
- Master it
- Let it go
- Enjoy flying again

DEALING WITH FEAR

By Heike Hamann

OVER the 17 years that I have been flying I've had my own share of fear to deal with. Between two accidents that resulted in hospital, and an incident that didn't actually result in physical injury but left me with emotional damage, I'd say it's been the biggest factor in my flying performance and pleasure, the piece that has taken the most ongoing work.

When I feel frightened in the air, it is debilitating. I spend most of my energy dealing with it, rather than the task at hand of observing what is going on around me, making tactical decisions and having fun. I land exhausted.

My first accident was landing on a powerline – a single strand running down the side of a rocky, tree-covered hill. Although this was probably the most dangerous and potentially fatal incident I've had, it had a happy ending, in that I started sliding down the line with my glider and eventually had the wing reinflated by a thermal coming through – and it left no long-term scars.

The second accident occurred on tow, when one of the tow-points unclipped and I was dragged into the ground. A few X-rays later I was released from hospital – nothing broken, but in pain all the same.

My most frightening incident occurred at 5,000m in Spain, at the seven-hour mark of an exhausting flight, when I was in danger of being sucked into clouds. I was on a new wing, and it went parachutal after an incorrectly exited B-line. The result was a long cascade of G-force and terror-inducing events and thoughts of promises made about coming home safely. Eventually, using the last of the physical strength I had left, I pulled on a full stall and held it on as long as I could. When the glider recovered, there was a moment of calm. A calm that I had experienced about four times in the previous minutes – only this time the calm remained. When I eventually landed safely, I broke down and cried. It then took about five hours before I was picked up by the retrieve bus. Five hours of being alone in the middle of nowhere, dealing with my trauma.

A month or so later, while flying in the high Austrian Alps, I had a huge collapse close to the trees and threw my reserve. It opened just in time, but my impact with the ground was hard.

After a ride suspended in a stretcher below a helicopter I found myself in hospital. Once again nothing broken, but almost, and internal organs shaken severely. Seven days later I emerged sorely from hospital. After much soul searching I decided to keep flying. Judy Leden's book, Flying with Condors, helped me decide.

Fear and fantasy

That all happened well over a decade ago – the fearlessness that marked my earlier flying days was gone forever. Since then I have come up with a strategy that helps me deal with fear. It is a synthesis of talking with people and working on myself.

Coming back from those two incidents took a year of focused effort, to get myself flying close to the levels I had before they occurred. Lots of short flights, so that my 'courage quotient' didn't get too drained – I found time on the ground built up the courage quotient, and time in the air drained it. A new wing. Studying myself using the skills I was learning in my psychology studies. Talking to other pilots. Sessions with a therapist and a sports psychologist to work through some of the trauma.

Years down the track I find myself going through phases of high levels of fear every now and again, and I do more work, study more, talk to more people until eventually I work through the next piece. Then I come back to loving being in the air again and being closely in touch with my glider when things get a little rough, rather than semi-freezing and just wanting to land.

The seven steps

I have seven basic steps I use to deal with fear. Five of them occur when I am in the air, feeling afraid, wanting to land to end the horrible experience. The final two steps take place on the ground.

Before I go into the seven steps I want to briefly discuss fear. A useful acronym often used by sports psychologists is FEAR: Fantasy Expectations Appearing Real.

However, in paragliding there is a real difference. Fear is not simply a fantasy. Sometimes it is, and I call that 'irrational' fear – others call it anxiety. Other times we really are in danger. There is no fantasy, there is no 'appearing real'. It's real. This fear I refer to as 'rational' fear.

1: Notice you are afraid

That might sound obvious, but unless you've just had a big collapse or find yourself without a glide out to a landing field, fear often creeps up on you. There were times that I did not realise I was afraid, until I found myself wanting to land. Get to know yourself: how do you know when you are beginning to feel afraid? Do you start breathing more shallowly? Do you tense up? Do you find yourself looking constantly at your wing?

One of the first signs for me is that I pull my feet up, so they are at right-angles to my shins. Or I find myself sitting more upright in the harness, rather than relaxing back and letting it hold me. Catching it early is important, so that you can address it before it's gone so far that landing is all you can think of.

2: Breathe deeply

We start breathing more shallowly when we are afraid, so breathe deeply right into your belly. Three times. This deep breathing will ease the tension somewhat, and once you've used this seven-step method a few times, will mark the beginning of the fact you are about to do something about your feelings of fear, rather than just ignoring them.

3: What are you afraid of?

Is it the bumps? Or the clouds? Is it that tuck you had? The rustle? Is it because you are so high? Or so low? Name it. Out loud, as though you were telling someone about it.

When I was first recovering from my accidents I would find myself having made the decision to land because I was afraid. But once back on the ground I couldn't actually say what I was afraid of. So for a while I took a voice recorder with me, and I would speak into it when I was feeling afraid.

Clarifying what the fear is about, rather than just leaving it as a nebulous feeling, is important. Even if it's just a vague feeling, concentrate on it, guess what might be causing it. Dismissing it as 'silly' or similar, without really knowing what is behind it, is not helpful.

4: Are you in danger?

Having named the fear, step four is to ask the question: are you actually in danger? An interesting discovery I made here is that

"Be nice to yourself - you are here to have fun"

sometimes I didn't know. After all these years of flying, I didn't actually always know where the 'danger zone' was.

Sure, being right under a big cumulonimbus cloud is dangerous. But how about if it's a cumulus congestus? How close is too close? How close is okay? Take the time to read the books and talk with experienced pilots about these things, and work out where your own safety margins lie.

There are three answers to the question am I in danger?

Yes

In this category I include big clouds, rain and the associated gust front, strong winds and no glide-out to a safe landing.

No

Being high and being alone however, fall into my No category. These are good examples of irrational fear, anxiety. I sometimes feel frightened in these situations because of past experiences I've had. The feeling of fear is just as intense as if I was really in danger. However, I am not in any danger – unless I stop thinking clearly as a result of feeling frightened and then do something that puts me in danger.

I don't know

This category can contain all of the situations included in the Yes category, if I don't know what my safety zone is. More about this shortly. I would also add strong turbulence into this category – others might put it in the Yes category. Each of us needs to find our own answers to this question.

5: What now?

Having established whether or not you are actually in physical danger, the next step is to come up with a strategy to deal with the situation you are in. If you are in danger then your highest priority is to get yourself safe.

If you don't have a strategy for dealing with these situations, make it a priority to find one, by talking to people and reading books, watching videos, attending pilotage or SIV clinics etc. This will not only make you a safer pilot, but will also give you peace of mind, which in itself may reduce your levels of fear. Some strategies of mine include:

Big clouds

Fly away from them, and if you need to land to be safe, fly away from them using speedbar and big ears. If you are under one, big ears and speed bar to the edge of the cloud, having taken a GPS direction reading so that in case you get into the cloud you know which way to keep heading.

Rain

I have a policy not to fly with a wet glider, however mild the rain is. So I land before it gets wet, and if it is wet, land ASAP, remembering the glider may become more prone to going parachutal, so keep the glider flying fast.

Gust fronts

If you can see one coming and can't land in time, one option is to stay as high as you can and ride it out that way. I don't even like to think too hard about that possibility – it's too scary. Yet think about it we must. Another option is to fly in the opposite direction of the gust front, and find the largest, widest part of the valley, if that's what you are in, and pick the biggest field free of powerlines that you can find to land in. Best of all however, don't get caught in a gust front – learn how to avoid that happening.

Strong winds

Landing safely here is the key. Find a big, obstacle-free field, free of powerlines, ideally with other fields downwind in case you get blown back. Set yourself up at the upwind end of the paddock, face into the wind, and fly from one side of the paddock to the other, as though you are ridge soaring – like a squashed figure 8. When you do land (and remember you won't need to flare), you need to be able to control your glider. Learn how to do that in strong wind.

No glide to a safe landing

If you have flown too deep into a hill and don't have the glide out, find the line to the closest field that maximises your chances of lift or finding a thermal – normally by flying down the windward side of a ridge. It is tempting to take the most direct route to the landing paddock, but that may put you in the heaviest sink. If there is no way out, and you are going to land in a tree, do the thing you learned at paragliding school – pick a big bushy tree and then land in it like you would on the ground.

The key in all these instances is to have thought about the scenarios beforehand, and the strategies for getting yourself safe again. In the moment of danger, you need to know what to do, so you don't add to the fear by needing to work it out at the time. Think and talk it through beforehand. This has the added advantage of probably putting you off getting yourself into such a situation in the first place. If you can, remember to breathe deeply and visualise yourself getting out of the situation.

Visualisation has a strong effect in the middle of a dangerous situation – it sets the determination to get yourself safe. It replaces the frightening images of what could go wrong with a positive one. My body immediately relaxes somewhat and the determination to find a safe way out increases.

Anxiety

Let's move now to those situations where you are feeling scared, but are actually not in any danger of physically hurting yourself. This is the situation I find myself in most often – and I have a routine (another seven steps!) I take myself through when I am aware this has happened.

1 Look around

When we get scared we can become fixated, so by forcing ourselves to look around the level of fear immediately reduces.

2 Breathe

Once again, breathe deeply.

3 Set myself a mini-goal

These are crucial. They shift your focus from whatever is frightening, to something positive. Examples of the types of mini-goals I

set myself are to core thermals well, get to the top of a thermal faster than everyone else or stick with pilot A – don't let them outfly me.

Focusing on coring thermals has the added advantage of keeping you in what is generally the most formed part of the lift. When we are half-hearted about thermalling we may find ourselves at the edges of the thermal, where it is roughest.

When I was coming back from my accidents, just staying in the air was an achievement. So once I noticed myself feeling uncomfortable, I would set myself a mini-goal of flying for another 10 or 15 minutes. And then go in to land. That way I could feel good about having achieved a goal, rather than just berating myself for landing early.

Similarly, I might say, I'll go and land after I've had two or three tucks, however small. This was a particularly good mini-goal to set myself if I was afraid of the wing collapsing because of the conditions. Inevitably I found that I wasn't actually getting any collapses at all!

4 Use my anchors

Having set a mini-goal, I then use anchors to change my state from a fearful state to a more desirable state. Anchors are words, sounds, songs, movements or specific physical touch that are associated to a certain, positive state in your body. I have two anchors that I use when I am frightened but not in any physical danger. The first are some words that get me into a calm yet focused state. The second is a song that I hum to myself, that reminds me of my connection with something bigger than myself – nature, spirit, whatever you want to call it.

To get an anchor, you must first access the psychological state you want to be able to reconnect with. It is important to really be in that state – for example, being calm yet focused. You need to feel it in your body, to look around at the world from that state, to walk around in that state. Then choose a movement, sound, song, visual image or some physical touch, such as pushing or pinching a certain part of your body, which somehow captures that state for you. Whatever you choose needn't make sense to anyone else – it's often an intuitive thing, that just works for you. When you want to re-connect with that state you just repeat the movement or touch, make the sound or sing the song, or look at the visual image – I have seen pilots with a smiley-face sticker on their vario, for example. Looking at it, using the anchor, brings the pilot back from the fearful state.

5 Visualise myself landing

I then visualise myself landing safely – I visualise myself coming in above the field, assessing the wind direction, deciding where and how I'm going to set myself up for a good landing, executing that landing approach, and flaring at the right time.

6 Talk to people on the radio

Talking to people is also a very effective way of moving through an irrational fear moment. Get on the radio and ask people how they are finding the conditions. Talk with them about what you are noticing and feeling, and ask them for their feedback or thoughts.

7 Remind myself

The last thing I'll do is remind myself that flying well sometimes means pushing myself out of my comfort zone. There are times when the air is rough, or the day is windy. I know I have the skills to handle the conditions safely – it's just uncomfortable. And chances are it will change, as I move to another part of the flight or as the day progresses. I'll do this more when I'm competing than when I'm free flying – when my desire to achieve a good finish outweighs the discomfort I am feeling in the moment.

These days, when I am free-flying, I will tend to go and land when I am flying outside my comfort zone – I am in the air to enjoy myself, so if I am not enjoying myself, why persist? This has been particularly important for me, as I have had a tendency to keep pushing myself, and then forget how much I love flying. It becomes more of a chore, another job I need to do, rather than something I love doing.

6: Back on the ground

If you've been scared in the air – either through irrational fear, you've been in physical danger, or you don't know – talk about it when you're back on the ground. Ask other pilots for their opinions about the conditions and find out how they dealt with them. Don't be shy here – people generally love helping out. And if you can, share your feelings: let someone you trust know what it was like and whether you were frightened or found it difficult.

Likewise, be gentle with yourself after such experiences. For the longest time I felt like I had to be strong and deal with them myself. Or, more like it, not deal with the feelings at all, and just move on.

Years after my cascades in Spain I realised my flying pleasure and performance were still being hampered by the experience I'd had eight years earlier. When I eventually let myself revisit that time, feel the feelings and have the associated emotions, and take care of myself around them, there was a marked change in both my flying pleasure and competition performance. Little did people know that the reason why I was standing on the winners' podium was because of the 'inner work' that I did.

7: Other strategies

I've already mentioned studying up about what is and isn't safe, and finding that line. Read and talk to people – increase your knowledge base, get the facts, come up with your own methods for working out where your safety line is.

Flying a glider you are comfortable on is also important. Flying a wing with less performance can greatly increase your sense of wellness and comfort. And it is surprising how much better you can fly when you feel like you are on top of things and in control of your glider: your own performance will probably increase, despite the glider's lesser performance.

Doing an SIV course is also a great way of becoming more comfortable on your wing and helps you get comfortable with rapid descent techniques. Knowing that you can get out of the sky quickly, if you need to, will increase your level of comfort and your physical safety when flying. And the controlled collapses will help you understand better how your wing reacts.

Reading sports psychology books and articles about fear and how to deal with it, may also help you work through your fears – both in flying and in life.

The more you think about your fear when you are on the ground, and the situations that cause it, the more you'll be able to deal with the fears, become a safer pilot and enjoy your flying.

NEED TO KNOW

- A bit of fear is good, it keeps you safe
- Too much fear is bad, it limits what you do
- The first step is to recognise you are feeling afraid
- Then breathe deeply, it relaxes you
- Work out what you are afraid of. Is there any real danger?
- If yes, move away from the dangerous situation
- If no, there are techniques you can use to bring yourself back to a level
- Fly a comfortable glider
- Consider SIV, pilotage and other courses
- Be nice to yourself. Talk it through, others will help. Lots of pilots have been there
- Remember, the reason you are flying is to have fun

HOW CBT CAN HELP YOUR FLYING

By Hugh Miller

IT'S A head game, flying – so why don't we delve inside and see what's going on?

Cognitive behaviour therapy is the current buzz treatment in psychotherapy – its effectiveness has been proved, and it's a recommended intervention for depression, anxiety and phobias. In my personal life and also day job as a psychotherapist, I've found it incredibly powerful. There's not much mystique to it though – CBT is just a really simple way of looking at what we're telling ourselves, and seeing how that makes us feel and behave. It's increasingly being used in sports psychology, and as we all know, decision-making and strong emotions are two big features in flying.

The concepts that underpin CBT are simple, and there's lots of crossover between the CBT model ("thoughts, feelings and actions"), mindfulness ("know and let be"), Buddhist psychology ("your mind creates your world") and mentalisation ("the helicopter view").

Essentially, it is a common sense model that doesn't take a huge amount of understanding to put to good use.

First steps

The first step in the CBT process is to stop and recognise what's happening. This is easier said than done. We are conditioned creatures, and over time we build up our own 'tapes' that we play to ourselves over and over again – often without realising it. Take public speaking, for example. Some of us don't mind it – but a lot of us are scared witless at the prospect. CBT would say that it's our thinking about our performance that leads to the fear. Common beliefs might be, "I have nothing interesting to say", "I'll look an idiot", or, "they'll see I'm anxious and it'll get worse." There's no evidence for this, but over time, that's what we end up telling ourselves.

Jane is a brilliant, natural pilot, and is often at the top of the stack. But on scratchy days, she used to find herself sat on the hill, unwilling to launch, letting the 'top guns' enjoy the light thermals out front. Her reluctance was holding her back, and I was intrigued by where it came from – as she so wanted to start knocking out some big distances.

I spent some time asking her to imagine sitting on take-off and work out what was happening for her. "I don't want to bomb out" was the first thing that came to mind – despite her proven thermalling ability. Then she admitted, "I don't want to mess it up for the better pilots." She didn't want to put herself out there – and not trying was better than failing. Jane realised she was putting the 'top guns' on a pedestal, and, equally, herself underneath looking up at them.

It wasn't long before Jane found herself realising she'd created her own glass ceiling. Ultimately, at some level, she felt, "I'm not good enough." Interestingly, one of the top female pilots of the 1990s used to feel the same way going into each new competition – she felt like a fraud. That's the power of our

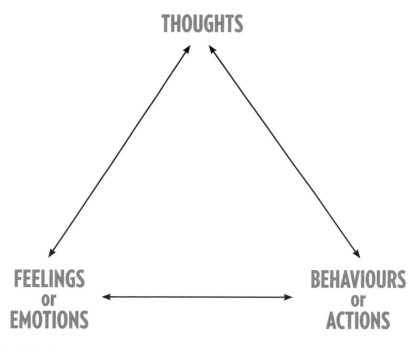

THOUGHTS

FEELINGS
or
EMOTIONS

BEHAVIOURS
or
ACTIONS

▲ CBT TRIANGLE
On paper separate out your thoughts, emotions and behaviours. You will then start to see how each affects the other. The basic premise is that what we think affects how we feel and act, while how we feel affects what we think and do – and of course, what we do affects how we think and feel.

thinking, right there: it creates our self-image, and can leave us literally glued to the ground.

Your core beliefs

The second step is to then check out the reality of the 'core belief'. Just ask yourself the simple question, "Is this true?" Having unearthed these beliefs, it became easier for Jane to challenge them, and funnily enough, her desire to improve her flying ran deeper than her fear of failing in front of others or getting in their way. Time after time, the habit got noticed and its power fell away. We don't have to be cowed by our unconscious beliefs.

Another example is the three o' clock space-out. I find it very hard to concentrate for more than two or three hours, and by mid-afternoon I usually go totally vacant for a short time – and land soon after. No doubt it's

a blood sugar low, but it really messes with my head. I generally start thinking irrationally – "wow, this lift line will go to the coast" usually leads to me racing myself to the ground. Or, "God I'm so stupid, what am I doing?" tends to see me drift aimlessly in zeroes for ages. With a bit more awareness, and checking out the beliefs, I can hopefully manage myself better in these situations in the future.

The CBT triangle

When you come across a situation where you feel like you're limiting yourself, but you don't know why, you could try out the CBT triangle exercise above – it works.

CBT can also work wonders with fears. Of course, fear is an integral part of flying. It kind of makes sense to be a bit on edge when you're dangling miles in the air from the contents of your rucksack. And if you don't ever get scared flying, there's something wrong. You may well be dissociated from your emotional responses – and that's dangerous, as they're there to help you survive: to warn you of rotor behind a ridge, or when to be really alert for example. Fear is a neurobiological response, and the cortisol that is released helps us be alert for action.

However, sometimes fears can get above their station. Perhaps you find yourself looking at your karabiners and suddenly thinking they can't be strong enough, and before you know it you're imagining them cracking and you falling through thin air. Or maybe you get a collapse or two exiting a climb, and next thing you know you're thinking, "my wing is a total death-ship and I'm not going to survive the next five minutes".

As SIV instructor Jocky Sanderson says, knowledge is power here: the more you can understand about your gear and the conditions, the better. Once you have that knowledge, you can use step two – Is it true? – to check out your fear, and make a more informed choice, rather than act out of sheer panic.

The jitters

As an aside, some of us suffer from anxiety and worry more than others. It doesn't matter what the situation or trigger, we just tend to get more worked up. If that sounds like you, then simply finding a more compassionate way of relating to the experience of fear and anxiety can be incredibly powerful.

The first step is acknowledging your fear. If you've got the take-off jitters, for example and there's nothing amiss, then just label it 'the jitters.'

This dis-identifies you and the actual situation from the emotion – the 'jitters', and this dis-identification frees you up a little space to reflect and re-centre. A lot of research has gone into this process: it works.

Be kind to yourself

The second step goes contrary to all the pop psychology advice of 'squashing the fear', employing positive self-talk and so on. In fact – a lot of that stuff can be counter-productive. Fighting a fear can make it feel ever bigger. Simply remain aware of the physical experience of fear – the knot in your stomach, the butterflies in your chest – and be kind to yourself as you experience it, and because you're experiencing it. Radical, but it works – as proven in the evidence-based 'Mindfulness-Based Self-Compassion' therapies that are now being developed.

Improve your flying

Another way of using CBT is to improve your actual flying performance. You can start to recognise the thoughts and self-beliefs that 'drive' your flying. We've all had those moments of euphoria two hours into the flight when everything's going amazingly well, we think 100km is in the bag, then five minutes later we're on the ground, scratching our heads.

From a CBT perspective, your focus has switched from the task of observing conditions, feeling the air and flying your wing and got totally swamped by feeling invincible: no wonder you land. Or alternatively, you might have a negative core belief, "I'm an average pilot / I can't climb as well as the others" that makes you stay in a weak climb when others are definitely going up better downwind. Again, it's a belief that, if checked out, might reduce in power and lead to more freedom.

Aim for fifth, not first

In 2010 Mark Watts was getting a little sick of always coming second. He'd flown numerous World Championships and World Cups. Most importantly, he'd flown the British Championships for 16 consecutive years and was always the pilot who should have

▲ MARK WATTS
Champion pilot. Photo: Marcus King

won – deserved to win, given his speed and confidence – but never had.

I was just finishing my psychotherapy training and Mark asked if I'd spend a couple of sessions with him to see if we could shine any light on what was going on. Before our first session I asked him these questions:

- What kind of pilot are you right now?
- What does it feel like when you place around 6th-10th in a task?
- What does it feel like when you win a task?
- What do you mean by going better – in what ways do you want to improve?
- Why do you want to go better?
- At the end of the year how will you know you have done better? How will you measure the change?

I had an inkling Mark was flying too fast and recklessly, but I had no idea why he was doing so – and nor did he. Over the course of just an hour, he recognised that he didn't want to be seen as a cowardly pimp – the kind of pilot who hangs on to the coat tails of others in order to place well. He also noticed how much frustration he felt staying back with the gaggle when all his instinct told him to push on ahead.

Mark is a brilliant pilot (Gin Seok Song rates him as one of the world's most natural) and he usually outclimbs everyone. But with this kind of psychological 'driver' – (in his words, "don't fly like a muppet") – it was no wonder he was so often out front, first, but often landing short of goal.

After our sessions, I wrote him a letter, which he re-read several times over the

▶ **IT'S PRECIOUS**
Keep your head in a helmet – it's the most important bit of
flying kit you've got. Babu Sunuwar at the start of the
Red Bull X-Alps. Photo: Roger Turner

winter. I wanted him to focus on a new goal: coming fifth. What actually happened is Mark stopped caring quite so much about winning at all – he just enjoyed the competitions for what they were. He bought a fast car and got his kicks out of that. In his flying, he also started applying more discipline, and told me he'd started enjoying hanging back up high and letting others glide off in front so he could pick and choose the best thermal without doing so much of the hard work.

In 2011 Mark won the British Championships and in 2012 he scooped the US Paragliding World Cup. Who knows whether that tiny bit of CBT helped at all; he didn't do any of the homework exercises I'd suggested, anyhow. Mark cites having a competitive wing and "just not caring about winning" as being the main reasons for his success. He also spent a lot of time flying with teammate Russ Ogden, a man who constantly bangs on about the need for "discipline" in reigning in your urges while competing. Maybe too, 16 years of making similar mistakes was enough time to want to try something different.

I'd still argue though that becoming aware and saying out loud that he didn't want to "look like a pimp", and then subsequently "giving up" on his desire to win, to prove himself in the eyes of his peers, may have been a useful turning point.

Centre yourself

Some pilots are lucky enough to be more 'centred' and balanced than others. I don't count myself among them. Far from it. That's probably what led me into retraining as a psychotherapist, but luckily there are some great ways of re-balancing the mind. CBT is by no means a fix-all, but it is a useful way of exploring what's going on and can open up some new options.

If you've ever met some of the greats – Chrigel Maurer or Manfred Ruhmer, for example – you'll realise what I mean by centred. They are totally unflappable, unfazed by success or failure. Their ability to step back from emotions, observe them, and make more informed choices is, I would say, at the heart of what it is to fly well – and CBT is a great way of developing the skill.

As neuroscience is now proving, our brains are incredibly elastic and can always be rewired. It just takes practice. As for me, well I'm sure I'll keep making the same old mistakes and banging my head against the same brick wall. I'm not saying it's easy!

NEED TO KNOW

- Try and become aware of any self-limiting beliefs or thoughts. Write them down, check them out.
- When you experience fear or strong emotions, let them be – label them, but don't necessarily act on them unless they are specific to a real and present danger
- Question any potentially irrational fears. Ask yourself, "is it true?"
- Work with another pilot or friend with this kind of stuff. The 'helicopter view' afforded by a shared perspective makes it all easier to work with.
- If you notice you tend to freeze in properly scary situations – try shouting out loud. This can change your response to 'fight' just when you need to take action!

FLYING YOUR FIRST COMPETITION

By Bob Drury

COMPETITIONS give you the opportunity to meet and fly with a group of like-minded people. The majority will be XC-hungry individuals who love exploring the limits of free flight and themselves. Only a very small bunch will be there to win, but you will get a chance to fly with them, talk to them and learn from them. Often much is learnt on launch or in the bar later.

Competitive or not, you'll get more out of the experience if you're flying well and are well prepared. Here's what to expect and how to tackle it.

Know where you're going

If you know where you are, you're halfway to getting to where you want to be. So if you can, choose a comp at a site you know. Nothing is better than flying the competition venue beforehand. The more you demystify the area the less daunting the competition will become.

Get a map or look on Google Earth and learn where the obvious flying features are. If you can't get there to fly, then learn where the long ridges, high peaks and wide valleys are. They will probably all feature on tasks so the knowledge will help you anticipate the challenges you'll be set.

Learn about the infrastructure on the ground too. It will make you less worried about bombing out if you know where the roads and railways are and how to get back to base.

Plan the obvious XC routes, or better still, go there and fly them. Look at tracklogs on sites like XContest.org to see the common XC routes. These can teach you where the house thermals and cruxes are (they'll be where lots of flights end). If you know what's coming up next you'll be better prepared to deal with it.

Know your gear

Success comes when opportunity meets preparation. Fly a wing you know well, with your normal XC harness and with instruments you understand and can use.

You'll fly better and focus more on the task if you are totally comfortable with your gear. Similarly, know your instruments and have them ready to use.

Trying to borrow batteries, fold maps or remount your reserve on launch all loses you crucial flight-planning time. Instruments can be complicated at the best of times. Learn how to program them before you arrive – wading through the manual on launch or pestering someone who's got the same model will waste more time and annoy others.

If you normally fly with a drink system, sweets or a teddy bear tied to your riser then make sure you do the same in the comp. Little things out of place will erode your focus.

Know thyself

Everyone approaches competition from a different angle. Knowing what you want, focusing on your goal and behaving appropriately will take you a long way towards going home satisfied.

If your aim is to fly with lots of great pilots and learn as much as you can, then don't charge off alone. If you want to fly as much and far as you can then make sure you get round the course everyday, regardless of the speed you make it at.

If socialising and having fun with like-minded people is a major factor then for sure stay up late at night drinking and partying, but if you want great flying then get to bed early and sober. If you love to party then remember competing tired or hungover is unpleasant at best and dangerous at worst.

On the day

Get up early and get your equipment sorted. Eat breakfast but avoid coffee – it's a diuretic and can ruin your flight. Then get up to launch. Comp organisations start transporting people to launch many hours before the window opens, as it takes a while to get 100+ pilots ready to fly.

If you're early you should be able to get a good place to lay out your wing or rig your hang glider. Don't be shy: claim your place on launch and get your wing ready, your harness totally sorted and your flight clothes either on or ready to put on. The more prepared you are now the less rushed you'll be after briefing.

Listen at the briefing. Tasks are often more complicated than you think. Timings are particularly easy to miss or get wrong. Write down the times (don't forget to take a pen or pencil), particularly the start gate and land-by times as they are the two that will ruin your score if you get them wrong. Make a note of any local rules the organisers announce, no fly zones or places you mustn't land.

Once briefing is over, plan your route. If

"Success comes when opportunity meets preparation "

you've done your homework you'll already have an idea of how to fly it. If you can discuss the route with anyone more experienced or local to the site then do so.

If it's going to be soarable when the window opens then be clipped in and ready to launch when it does – you are better off getting in the air early and settling in while you wait for the start gate to open. It gives you a chance to get a feel for the conditions, sort out any problems with your kit and look ahead at the route.

In the air

Try to be as high as you can when the start gate opens – rushing off low will only ruin your day. Once everyone gets on their way, the field soon splits into gaggles and you'll find yourself naturally flying with certain pilots.

If you are with an early gaggle chances are they're good pilots, so try to stick with them. If you're getting outclimbed all the time then accept that and let yourself slip from the gaggle. Don't keep leaving each thermal lower and lower to catch up. Your main objective is to fly the course, learn as much as possible and have the best day out; you won't have that on the deck.

Stay focused and believe you can get round the course. Task setters typically choose courses that most of the field can get around, so stay positive, even if you get stuck for a while.

Avoid taking risky glides. You want to get to goal so give yourself a big margin for error on each big glide and let a few others go ahead.

If others take different routes then question why. The more you analyse the decisions others take the more you'll learn yourself.

Don't blow it right at the end. The thought of completing the task is enough to send some competitors into a 'goal frenzy'. Charging ahead to shave mere seconds off their time they leave the last thermal too low, hit full speed on their final glide and blow all their hard work by landing short. If you've got to your final glide, make sure you climb high enough to get in with ease. Wingovering down to the goal is so much nicer than doing the walk of shame from one field short!

Be consistent

Congratulations! You've completed your first comp task. Most scoring systems reward consistency, so do that every day and you'll suddenly find your name jostling near the top of the scoresheet. Better still, you'll have had more flying than most and hence have almost certainly done what you went there to do: have fun and learn lots.

NEED TO KNOW

- Flying competitions helps you learn more about flying XC
- Most pilots are there for fun, very few are there to win
- Choose a competition at a site you know
- Study maps and tracklogs online before you arrive
- Fly a glider and harness you know well
- On launch get ready in good time
- In the air get high and focus on flying the task, not racing to goal (or most likely the deck)
- Fly consistently, and have fun

COMPETITION FLYING

By Bruce Goldsmith

IT CAN be quite hard to know where to start when you turn up at your first competition. The talk is all about racing into goal at high speed and the technicalities of the scoring system, when what you really need is simple direct advice that cuts through the hype, goes back to the basics and gets you through the event unscathed and with a satisfactory result. From there on in, your competition career will flourish or fail depending on how you approach it and the racing game in general.

By far the best way to start in competitions is to get to goal every time. Clearly, if nobody gets to goal at all then it is an impossible task, but if only one person gets to goal it isn't, so you need to make sure it is you. If you can't complete the task and get to goal every time, then there is no point in racing at all. Only when you are confident in your ability to get to goal is it worth starting to improve your times into goal by racing.

Getting to goal every day is a surefire way to push yourself to the top of the rankings. Consistent top-twenty places over a week-long event will quite often put you in the top five if not on the podium. This was very well demonstrated in the 2007 World Championships when I was the only pilot in the whole competition to get to goal every day. I won the competition as a result.

Recent scoring systems often try to reduce this effect to encourage racing and in some competitions dropped tasks are allowed, allowing you to discard your worst task result from your overall cumulative score for the event – often one when you didn't get to goal. However, this does not really change the fundamental rule that getting to goal is more important than racing.

Learning to fly fast

Learning to fly fast is a skill that takes years to learn. The best way to learn is from top pilots, who themselves will have learnt it from years of competition flying.

Slow pilots are normally unaware that they are flying slowly and inefficiently, and there is an incredible difference between a slow pilot and a fast one – a slow pilot might take two hours to fly a course that a fast pilot can fly in half an hour. The first time you fly in a top-level competition, be prepared to be left far behind very quickly! It can be quite a big shock.

Here are some top tips to help you master flying quickly.

Stay with the lead gaggle

It's highly advantageous to be flying with the best pilots in the race, so try taking off before them and placing yourself in the best position to be with them when the race starts, which is normally as high as possible at the edge of the start gate. Once the race starts, stick close to the top pilots as they head off along the course and watch what they do.

At first you may only stay with the lead gaggle for the first thermal. But, as you have to be in the race to win the race, you need to keep practising this until you can stay with the lead gaggle for the whole task. This can take years of practice and some pilots

66 Racing with the lead gaggle can be quite a buzz 99

never manage to stay with the lead gaggle for long.

Pimping

Racing along up front with the lead gaggle can be quite a buzz. If you're now flying fast enough to stay with the lead gaggle you've already achieved a lot. Many pilots take years to get to this stage and some never make it at all. You are now at a stage of your competition career that many pilots never leave.

They just stay with the lead gaggle as much as possible and never move on to make decisions themselves or take any risks. It's possible to do quite well in competitions flying like this, but you're not likely to win any, nor likely to make many friends if you only ever fly like this. Because 'pimping' – the act of trailing better pilots and feeding off their decision-making without ever contributing to the gaggle's success yourself – is generally sneered at in competitions.

However, everyone pimps to some extent – at the beginning it's part of how you learn to stay with the gaggle. But, sooner or later you have to use the knowledge and confidence you've gained to the greater advantage of the pack and then others will pimp off you.

ORM: One Right Move

Once you're good enough to hold your own in the lead gaggle you can start to implement the ORM, or 'one right move', a technique that I'm

quite fond of. This technique involves staying with the lead gaggle for 90% of the time, all the time carefully watching every move they make to spot an error and hopefully spy a better route. Then, when the lead gaggle has gone off, you make the cleverer move and beat them all. Remember that you only need to do this once in a competition to win it, as long as you are right up there at the top on every other day. Pulling off a successful ORM requires you to first be able to spot the gaggle's error; secondly you have to have enough confidence in your decision to avoid the gaggle-drag yourself and break away from the pack; thirdly you have to have the skill and continued confidence to go it alone, possibly all the way to the goal line.

Climb fast

The best way of racing is of course to climb fast. You gain much more time by climbing fast than by gliding fast. How many times have you heard pilots say, "I could only find 2m/s climbs at best today" when you have just been flying in thumping 5m/s lift? Lots of pilots find a small weak core and are content to climb in it. But flying fast is all about flying in the best lift available. If you're climbing in 2m/s and someone else is in a 5m/s pumping thermal nearby then you have to either get in the stronger lift immediately or accept you'll get left behind. A successful comp pilot is searching and observing all the time to make sure nobody ever outclimbs them, not even a bird or a plastic bag.

Gaggle flying

Much of competition flying is about flying in gaggles. There are both good things and bad about gaggle flying, so let's start with the good.

When you fly in a gaggle your search power is increased. A good gaggle will spread out and cover a wider area of the sky, which is a major help when looking for elusive thermals. Being in a gaggle is especially useful if the thermals are weak and far apart. Gaggles are particularly useful in flatland flying because the location of thermals is less predictable. In weak conditions a gaggle can help you find the only thermal and can therefore help you to stay up. In stronger conditions the gaggle can help you find the best core and thus help you climb faster.

However, gaggle flying means you are compromised as well. You can't just fly wherever you want, as with so many pilots in close proximity, the chance of collision is high. Instead you have to join the communal merry-go-round as it ascends as one mass.

Once you're settled in the gaggle study all the gliders around you and try to anticipate their moves so you are able to keep yourself in clean air if they turn toward you. Look for anyone climbing faster than you, particularly from below. If you spot someone in better air adjust your circling to take you into their part of the thermal. If there's enough room you may even get an extra 360 in it and gain valuable height on the others. Even though your ability to move freely within the thermal is compromised, with so many good pilots in one thermal the gaggle is unlikely to ever lose the climb. Unless you have a task-winning ORM up your sleeve it's worth sticking with it.

The quality of the gaggle

But be warned, all gaggles are not equal. The quality of a gaggle is only as good as the quality of the pilots in it. This means there are slow gaggles as well as fast gaggles. Obviously the lead gaggle, the one you want to be in, is always the fastest gaggle. The lead gaggle in any competition will both climb faster and glide faster than the other gaggles. The pilots in the lead gaggle are also more adventurous and will do more searching thus finding the strongest lift quickest.

Beware of gaggle-drag

Conversely, slower gaggles can suffer badly from what is known as 'gaggle-drag'. Less skilled or experienced, the pilots in the slow gaggle may be indecisive and hang on in weak lift or not leave the thermal quickly enough when it tops out. Once you are in a slower gaggle it's very difficult to leave the gaggle behind and leapfrog forward to the faster gaggles in front. The best way to learn to fly faster is to get into the lead gaggle and then try to stay with it.

Know when to race

Once you're a good competition pilot, who's learnt to race efficiently, and can get to goal nearly every time. The final stage in your apprenticeship is knowing when to race.

The obvious answer is only to race when you're certain you'll not go down. Obvious, yes, but the trick is knowing when you're definitely not going to go down.

The risk of going down is less the higher you are, so race fast when you're high and slow down when you're low. If you are so low that you're on the point of landing then stop racing completely and work at just staying in the air. It sounds simple, but I've seen many a hot-headed pilot race themselves all the way into the ground when they should have slowed down and just stayed airborne.

Anticipate what's ahead

Look at the weather, the terrain and the task. If there's a sheet of cirrus coming in then you'll

▲ **GET TO GOAL**
Consistency is key in competition flying.
Photo: Martin Scheel

need to be high and prepared to slow down as the shadow arrives. If there's a crux move like a difficult valley crossing or an unavoidable blue hole ahead, you probably want to slow down and gain height too. How far you are down the course matters too. If you are on final glide to goal you don't need any more thermals, so the risk of going down gets less the closer you get to goal. Only if there's a clear line of thermal-producing terrain ahead, that you are confident you will find thermals all along, should you be in full race mode.

Switching instinctively between the two flying modes – race and survival – can be what makes a great competition pilot.

The winning pilot in a task is normally the one who sticks with the lead gaggle the entire task before making an ORM right at the end to outfox his competitors, or who times their final glide to utter perfection and leaves the last thermal at exactly the right height. But be warned, leading out too early can be a very expensive mistake, as many have found.

NEED TO KNOW

- Learn how to get to goal every time before you start racing in competitions
- Consistency is key – coming tenth every day is better than winning one day and bombing the next
- Understand gaggle flying – try to stay with the lead one, it's got the best pilots in it
- Learn to change gear – know when to stick with the pack and when to push
- Don't race into the ground – you won't win unless you stay in the air

TURNING PROFESSIONAL

By Bruce Goldsmith

IT goes without saying that a pilot who intends to be a top competition pilot needs to have fantastic flying skills. Flying needs to be second nature to him or her. He needs to be so confident with his flying that he can concentrate on the other factors that make a top comp pilot, such as tactics, rules and navigation. This can only be achieved with a lot of practice both in and outside competitions.

Generally speaking you need to have been flying two to three years before you are ready to start competing at the most basic level. Then it takes another two to three years to fight your way up the competition ladder.

The first level is club competition and this is a very gentle introduction. Here you will learn the basics of how to use your instruments, how to follow a task and how to get to goal. At this level the tasks are normally XC tasks rather than racing tasks. It's all about flying far and reaching goal.

If you progress quickly then by the second year you will be flying in national competitions. If you are a real star you may be ready for international competition in the third year. By this time you should be getting to goal on a regular basis and can actually start to race and improve your times.

Don't expect to be on top in your first year of international competition either, even if you are national champion. International competition is a whole different ball game and you need to do enough competitions so that comp flying becomes second nature.

Because it is difficult to enter the Paragliding World Cup directly, you will need to do Pre-PWCs or easier events before flying in the PWC itself. If you are doing well in international competition in your second year, then you are doing very well. The fast track to becoming a top comp pilot is five to seven years from learning to fly.

Finance and sponsorship

Competing is an expensive business. Most competition pilots earn their money doing regular jobs and compete in holiday time. (Incidentally, this is why the main objective of competitions is to provide enjoyment for the competition pilots, and is consequently the reason why the pilots do not want to do tasks intended for the media or the public. They are on holiday and they want to enjoy themselves as much as possible!)

However, there is a big problem with competing like this. With a normal job you cannot really get enough time off to compete often enough to become really good. Ideally you need to compete around 50% of the time. Even better is to compete full-time as there are so many competitions: just follow the summer season around the hemispheres of the world.

Professional pilots in major sports such as golf or tennis manage to earn enough money though prize money to compete. In paragliding (or hang gliding) you can forget this option. The prize money is simply not enough to pay for the cost of competing. A one-week international competition will typically cost between €1,000-1,500 if it is in Europe and you live in Europe. This includes travel, entry fees, accommodation and some money for equipment. It is very rare to find a competition with a first prize above €2,000. So even if you were the best pilot in the world and won every comp you entered you probably wouldn't earn enough to pay your way with prize money alone.

Next comes national sponsorship. If you are a top competitor and represent your country then some countries will help support you financially. In the UK such funding has dropped steadily over the last few years, and now you only get some of your expenses paid at certain really major competitions.

However, the news is not so bad for other countries. Switzerland has the highest level of sponsorship for top comp pilots, and this quite likely has contributed to their success over the years. The French too.

When I started competing one of the first things I did was get to know John Pendry and Judy Leden. Both had major independent sponsors that paid their competition expenses. John was sponsored by Planters and Judy by Citroën. I quickly learnt from them that sponsorship was not simply a gift, but was money that had to be earned. The pilot needs to show to his sponsor, through a sponsorship proposal document, how the sponsor will get good value for money by sponsoring the pilot. You need to log the media exposure you have had in the past and expect to get in the future and then put a price on it. Your aim is to prove to your potential sponsor how they can actually get better coverage by sponsoring you rather than using some other form of advertising. This is not easy and can be a full-time job in itself.

Major sponsors in paragliding are few and far between, but they do exist. You are most likely to be able to go down this route if you already have a contact with a company. I don't really include paragliding companies here because generally they don't have the money to provide much sponsorship to pilots except through equipment.

The best way to earn enough money to compete and fly then is to work for a paragliding manufacturer. And indeed a significant proportion of top comp pilots work for paragliding manufacturers, either as test pilots, designers or dealers.

Equipment

Choosing the right equipment is a very important part of competition – and it gets increasingly important the higher up the competition ladder you go. I cannot emphasise enough that it is the glider that is the most important part of the equipment.

In the days of Open Class it was very similar to F1 racing. You needed the best glider and also to be one of the very best pilots flying it. So you were only likely to get the very best prototypes if you were the top sponsored pilot, or actually worked for the brand that is producing the top proto.

With some type of certification arriving for competition – EN D or EN 'comp class' – this has changed. Now anyone can buy a top glider. However, being close to the manufacturer means you are more likely to get hold of the first glider off the production line. This can make a difference as making a competition glider takes a lot of time and waiting lists can be long. You need to be in with the manufacturer, either as a sponsored pilot or otherwise actually working for them.

Advertising and PR

Before embarking on my competition career I took a lot of advice from Brian Milton, who was British team manager at the time. He advised me to manage my own PR and to get as much magazine coverage as possible and

▲YES-LOGO
Look for sponsors outside the sport.
Photo: Martin Scheel

not to just rely on competition results to boost my competition career. So I did everything I could to make sure that I appeared in every single issue of Skywings, the magazine for the British national association. It was not important what I was in there for – just to have my name mentioned in every issue was what I was after.

Today, professional pilots do a lot of their own publishing: on Facebook, blogging and other social media, both writing, photography and video. Most manufacturers and sponsors will expect you to do this if they sponsor you, and many will want to see evidence that you can. You can build a profile and a following very quickly if you are smart at this. Once you have that, you are well on your way to becoming a mini brand, and that means you've turned pro.

NEED TO KNOW

- Build your competition profile: start local and aim for international comps
- Getting good international results takes a minimum of five to seven years
- Competing is expensive and sponsors rare – look outside the sport for cash
- Get close to a manufacturer if you want to fly the top wings first
- Work on your media profile, website and social media – engage

INDEX

GLOSSARY

Acro: Acrobatic flying

Active flying: Responding to what the glider is doing by using brakes and weightshift

Aerofoils: The shape of a wing in cross-section

Airspace: Controlled airspace, the part of the sky that is governed by laws

Altocumulus: Mid-level heaped cloud

Anabatic flow: Wind flowing up a hillside caused by the sun heating the land. From the Greek anabatos

Anchors: A technique used in sports psychology designed to put you in a good frame of mind

Angle of attack: The angle between the glider and the airflow

Arc of slack: The shape of the brake lines on a paraglider when the hands are up

Asymmetric collapse: When one side of a paraglider deflates

Asymmetric SAT: An acro manoeuvre

Asymmetric spiral: An acro manoeuvre

Averager: Instrument that averages out your climb rate in your vario

Ballast: Extra weight, usually water

Bank: The angle between the glider's normal axis and the horizon

Big ears and speedbar: Fast descent technique of folding in the paraglider wingtips and pushing the accelerator system (speedbar)

Bite: How a glider feels when it hits a thermal or in a turn – biting in, like crunching on an apple

Blue days: Days when there are no clouds – tricky as cumulus clouds show the thermals

Blue holes: Areas where there are no clouds in an otherwise cumulus-filled sky

Bolster eddies: Areas of turbulence in front of an object, caused by the wind hitting it

Boundary layer: The bit of the atmosphere in which we fly

Brakes: The two lines that go to the back of the paraglider, controlled by the pilot through the brake handles

Breakaway points: Where a thermal leaves the ground, or where a racing pilot breaks away from the gaggle

Bridges: Areas of lift or routes through the air that allow pilots to make otherwise difficult transitions, eg using convergence to cross a valley

Cascades: A dramatic sequence of collapses on a paraglider, each worse than the other

Changing gear: The ability of a pilot to slow down or speed up in response to changing conditions

Chequerboard theory: A neat way of looking at the sky: blue bits are no-go zones, you can only move from white puffy cloud to white puffy cloud

Chord: The width of the glider from front to back

Cirrus: High cloud

Cliff bands: Rocky outcrops, often good places to soar or find a thermal

Climb rate: How fast you are climbing in a thermal. Varios average out the speed over time so you get a true picture. Measured in metres per second (m/s) or thousands of feet per minute (3-up).

Climbing: The art of going up in a thermal

Cloud development: How clouds change during their life cycle and over the course of a day

Cloud flying: Flying in cloud

Cloud suck: Strong, consistent, smooth lift near the base of and inside some cumulus clouds. Technically the same as strong lift but can be dangerous as it will pull you into the cloud faster than you can spiral down

Cloud streets: Cumulus clouds in a line. Very good for flying

Cloudbase: The bottom of a cumulus cloud

Collapse: When a part of a paraglider deflates

Col or pass: Geographic feature between two hills

Comfort: An important aspect of flying and glider design, often overlooked

Competition gliders: Generic name for high performance gliders used in competition

Confidence: Important to have

Conical hill convergence: Where two winds divide around a hill and meet on the other side creating lift

Conservative flying: Staying high and not going too fast or taking risks that might put you on the ground

Convection: The process of the air being heated by the ground and rising

Convergence: Where two or more winds meet

Core, the: The central part of a thermal, where you want to be

Coriolis effect: The effect of the Earth's rotation

Countering the turn: Technique of maintaining direction following a collapse

Crashing: Try not to. If you do, PLF (and keep legs together when coming down through trees)

Cravat: Where the wingtip of a paraglider gets caught in the lines

Cumulonimbus: A large cloud that will rain or storm. Generally higher than they are wide

Decision-making: A crucial part of flying

Deep stall: When a paraglider stops flying normally and descends vertically, also known as going parachutal

Deflation: When part of the paraglider collapses

Dolphin flying: The technique of flying from cloud to cloud in a cloudstreet with minimum circling, slowing down in lift and speeding up in sink

Downbursts: A burst of rain, virga and wind from a cumulonimbus cloud

Downwind: Going with the wind

Drag: Resistance through the air caused by the glider, the pilot or the lines

Drift: Floating across the landscape underneath a cloud. Also the direction you are blown in the wind.

Dust devil: A small whirlwind caused by thermal activity, visible because of the dust it picks up

Dynamic turns: The technique of using the energy of a dive to turn

Efficiency: Efficient flying is fast flying

EN A / B / C / D: EN means European Norm. It's the almost-universal system of testing and rating paragliders. It measures responses to induced collapses and other manouevres. A requires the least time or pilot input for the glider to regain normal flight, D requires more time or pilot input

Energy flow: Lift and lines of lifty air in the sky

FAI: Fédération Aéronautique Internationale, the World AirSports Federation. Oversees many competitions and all world records

Fear: Normal, useful, necessary. Too little or too much can be a bad thing.

Feedback: The feeling you get from what the glider, and therefore the air, is doing

Feeling: Sensitivity to lift, the glider's movements and the air

Final glide: The last glide of the day, or the glide into goal in a competition task

Fisherman's technique: The technique of resting a finger on the brake line so you can feel the glider

Five star system: A techniqe of assessing the potential of a possible thermal source from looking at the Sun, the wind, the terrain, clouds and other gliders or birds. Award one star for each

Flatland flying: Flying in relatively flat terrain

Flow: Taking advantage of the flow of the day means getting the best from the day, efficiently. Eg, flying easterly faces in the morning, southerly ones in the afternoon and westerly ones in the evening

Freeze-frame technique: Taking a mental snapshot of a developing cloud on each turn, in an attempt to discern whether it is growing or collapsing

Full frontal: When the glider collapses at the front, symetrically

Fun: The point of it all

G-force: The feeling you get in a spiral dive or other strong manouevre. Some love it, others hate it

Gaggle drag: When you get stuck with a load of bad pilots in a gaggle and the whole gaggle slows down because no one is willing to lead out or make a decision. Leave it and fly your own flight

Gaggle flying: Flying with a group of pilots

Gaggle: A group of pilots in a thermal

Getting stuck: To avoid

Glide angle: The angle of your descent through the air

Glory: An optical phenomenon. A rainbow halo with you in the middle. Visible below you when the cloud is below you and the Sun is above

Goal: The end-point in a competition task or defined cross country flight

Goals: Things you adopt to help focus your flying, eg "I'd like to fly 100km"

GPS: Electronic instrument that uses Global Positioning System to give us speed and position info

Groundspeed: How fast we are travelling across the landscape

Gust front: The outflow of air that precedes a cumulonimbus

Hail: Ouch. Should have landed ages ago.

Headwind: When flying directly into wind

Hedge-line: A ground feature created by hedges, useful when thermal hunting in flatlands

Helicopter: An acro move

Hexagon theory: Open cell convection. Where on a still day clouds form in a polygonal or fish-net pattern

High pressure days: Blue skies, light winds, high cloudbase

Honey theory: Imagine the landscape covered in honey. Turn upside down. Where the honey drips off, that's where your thermals are

Hook-knife: A special knife with a protected blade for cutting lines

Hotspots: Cores within a core in thermals

Infinite tumble: Successive upside-down turns on a paraglider

Instability: Air that is unstable and good for thermals

Intermediate gliders: A glider aimed at recreational pilots who fly 50-100 hours a year

Inversions: A temperature boundary in the air, where warm air overlies cooler air. Stops thermals

Katabatic convergence: Where two downslope winds meet and create lift, often in the centre of a valley

Katabatic flow: Downlope breeze caused by cooling air in the evening

Kiting: Playing with your paraglider on the ground

Latent energy: The heat released during the process of condensation and cloud building

Leading edge: The front edge of a paraglider

Lee-side convergence: Where winds meet on the downwind side of a hill or mountain

Lee-side flying: Flying in the lee of the meteorological or valley wind

Lenticulars: Flying-saucer shaped clouds, caused by wave or strong wind in the mountains

Lightweight gear: Made with light materials, often less hard-wearing but much easier to carry up the hill

Lines: The string bits on a paraglider

Load tests: A test, often to destruction, of equipment including harnesses, paragliders, lines and karabiners

Low saves: Catching a thermal close to the ground

MacCready Ring: A mechanical ring that tells you what speed to fly, primarily used by sailplane pilots. Nowadays incorporated into electronic flight instruments

MacTwist: An acro move

Magic lift: Lift that is smooth and going up everywhere. Often in the evening, often restitution

Maximum glide: The best glide you will get from your glider

Micro-cores: Small cores within a core in a thermal

Mid-air collisions: When two gliders hit each other in the sky. Avoid

Minimum sink: The airspeed of a glider at which the glider reaches its lowest rate of descent, and will therefore stay in the air for the longest time possible

Misty Flip: An acro move

Moonbeams: A beautiful thermal that feels like it will take you into Space

Motorways: Well-used flying routes, usually in the Alps

Mountain flying: Flying in the mountains

Multi-cores: A large thermal with many cores

Observation: One of the most important skills you can develop in flying. Observe more, fly better

One right move technique: A technique in competition where, if you make one right move, it will put you ahead of the gaggle and win you the task

Open class: Paragliders that have not been through the EN certification system

Open-cell convection: Hexagon theory

Orographic cloud: Cloud that forms when moist air is pushed up over an object or hill

Over-accelerated progression: Learning too quickly so the pilot is in danger of over-reaching themselves

Overcontrol: Controlling the glider too much, with potentially unintended results

Overdevelopment: When clouds develop into storm clouds, or when the sky fills out with 'spreadout' cloud

Parachute landing fall (PLF): Landing with legs together and rolling on your side

Pimping: Profiting from the good style of other pilots without putting the effort in yourself. Bad form

Pitch: An aspect of flight dynamics. Forward and back motion.

Polar curve: A graph which contrasts the sink rate of an aircraft (typically a glider) with its horizontal speed

Pressure, high and low: Refers to the air pressure of a particular day

Pumping out deflations: Technique of using the brakes to push air through a paraglider to remove collapses

Rear-riser control: Controlling a paraglider while on glide and speedbar by using the back risers

Red Bull X-Alps: Adventure race through the Alps

Reserve parachutes: A parachute carried by pilots in case of emergency

Restitution: Evening lift 'everywhere'

Reynold's number: Used in fluid mechanics

Ridge soaring: Flying up and down a ridge in dynamic lift (the wind)

Rodriguez brothers: Acro masters from Spain, Felix and Raul

Roll: An aspect of flight dynamics. The rotating of a wing on its longitudinal axis

Rotor: Turbulent air in the lee of (behind) an object

Rythmic SAT: An acro move

S-turn: Turning the glider in S-shapes, often used to lose height on approach to landing

Safety: Very important

Sailplane: A glider – the white plane-like ones with long wings

Sanderson, Jocky: SIV guru

SAT: An acro move

Scratching: Trying hard to stay up in meagre lift

Sea-breeze convergence: When a sea-breeze meets an offshore wind and creates soarable lift. Not a cocktail

Sea-breeze: A regular pattern of wind that sets up along coasts caused by the heating of the land during the day which pulls in air from the sea

Shear: A difference in wind speed or direction between two air masses, often turbulent

Sink: Going down

Sink rate: The speed at which you are going down

SIV: Simulation d'Incident de Vol – simulated flight incidents. A post-qualification piloting course where you can safely test the limits of your glider. Always over water and under instruction, please

Snow-line: Where the snow ends in the Alps. Often a good trigger for thermals

Solar heating: The Sun heating the ground

Sources and triggers: The source is where the warm air is from, the trigger is what sets the warm air off so it rises. For example, a brown field is the source, the treeline downwind of it would be the trigger

Speed-to-fly: A theory of how fast you should fly according to conditions for maximum efficiency

Speedbar: The accelerator system on a paraglider. Applied by the legs

Spin: Oops. Occurs when one side of the wing is stalled, and the wing rotates

Spiral dive: A series of steeply banked 360 turns

Stable days: Days where the air mass and air pressure coincide to mean an absence of thermals, despite sun

Stall: Applying the brakes so the glider stops forward flight and collapses behind you

Stratus: Cloud characterised by horizontal layering with a uniform base

Test flying: Flying a new glider to try it out. Or, a test pilot flying a prototype glider for the EN test

Thermal: What we love. Rising columns of warm air topped by a perfect cumulus cloud (in theory)

Thirds rule: A flatland flying theory. If you are in the top-third of the sky fly by the clouds, if in the bottom-third fly by the terrain, if in the middle-third use both.

Thunderstorms: Avoid

Trackers: Electronic gizmos that track pilots, often uploading the data regularly to the internet

Trailing edge: The back edge of a paraglider

Tree-line: A line of trees, useful in flatland flying as possible triggers. Or the altitude that trees grow to in mountainous terrain

Trim speed: The speed of a paraglider when flown 'hands-up', ie with no brake input

Trimmers: Adjustable webbing on a paraglider's risers that allow the pilot to adjust the profile of the wing to increase or decrease trim speed

Tumbling: An acro move

Turbulence: Air that is not smooth

Turnpoint: Used in competition and in defined cross country flying. A dedicated point, physical like a building or simply a GPS point in the air, that pilots must reach before carrying on

Valley crossing: Crossing a valley, often the crux of a cross country flight in the mountains

Valley wind convergence: Where two valley winds meet, creating lift

Valley winds: The system of winds and airflow that sets up during the day as mountains heat up and draw air in. Can be strong. Essential to understand for mountain flying

Vario: Electronic instrument that tells a pilot if they are going up or down

Venturi: Where air speeds up as it passes through a gap or narrowing

Virga: Rain that falls from a cloud but doesn't hit the ground

Visualisation: A sports psychology technique that helps you imagine what is going to happen so that when it happens you are prepared

Vortex, leading: The top of a thermal

Wave: A type of lift

Weightshift: The technique of shifting your bodyweight so the glider turns

Wind shadow: An area that is protected from the wind by an obstacle, eg trees, a building or a mountain

Wing loading: The loaded weight of the glider divided by the area of the wing

Wing-watching: Looking at your wing while in flight. Not as bad a habit as some will tell you

Wingovers: Rubbing your tummy while patting your stomach, but in flight. A series of smooth, coordinated dynamic turns

Wingtip: The end of your wing. Gliders have two of them

Wraps: The technique of shortening the brakes on a paraglider by wrapping the brake lines around a hand

XC: Cross country flying

Yaw: The rotation of a wing from side-to-side, as if around a mast on a yacht

Zeroes: A thermal that means a glider maintains altitude, neither losing or gaining height. Actually rising air. Stick with it, you can drift a long way in a zero and it might just develop into a proper thermal

UNITS

1m = 3.28ft	0.5m/s = 98.5 ft per minute	1km/h = 0.54 knots = 0.62mph
100m = 328ft	1m/s = 197 ft per minute	1 knot = 1.15mph = 1.85km/h
1,000m = 1,093 yards	2m/s = 394 ft per minute	1mph = 0.87 knots = 1.61km/h
1km = 0.62 miles	3m/s = 591 ft per minute	
100km = 62.14 miles	5m/s = 984 ft per minute	10km/h = 5.4knots = 6.2mph
10ft = 3.05m	10m/s = 1,969 ft per minute	15km/h = 8.1 knots = 9.32mph
1,000ft = 304.8m		32km/h = 17.3 knots = 20mph
1 mile = 1,609m (1.6km)		50km/h = 27 knots = 31.07mph
100 miles = 160.94km		

THE AUTHOR

Photos: Roger Turner

BRUCE GOLDSMITH was born in Hemel Hempstead, England in 1960 and trained as a civil engineer. He first saw hang gliding as a child and learnt to fly while at the University of London. In 1986 he became a member of the British Hang Gliding team and one year later turned professional when he landed a major sponsorship deal with Newsweek magazine. His successful hang gliding competition career culminated in winning the Hang Gliding World Cup in 1990. He designed hang gliders for Airwave from 1986-89, before founding the paragliding side of Airwave in 1990. He was a director and designer there until 1998. The following decade saw him help found Ozone, before working again as a paraglider designer for Airwave. In 2007 he won the Paragliding World Championships in Manilla, Australia, on a paraglider that he had designed himself, the first pilot to do so. He has been multiple British Champion in both hang gliding and paragliding and flew at the highest level in international competition for decades. In 2013 he founded BGD – Bruce Goldsmith Design GmbH. He lives in the south of France with his Icelandic wife Arna (also a pilot) and their three children Tyr, Freyja and Gunnar.
www.flybgd.com

THE JET STREAM
Narrow bands of high wind of up to 450km/h

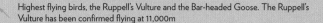

Highest flying birds, the Ruppell's Vulture and the Bar-headed Goose. The Ruppell's Vulture has been confirmed flying at 11,000m

AIRLINE CRUISING ALTITUDE, 10,000M

9,947M
On 14 February 2007 Ewa Wisnierska was sucked into a cu-nim near Manilla, Australia at 20m/s and reached 9,947m. She blacked out for about an hour before waking up again at 6,900m. Covered in ice from the subzero temperatures she found sink and flew down to land normally in a farmer's field. She was taken to hospital where she was treated for frostbite.

9000m

8,848M MOUNT EVEREST
First summit flight flown by Jean-Marc Boivin on 26 April 1988. Also flown by two tandem pairs: Bertrand (Zeb) Roche and Claire Bernier on 21 May 2001; and exactly a decade later, Babu Sunuwar and Lakpa Tshering Sherpa on 21 May 2011. Pilots regularly fly XC at 7,000m and above in the Karakoram, Pakistan.

8,811M K2

7000m

CIRRUS
Short, detached, hair-like clouds found at high altitudes. These delicate clouds are wispy with a silky sheen and can indicate a change in the weather as a warm front approaches.

CIRROCUMULUS

6000m

5,893M KILIMANJARO

CIRROSTRATUS

4,810M MONT BLANC
In the Alps pilots often fly at 3,000-4,000m and on exceptional days can go higher. Mont Blanc, Western Europe's highest peak, has been top-landed several times after pilots took off from the Chamonix Valley. Most famously well over 50 pilots top-landed on 19 August 2012 with many more soaring above the peak at over 5,000m.

ALTOCUMULUS

4000m

ALTOSTRATUS

CUMULONIMBUS
Commonly known as a thundercloud, the base of a cu-nim is often flat and dark and may only be a couple of hundred metres above the ground. However, the top of the cloud can extend to 10,000m forming classic towers and the anvil shape. Lightning, heavy rain, thunder, hail and torna-does are all associated with cu-nims.

NIMBOSTRATUS
Dark grey or bluish grey featureless layers of cloud, thick enough to block out the sun. These mid-level clouds are associated with continuous heavy rain or snow and cover most of the sky

3000m

CUMULUS
Free-flight pilots depend largely on cumulus clouds to fly cross country, which makes us a patient bunch and is why we're willing to travel thousands of kilometres in search of the perfect sky. In hang gliding the world record stands at 764km, set by Dustin Martin (US) on 4 July 2012 in Texas, USA. In paragliding Nevil Hulett (ZA) flew 502.9km in South Africa on 14 December 2008. These records will no doubt fall to others.

1500m

STRATUS

World's tallest building, Burj Khalifa, 828m

JOIN THE FAMILY

+ Each new 100 page issue delivered every two months
+ A 100+ page Travel Guide to the world's best flying sites
+ Entry into our win-a-paraglider prize draw

SUBSCRIBER BENEFITS:

FREE TRAVEL GUIDE

New subscribers receive our latest international Travel Guide, absolutely free.

FREE LEARNING

Keep up to date with current techniques and knowledge from some of the best in the sport. Each issue is packed full of learning and technique articles.

EXCLUSIVE REVIEWS

Each issue we review gliders, harnesses and technology in a dedicated 10-page section. From the latest crop of sporty EN Bs to the sharpest EN Cs. Our reviewers are highly experienced pilots, out there flying. Often we'll give the equipment to a pilot for a whole season so they can really take it apart. This means they're free to give their honest considered opinion after many hours of fly-time.

EXCLUSIVE INTERVIEWS

From the latest World Champion to the Red Bull X-Alps athletes, we speak to the leading lights in our sport on a pilot level and find out exactly what makes them tick and what it takes to fly like they do.

BRILLIANT PHOTOGRAPHY

We draw from a wide pool of talented international pilots, photographers and writers every issue. Nearly all of what they create for us is exclusive to us.

ADVENTURE, TRAVEL AND LEARNING

Those are the three things at the heart of Cross Country. Each issue we bring you a crafted package of the best of free flight that includes amazing flying destinations and beautiful locations all backed up by a powerful learning and 'How to' section.

BY PILOTS FOR PILOTS

Since being founded in 1988 Cross Country has been written by pilots, for pilots. It's still the same.

HOME DELIVERY

The magazine is delivered to your door or tablet six times a year.

YOU STAY IN CONTROL

Subscriptions can be billed issue by issue or annually and can be cancelled any time. Opt for auto-renew and save money.